AF559977

INDIA'S ASIA-PACIFIC ENGAGEMENT

India's Asia-Pacific Engagement

Impulses and Imperatives

Edited by

AMAR NATH RAM

MANOHAR
2015

First published 2015

The responsibility for facts and opinions in this book rests exclusively with the authors and their interpretations do not necessarily reflect the views or the policy of the Indian Council of World Affairs, New Delhi.

ISBN 978-93-5098-080-4

Published by
Ajay Kumar Jain *for*
Manohar Publishers & Distributors
4753/23 Ansari Road, Daryaganj
New Delhi 110 002

Printed at
Salasar Imaging Systems
Delhi 110 035

To

the pioneers and visionaries of ancient India
and her extended eastern neighbourhood who inspired
succeeding generations to believe in our shared destiny.

Contents

Foreword

Over the years, there has been steady and substantial progress in the realization of the objectives and vision of our Look East Policy. Interaction with individual ASEAN member countries – the prime movers of the ASEAN totality, has developed very satisfactorily, with pragmatic emphasis on mutually beneficial cooperation in leading functional sectors. There is active leadership contact, supported by structured exchanges at Foreign Ministry and other expert levels. The parallel, overarching engagement with the ASEAN collective enables a qualitatively enhanced relationship reflected in the Dialogue partnership, now appropriately at Summit level. The FTA has stimulated trade growth and the expected parallel Agreement on investment would be a high point. Multimodal connectivity is an important part of the agenda, crucial not only because of the requirements relating to our Northeast, but also as a potential game changer on a large scale for both India and SEA. Also of note is the attention devoted to a complex of critical global challenges – economic, social, the environment, transnational terrorism, the all important maritime dimension as well as non-traditional security issues. There is a business-like prioritization of sectors taken up in the Dialogue mechanism. Significantly, defence related areas have acquired progressively greater focus in recent years – as indicated in our purposeful participation in ADMM+. Not least, the relationship has been enriched by lively exchanges in culture and the arts.

India's membership of ASEAN-driven regional fora, beginning with ARF and subsequently, ASEM, underlines ASEAN centrality to LEP; it has also prepared the way for closer engagement with the larger Asia Pacific region, which is the essence of the policy. The initial focus in the nineties on ASEAN was accompanied by renewed contact with countries in East Asia and Oceania. Our traditional relations with them should be seen in a new light, in the LEP frame-work. India's EAS membership is an important stage in the full realization of the LEP vision. This is reinforced by our involvement in Asia-Pacific – wide multilateral arrangements for Trade and investment, including the embryonic RCEP. Whether this or a variant presages an eventual Asian Economic Community or Common Market, is an open question, but the prospect should be kept alive. Of more immediate relevance are Asian affinities – rooted as they are in history and geography. LEP represents a rediscovery and reaffirmation. Nalanda II, recently inaugurated, reflects a regional consensus on this idea.

LEP should be seen holistically as one major element in our opening up to a larger extended neighbourhood, embracing not only the Asia-Pacific but West Asia, Central Asia and the IOR as well, regions which are again linked to us through history and geography. This spatial continuum which also includes our immediate neighbours in the SAARC region also brings home the great importance of and potential for connectivity.

Track 2/1.5 processes including those which involve Universities and think-tanks, e.g. CSCAP, Shangrila dialogue are playing an important role in bringing clarity to the discourse on these issues.

While the first steps were expeditious, LEP's progress thereafter has been gradual rather than spectacular. What matters is that key, relevant structures and mechanisms have been put in place. India is very much in the Asia-Pacific arena, and has gone beyond merely looking East, to purposefully engaging the East – in keeping with the much quoted exhortation. Moreover, the ground has been prepared for further growth. LEP has come of age, is a going concern and, indeed a historic endeavour.

While we rightly celebrate LEP's successes, a hard-headed evaluation is also essential. Progress – yes, but is it optimal? How substantive is the engagement? India is intrinsically a strategic player in the region – but how effective are we in this role? Has the promise and potential envisaged in the policy been fulfilled?

The imperative requirement for an effective foreign policy is adequate national strength – a composite of economic, political, defence, social, human resources, governance quality of life and other elements – translated into capabilities and competitiveness, brought to bear on specific external relationships and situations, it also demands openness to learning from best practices elsewhere, and to using strategic opportunities presented by the outside world so as to reinforce our own strenghts. Only by meeting these requirements can we build the substance and traction, as well as a compelling mutuality of stakes and commitments, which are essential for any stable and dynamic external relationship.

No doubt, there is ample awareness of and a vigorous effort to apply these home truths to the conduct of LEP. However, the record of missed opportunities, tardy execution of projects – especially infrastructure and connectivity, as well as insufficient progress on certain other items of cooperation, indicates that this effort is not optimal. Policies of our partner countries are a major factor in shaping relationships, but this does not diminish the need to examine and rectify our own shortcomings.

These considerations are crucial, because the state of progress in economic and related areas, to a large extent sets the tone for the overall relationship. The core lesson is that if LEP is to attain critical mass and cutting-edge effectiveness, and full credibility, it is essential that we mobilized our resources and requisite capabilities, and deploy them with focus to serve the needs of the policy.

Efficiency in economic and related sectors is an imperative but not sufficient condition for ensuring interests regarding the political and security aspects of a relationship. The latter demands its own mix of capabilities which need to be identified and cultivated. This is all the more essential because of the complex, emergent political and security challenges we face in the region, relating, above all, to the building of an inclusive security architecture, which would allow legitimate space for all, and provides a milieu for peaceful national development. This is vital to our interests. This task is facilitated by the inherent trend to multipolarity inspired by regionwide national resilience and economic success. ASEAN, is an example. At the same time we have to take into account, the asymmetrically large power of China. We should support the time effort to reconcile these trends, and at the same time continue to develop meaningful cooperative linkages within the region and beyond – bilateral and multilateral, along with CBMs and dialogue systems, even as we also build good fences. All these operations require mobilization of national strength and capabilities: this applies to cooperation and confidence building as much as to competition. This exercise has to be carried out realistically.

These imperatives would also be relevant to our responses to the political and security agendas of other countries in the region, and larger powers, as manifested in their proposals for regional, sub-regional groupings and coalitions – including the high-profile US enunciation of a pivot strategy in Asia. This is particularly so at the time when we are seeking to define our growing defence and security interface in the region.

In this context, the 'Indo-Pacific' paradigm significantly modifying the canonical 'Asia-Pacific', an idea authenticated by the interconnectedness of the Oceans, is of vital interest to us given our geo-strategic location. We should be active participants in its ongoing actualization, as indeed in shaping other similar strategic trends in the region.

Yet another challenge is working out our position on proposals for multilateral economic arrangements (trade and investment), put forward by countries in the region and by the US (TPP). This would require initiatives from us.

These processes – often conflicting – are growing at a quickening tempo. Hopefully, they will be harmonized, to some extent through the force 'of globalization and more specifically, of convergence'. A confident, pro-active approach can help strengthen this prospect. In its totality, this complex of political security economic and other issues makes for a dynamic transformation, worldwide, which is being played out in the Asia-Pacific region in particular. It would not be an exaggeration to say, that given this milieu, LEP is entering a critical new phase.

This is the setting for the present volume – a logical sequel to the 2012 compilation – also published under ICWA auspices, with the same editorship. As in the earlier book, the story is told through the reminiscences, detailed analytical comment and in-depth history, recorded by several of our highly competent diplomat-practitioners, who have been closely associated with the evolution of LEP at different stages, as well as eminent and very knowledgeable experts on strategy and foreign policy. This is a comprehensive work, which besides updating the narrative, breaks new ground, revisiting the perennial questions and addressing new ones, and also providing thought-provoking insights. The text makes the LEP saga come alive, recapitulating its successes and also candidly identifying inadequacies and remedies, charting the way ahead. The result is a book that is scholarly, rigorous and readable as well.

Reflection on this work confirms the sense that LEP is more than a Strategic Option; it is in fact, central to our foreign policy. Throughout the last two decades, our political leadership has clearly recognized this vital fact and has provided purposeful direction. A strong new impulse has now been given by the new government, beginning with intensive and wide ranging high-level contact with countries in the ASEAN region, East Asia and Oceania. It is imperative that this we sustain this momentum and build further on the foundations already laid.

We must thank all the contributors for sharing their knowledge and experience, and their dedicated quality effort. The editor, A.N. Ram is a distinguished colleague with close and continuous contact with LEP right from its inception down to the present – and widely respected for his experience and scholarship. I appreciate his energy and initiative in following up on the 2012 volume, with editing this exhaustive new compilation. We should be grateful to ICWA for their foresight in prioritizing this work in their research programme, and DG, Rajiv Bhatia for his keen personal interest. Appropriately, he has also had long professional contact with the region, great expertise and a feel for the subject.

I have no doubt that this volume will be well received and will help enlighten our public on the LEP.

New Delhi
September 2014

AMBASSADOR K. RAGHUNATH
Former Foreign Secretary,
Ministry of External Affairs
Government of India

Message

The focus of global politics has shifted towards the East. In the emerging geopolitical dynamics, India has a significant role to play. Initiated in 1992, India's Look East Policy has been lauded as one of her most successful initiatives in the post-Cold War world. While India's relations with the Southeast Asian countries are deep rooted in history, over the past two decades they have crossed several milestones in terms of engaging with the Southeast Asian countries and their flagship organization – ASEAN. The milestones include India's membership of ASEAN Regional Forum (ARF), Bay of Bengal Initiative for Multi-Sectoral Technical and Economic Cooperation (BIMSTEC), Mekong-Ganga Cooperation (MGC), East Asia Summit (EAS) and ADMM (ASEAN Defence Ministers Meeting) Plus. In 2012, the twenty-year old Indian-ASEAN relationship culminated into the launching of Strategic Partnership. Additionally, the finalization of India-ASEAN Free Trade Agreement (FTA) in goods in 2010 has opened new vistas for regional cooperation.

This aptly sets the stage for a first-hand account of the evolution of Look East Policy entitled 'India's Asia-Pacific Engagement-Impulses and Imperatives', which is a follow-up publication to our previous offering – *Two Decades of India's Look East Policy: Partnership for Peace, Progress and Prosperity.* The present volume covers a much wider horizon and underscores the subtle and significant changes in India's Look East Policy in the recent years.

We gratefully acknowledge the contribution of Ambassador A.N. Ram who conceptualized the idea of this book and led the project with incredible professionalism and creativity. We also thank all the contributors who have shared their perspectives on India's eastward engagement.

At ICWA, we have been consistently engaged in policy-oriented debates with a view to bringing out sharp and focused cutting-edge ideas on India's foreign policy and the country's role in world affairs. I hope the present volume will be a valuable addition to the existing knowledge on the subject.

New Delhi
20 August 2014

AMBASSADOR RAJIV K. BHATIA
Director-General,
Indian Council of World Affairs

Preface

This volume, essentially, is meant to be a sequel to the earlier compilation of essays titled *Two Decades of India's Look East Policy: Partnership for Peace, Progress and Prosperity* published by the Indian Council of World Affairs in 2012. The earlier volume was well received and found to be useful by scholars and students alike, leading to suggestions of bringing out a sequel, updating the earlier discourse, containing the views and impressions of practitioners who had helped shape the Look East Policy from the field and other opinion moulders who had meaningfully impacted the policy by providing significant inputs. The effort, in this volume, is to introduce an added perspective relating to the evolving Look East Policy, updating and assessing developments beyond the first two decades of the policy and looking into the future of India's growing and deepening engagement with the larger and rapidly changing geo-political space of the Asia-Pacific region, which some now have begun to describe as the Indo-Pacific. By including a few essays by non-practitioners who have significantly added value to the discourse on the evolving engagement, this volume seeks to present a broader and a more comprehensive discussion on this important foreign policy initiative which, now in its third decade, has become an integral, inseparable and irreversible part of our foreign policy objective in this complex region.

The essays in this compilation cover various aspects of our evolving engagement with the Asia-Pacific, going beyond the ASEAN geo-political space and the hitherto traditional areas of focus, namely, trade and commerce, investments, science and technology, tourism and culture and, to a limited extent, bi-lateral political exchange of views. The now enlarged dialogue, both at the bi-lateral and regional levels, includes strategic, security, defence, political, economic, commercial, cultural, science, technology, diaspora and other aspects of our rapidly growing and deepening institutionalized engagement which, importantly, now also seeks to derive strength and irreversibility from people-to-people relationships premised on the imperative of mutuality of interest, integration and interdependence. The essays, especially in the concluding section, seek to peep into the future and suggest a roadmap and the next steps for taking forward the needed policy initiatives in the coming crucial decades which could shape and define the evolving regional strategic and economic architecture and India's role and responsibility in it. The other essays, under different heads, seek to do the same.

However, I am acutely conscious that no work of this nature can ever hope to be complete in all respects: there are bound to be shortcomings and gaps which can only be addressed by more in-depth research and work by scholars. Notwithstanding, this volume attempts to complement, in a peripheral way, the work initiated in the earlier compilation of essays, mostly by practitioners who had implemented and helped formulate the policy from the headquarters of the Ministry of External Affairs. This effort, like the earlier one, does not claim to be a product of deep research or study, for that is not the intention. Its value addition, essentially, is derived from the unique and rich experience of the essay writers who provided policy inputs and meaningfully carried forward a new foreign policy initiative. By sharing their perspectives, insights, experiences and expertise, they have greatly influenced policy making in their spheres of competence. This compilation, like the earlier one, in that sense, can be said to be unique.

I am grateful to Shri Rajiv K. Bhatia, Director-General, Indian Council of World Affairs, for readily agreeing to sponsor, encourage and support the project to bring out this sequel to the earlier volume on the Look East Policy. I have greatly benefited from his wise counsel. Former Foreign Secretary and a key participant in the early years of the Look East Policy initiative, Ambassador K. Raghunath, in his substantive and illuminating Foreword, has clearly identified the issues, challenges, constraints, opportunities and prospects that surround India's deepening and expanding all-round ties with the region. Indeed, he has lucidly and clearly spelt out the contours of the discourse from India's perspective. My special thanks go to the very worthy contributors who, in spite of other competing demands on their time, unhesitatingly agreed to my request. The candour, depth and seriousness with which they have shared their insights and discussed the issues should be of immense value to scholars, researchers and students. I would also like to thank Shri N.K. Saxena, Deputy Director-General, Indian Council of World Affairs and Shri Pankaj

Jha, Director (Research), for their untiring assistance and support. Ms C. Lalpekhlui, Research Intern, Indian Council of World Affairs, has been of immense help in providing logistical support and checking the minutest details. But for the publishers, Manohar, this book, like the earlier volume, would not have seen the light of day. I thank them for their fullest cooperation. However, I alone am responsible for any failings, shortcomings or inadvertent slip-ups.

I hope that this volume will motivate scholars, students and experts to delve deeper into India's evolving engagement with the Asia-Pacific, now an irreversible plank of our foreign policy, and to research and write more comprehensively on this important facet of our engagement with our extended eastern neighbourhood. It is equally hoped that this compilation of essays will add value to the discourse on the subject and provide fresh ideas and perspectives into future policy formulation initiatives.

New Delhi
1 September 2014

AMAR NATH RAM
Editor

Introduction

AMAR NATH RAM

India's Look East Policy (LEP), initiated by former Prime Minister P.V. Narasimha Rao in 1992, arguably, has now entered a crucial phase in which, conceivably, it has the potential to catapult our bi-lateral and regional macro-level relations with the Asia-Pacific to new heights of mutuality of interest, cooperation, integration, opportunity and irreversibility. In the first two decades, from 1992 to approximately 2012, the process of integration with Southeast Asia and the Asia-Pacific can broadly be said to have passed through two distinct phases.

II

In the first phase, roughly from 1992 to 2002, the thrust of our LEP, many believe, was largely confined to trade and economic relations with Southeast Asia (ASEAN), with our bi-lateral relations with the now ten-member ASEAN grouping receiving priority and impetus. In the first years, they argue, there was little overt strategic or holistic content in this relationship. At the same time, at the regional level, our institutional links with ASEAN were growing rapidly from sectoral dialogue partnership in 1992 (in four sectors of trade, investment, tourism and science and technology) to comprehensive full-dialogue partnership (ASEAN + 1) in 1995, followed, in 2002, by summit-level dialogue and, later in 2012, to strategic partnership which brought us to a much higher level of cooperation in our now enlarged dialogue arrangements with the ASEAN. The mechanism of regular meetings of senior officials at the Secretary level (SOMs) ensured proper preparation, substance and monitoring. The dialogue, now expanded and intensified, covered issues beyond trade and economic links. In 1996 India was included as a full member of the ASEAN Regional Forum (ARF), an overarching security dialogue platform driven by the ASEAN countries and, subsequently, in other non-economic fora as well. Our participation in the ARF Eminent

Person's/Expert's Meetings, later, gave us another platform to project our point of view on issues of regional concern impacting on our own security interests. The delayed BIMSTEC Agreement for sub-regional cooperation amongst two ASEAN (Thailand and Myanmar) and, eventually, five South Asian countries (India, Sri Lanka, Bangladesh, Nepal and Bhutan), signed in December 1997; the Mekong-Ganga Cooperation (MGC) arrangement/corridor (November 2000); the Indian Ocean Rim Initiative (IOR–ARC, 1997) – in 2012 rechristened as the Indian Ocean Rim Association (IORA) whose membership comprises several ASEAN and Indo-Pacific countries; the Bangladesh, China, India and Myanmar (BCIM) cooperation initiative and other trans-Asian connectivity/corridor projects were conceived but needed to be given shape and operationalized purposefully. While India's unsuccessful bid to join the Asia-Pacific Economic Community (APEC) was blocked due mainly to a technical moratorium, India earlier did participate in some APEC Working Groups briefly. Several other multilateral economic and connectivity projects, however, remained moribund. At the cultural level, India has had inter-governmental agreements with most Southeast Asian countries, many of which were given a new institutional thrust during this phase with cultural exchanges gaining strength. There were several track II initiatives as well. Cooperation at the business and industry levels through the apex chambers of commerce, ASEAN-India Business Council (AIBC), ASEAN-India Economic Cooperation Committee (AIECC) and the Joint Business Council (JBC) mechanisms also, haltingly, began to gain autonomous momentum. Additionally, in 2000 at the track II level, India was admitted as a full member of the security dialogue forum Council for Security Cooperation in Asia-Pacific (CSCAP). The LEP also provided value addition to and reinforced our participation in the work of United Nations Economic and Social Commission for Asia-Pacific (UNESCAP), the Asian Development Bank (ADB) and, perhaps, other inter-governmental regional bodies, including under the aegis of ESCAP, such as the Asian Highway Project, Asian Rail Network, Asian Telecommunications Union (ATU) and the not-so-successful Asian Clearing Union (ACU).

III

In the second phase (from about 2002-12), as our bi-lateral and regional relations with ASEAN and the Asia-Pacific countries developed rapidly (several strategic dialogue, transnational connectivity, cultural and free trade agreements were initiated and entered into), we saw a clear consolidation and expansion of our links with the region to now encompass, among others, political, strategic, defence, economic, science and technology and cultural areas of cooperation. It is important to recall that Prime Minister P.V. Narasimha Rao's path-breaking visit to Thailand in 1993 (his first as prime minister to an ASEAN country), followed by visits to some other countries in the region, particularly his defining lecture at the Institute of Southeast Asian Studies (ISEAS) in Singapore in September 1994, had clearly spelt out the rationale, contours and purpose of our contemporary Asia-Pacific engagement. This early phase was also marked by a large number of high and expert level visits and greater institutional linkages, signifying the importance of the Asia-Pacific in our foreign policy calculus and the imperative and compulsion of ASEAN's own developing look west policy, said to have been mainly directed towards India. To address ASEAN's core sensitivity, Prime Minister Vajpayee, at the Bali Summit in 2003, formally endorsed ASEAN's Treaty of Amity and Cooperation (TAC) and its Zone of Peace, Friendship and Neutrality (ZOPFAN) declaration. It is at Bali that India entered into a framework agreement with ASEAN for a free trade agreement to be operationalized within a short time. Another notable initiative was to promote 'open skies' for freer aviation links between India and ASEAN to facilitate business, tourism, people-to-people contacts and pilgrimage. A declaration on cooperation in combating terrorism was also agreed upon. A year later, at the Laos Summit of 2004, India and ASEAN agreed to a Vision Document outlining the road map for future cooperation up to 2020. Prime Minister Vajpayee's bi-lateral meetings with ASEAN partners and summit interface were very productive, opening doors to new levels of all-encompassing partnership between India and ASEAN. These were notable developments, perhaps, making Bali a landmark summit for India-ASEAN relations.

IV

Many experts see the last years of phase I (approximately 1997-2001) as reflecting our inability to fully grasp the economic opportunities (e.g. TATA-SIA airline project, Singapore investments in technology and IT parks, Malaysian investments in infrastructure and the Thai CP group's FDI in certain aquaculture related areas), causing avoidable loss of foreign investments, trade and technology at that crucial time, even as Southeast Asia's interest in India was pushed somewhat to the back burner, due mainly to its own preoccupation with the economic crisis of 1997-8 and its fallout. This phase, unfortunately, was marked by poor, delayed or inadequate implementation of agreed goals. The slowdown in India's exports and investments in the ASEAN region also reflected this trend. Some in ASEAN even began to describe India as a reluctant partner and drew comparisons with China. A period of hiatus followed, also possibly because of India's Pokhran nuclear tests of 1998 which temporarily caused unease in some ASEAN quarters. However, importantly, the institutions and arrangements remained in place and regular interaction continued, notwithstanding these hiccups.

V

The summit-level dialogue with ASEAN, launched at the Phnom Penh Summit in 2002, effectively ended this temporary hiatus and reaffirmed ASEAN's recognition of India's emergence and importance as a significant player in the region which now many had begun to describe as the Indo-pacific. The fallout of Pokhran was behind us and ASEAN too, now recovered from the economic crisis of the late 1990s, seemed to be more assured. In some quarters, India's emergence as a strong regional military and economic power, indeed, was welcomed. The countries of the region now, generally, seemed to recognize that India is integral and, perhaps, indispensible to any new strategic or economic arrangement that may emerge in the rapidly evolving but still fluid scenario. Some scholars in Southeast and Northeast Asia had begun to see India as a potential benign balancing force in this region, without any territorial or other designs, with whom there were no significant political differences; indeed, the areas of strategic convergence and congruence had become self-evident to many, albeit not without reservations from others overawed by China's growing presence and influence in the region. It is noteworthy that today India has strategic dialogue arrangements with ASEAN and other major Asia-Pacific countries like Japan, China, South Korea and Australia, among others, and foreign office/expert-level consultative mechanisms with almost all the major countries of the region. India also has or is in the process of discussing potential free trade/comprehensive economic cooperation agreements/

arrangements with ASEAN (covering goods and services, signed in 2009); Bay of Bengal Initiative for Multi-Sectoral Technical and Economic Cooperation (BIMSTEC); Thailand, Singapore, Indonesia, Malaysia, Japan, China and South Korea, among others. At another level, India is a founder member of the UNESCAP-sponsored Bangkok Agreement, 1976 (now called the Asia-Pacific Trade Agreement); an important member of regional organizations/ arrangements like the ASEAN Economic Ministers + 1 Consultations, the East Asia Summit (EAS), ASEAN Post-Ministerial Conference (PMC) + 1, ASEAN Defence Ministers' Meetings + (ADMM PLUS), Expanded ASEAN Maritime Forum, Track 1½ Asian Cooperation for Development (ACD), the IORA and the Asia-Europe Meeting (ASEM). India is also an interested key participant in the proposed mega Regional Comprehensive Economic Partnership (RCEP), thought by some to be a counter to the US-sponsored Trans-Pacific Partnership (TPP), for which difficult negotiations have commenced; in 2012/13 India, in principle, agreed to upgrade her FTA with ASEAN to include in its enlarged ambit investments and services and set a new ambitious target of US $100 billion for bi-lateral trade turnover to be achieved by 2015. India's deep and abiding interest and pioneering efforts in conceptualizing and working towards an Asian Economic Community (AEC) – which she regards as an 'arc of advantage' – has been strongly reflected in track II conclaves as well. The Memorandum of Understanding (MOU) to set up the Nalanda University with the support and participation of several Asia-Pacific countries approved at the East Asia Summit in 2013 is a significant step in reviving ancient academic and cultural ties that India has enjoyed with her eastern neighbours (the Parliament of India had earlier approved the establishment of the revived Nalanda University in 2010). This phase can be said to characterize the consolidation of India's expanded and deepening links with the Asia-Pacific, going beyond the Southeast Asian geographical space and the predominant economic focus, signifying India's growing role and potential as an important partner in the region.

VI

Having acquired the necessary critical mass in the first two decades of our engagement, the relationship with the extended eastern neighbourhood, now in the third decade of our evolving LEP (from about 2012-22), will need to be further deepened, expanded, consolidated and given a new irreversible mutually self- reinforcing direction and content. Initial signals suggest that Prime Minister Modi's foreign policy will accord high priority to relations with the countries of the Asia-Pacific extended neighbourhood, especially Japan, ASEAN, China, South Korea and Australia. In strategic terms, our security and political links, clearly, will need to address our larger geo-strategic concerns, including domestic concerns, especially because of China's lengthening shadows over the entire region, causing both the ASEAN and the other regional countries palpable disquiet. The important issues of maritime security, trans-national crime, terrorism, cyber security, energy, environment and disaster management must become integral to this process, as also our commitment to democracy, disarmament, development and human rights. In political terms, a benign and friendly extended neighbourhood in the Asia-Pacific has to be an overriding objective, especially in the context of the recent tensions and the presence, in a new avatar, of extra-regional powers seeking to re-engage by carving out a new security architecture, not without serious implications for the region and India. In the economic space, we will need to ensure that our long-term interests intermesh and converge to provide us incremental opportunities, protection and an assured, stable and predictable environment in an increasingly competitive and interdependent scenario. In advancing our core competencies, we will need to prioritize and focus on optimizing all-encompassing socio-economic connectivities, supported by more than adequate and dependable infrastructure, cooperation, convergence and avoiding impediments. The greater the connectivity and intermeshing of our economic systems leading to mutual advantage, the sooner will economic links, hopefully now on 'auto pilot', drive the other parameters of enduring policy positively. This should also have the desired multiplier effect on our economic links. However, effective monitoring and time bound and full implementation of agreed decisions has to be ensured if the potential and promise are to be optimally realized.

VII

The imperatives of our domestic concerns and priorities, particularly in our northeast, peninsular India and in the Andaman Sea – and in the Indian Ocean and Indo-pacific space – will, above all, need to be increasingly factored into our LEP, as it acquires irreversibility and a more focused mutually supportive content. The socio-cultural dimension of our engagement should increasingly derive strength from people-to-people and institutional links in a region which the eminent scholar G. Coedes had aptly described as the 'Indianized' part of our extended eastern neighbourhood. In other words, we need a new, pro-active and a more imaginative road-map, anchored on the building blocks of the first two decades of LEP, for taking forward our important relations with this region in the next two decades and beyond.

VIII

The agenda for Indian diplomacy for the current decade (2012-22), at the strategic and political levels, first and foremost, will need to focus on issues of security, specially maritime security, cooperation in countering terrorism and trans-national crime, gradual and verifiable elimination of weapons of mass destruction, materials and technology, particularly in the hands of non-state actors and in promoting democracy, development, disarmament and human rights. The establishment of macro and bi-lateral level institutional and legal framework arrangements with the countries of the region to deal with issues like terrorism, extradition, money laundering, trafficking in humans, drugs and small arms, cooperation in energy, environment and disaster management, will inevitably help create and sustain a stable environment. Mechanisms for peaceful and non-intrusive dispute resolution and confidence building will also need to be worked out. The ARF, India-ASEAN Eminent Persons Group and the track II CSCAP have been engaged in some useful work in these areas which now need to be given formal shape.

IX

India will need to accord the highest priority to relations with her immediate ASEAN neighbour, Myanmar, with whom she not only shares a 1600-km long land boundary, but also a maritime boundary (and other close ASEAN neighbours, specially, Thailand and Indonesia). Relations with Myanmar are of vital importance in securing our political, strategic and security, including internal security, interests. Our northeast is linked to this region through history, tradition, custom, ethnicity, culture and economics. In that sense, Myanmar, perhaps, is one of our most important neighbours.

Thailand, in a sense, is our gateway to Southeast Asia and home to a large dynamic Indian diaspora, apart from being a country with very close traditional links with India. Indonesia is the largest ASEAN country with whom our economic and political links are important and growing. We also share a strategically important maritime boundary. Singapore, though a small nation, is influential beyond its size and has, from the very beginning, been highly supportive of India's close links with ASEAN, recognizing her potential to help enhance peace, prosperity, security and stability in this as yet vulnerable region. She is also a major economic and technology partner and host to an influential Indian diaspora. Malaysia, apart from Singapore, Thailand, Indonesia, Fiji and Myanmar (and now Australia and New Zealand) is host to a large Indian diaspora and is an important partner with enduring affinities, having excelled in infrastructure development. India has enjoyed a very special historical and cultural bond with the Cambodia, Laos, Myanmar and Vietnam (CLMV) countries and would like to strengthen these in the contemporary context. Japan's recent focus on strategic and all-round close relations with India is a significant and welcome development which, happily, is being fully reciprocated by India. This is all the more significant in the context of the evolving developments in the region; both are democracies sharing similar perspectives on regional issues; there are virtually no bi-lateral issues separating the two. Japan is also one of the most important sources of trade, investment, technology, tourism and economic assistance, on soft terms, to India. The Modi government's special focus on developing strategic relations with Japan is expected to give a further boost to Indo-Japan relations, making them an important plank of our foreign policy. The pacific space has been a somewhat neglected area of our diplomacy which needs a new look. Australia, in spite of ups and downs in our bi-lateral relations, has the potential of emerging as an important partner with whom we share much. We need to give a mutually beneficial content to this promising relationship. However, Australia, perhaps, now needs to show somewhat greater sensitivity to India's core concerns.

X

The implications of the rise of China, her increasing assertiveness and growing influence in the region, above all, will continue to occupy serious attention in our engagement. Sino-Indian bi-lateral relations will inevitably be a factor. Our diplomatic efforts, through dialogue and engagement, will have to neutralize and blunt those forces that seek to cause India discomfiture, even as we pursue a policy of friendship with all, including China. There should be no insurmountable reason for India and China not to be able to work together for our mutual benefit – and for the region's benefit – in this area as there is enough space for both to pursue and advance their legitimate interests. The Asia-Pacific and India will need to see some evidence of benign Chinese policies in this region and beyond. It appears that both China and India, under the new government in Delhi, are keen to give a new pragmatic thrust to our somewhat troubled relations with a view to furthering our bi-lateral relations, managing conflicts and providing stability in our extended neighbourhood, including in the Asia-Pacific. The beginning made augurs well, though we can at best be cautiously optimistic at this stage.

XI

India's non-traditional security threats such as terrorism, extremism, transnational crime, trafficking in drugs and small arms, natural disasters, environment, activities of non-state actors inimical to our interests, maritime and piracy related issues are closely interlinked to the ASEAN region and beyond. We need to evolve both institutional and legal mechanisms to jointly combat and counter these common threats. Our participation in regional security dialogue fora like ARF, ADMM+, an expanded ASEAN Maritime Forum and, at the track II level CSCAP, reinforcing our track I bi-lateral arrangements with the countries of the region, could go a long way in evolving regional and bi-lateral frameworks for meeting these challenges.

XII

At the economic and commercial levels, the ultimate goal and priority, no doubt, will have to be of integrating and intermeshing our economic policies, structures and systems with those of the Indo-Pacific and working towards a mutually reinforcing pan-Asian economic community, selectively and step by step harmonizing our approaches and policies based upon the free trade and comprehensive economic cooperation arrangements we have entered into. The vision of an 'arc of advantage' will need to be pro-actively pursued. Promoting time bound all-round regional connectivity and networking, particularly with our close neighbours, is integral to this process as it could act as a force multiplier. Such integration, connectivity and intermeshing is the best insurance against political vicissitudes, provided mutually agreed decisions are implemented in a strict time line. Good economics also makes good politics.

XIII

ASEAN, over the years, has acquired valuable experience and expertise in areas such as managing and carrying forward economic and social reforms, successfully dealing with financial upheavals, delivering socio-economic services at the grassroots level, population control, high-end and budget tourism, services and hospitality, agriculture and agro-industries, quality infrastructure and some high-technology applications in industry. Even as we promote and share our own unique and varied experience and expertise in areas of our core competency, particularly such as HRD, science and technology, information and cyber technology, communications, research and development, higher education, medicine, engineering and frontier areas of space, oceanography, bio-technology, ecology, energy and peaceful uses of nuclear science, we will consciously need to promote integration, intermeshing and interdependence through a process of two-way exchange of experience, best practices and expertise on a self-sustaining and enduring basis.

XIV

The implications of the increasing domination of China, in its economic dimension, will need to be constantly monitored and, if necessary, balanced through cooperation and dialogue with the concerned. The Asia-Pacific is a large enough space to accommodate the legitimate interests of all but will not accept domination of any single country. India's growing 'soft power' and our unique cultural links and diaspora, additionally, are our strengths and must be optimally used and factored into our policy. The recently set up ASEAN-India Eminent Persons Group (AIEPG) and tested fora like the India-ASEAN lectures, Delhi Dialogue, ASEAN Car Rally and networking of ASEAN-India Think Tanks (AINTT), no doubt, will strengthen this process. The ASEAN Centre recently set up at the Research and Information System for Developing Countries (RIS) and the proposed ASEAN-India Trade and Investment Centre could become catalysts in this process. The theme and the discussions at the recently concluded Delhi Dialogue VI, sponsored by the ICWA and the Ministry of External Affairs, focused on some of the areas covered in the preceding paragraphs and arrived at similar assessments and conclusions.

XV

One does not need a crystal ball to see that the Indo-Pacific landscape is undergoing a reconfiguration of the tenuous post-Cold War political equilibrium, strategic balance, military and maritime positioning and economic expansion and competition, giving rise to new concerns, paradigms, opportunities, arrangements and even strategic alliances. At the political level, some experts argue that ASEAN's centrality in the region may be getting somewhat diluted or reduced with ASEAN itself, often propelled by extra-regional considerations, looking beyond its boundaries for security, comfort and reassurance in a rapidly changing political environment. At the strategic level, US's 'pivot' to Asia or 'rebalance' policy, as it is called now, arguably largely in response to China's growing strength and influence and her increasing domination and assertiveness, has meant a new kind of imperative forcing the countries of the region to be sucked into a not-so-subtle rivalry with implications for future security and stability. The disputes in Northeast Asia, East and South China Sea, Southeast Asia and the Taiwan Straits, not to speak of other disputes involving a rising and a somewhat belligerent China, have aggravated uncertainties and anxieties, with both China and the US engaged in a diplomatic war of words and proxy confrontation to counter each other, often impacting on ASEAN's unity and the region's security reassurance. President Obama's recent pronouncements (April 2014) in Tokyo and Seoul demonstrate this attrition and reflect US compulsions arising out of the need to balance her security commitments to her allies. Are there shades of an undercurrent of the Cold War to be seen again in a new form?

XVI

At the economic level, the US proposed trans-pacific partnership (TPP), arguably meant to circumvent the fledging EAS process and the other existing/currently under discussion, regional arrangements (possibly not viewed with favour by the US), has created a new challenge for the Asia-Pacific countries forcing them to choose between their own agreements and arrangements and the new US-led partnership, which at present excludes China and some others. Even as negotiations to establish an ASEAN Economic Community (AEC) by 2015 are bogged down by differences, some ASEAN countries may have expressed their preference for the US-led initiative and some others, mulling their options, may not like to be left out. China too, apparently, is evaluating its strategic and economic options. India, obviously, has a vital stake in this evolving scenario and will need to take steps to safeguard and further her core regional interests, so far anchored on the hope of a proposed mega regional economic community (RCEP). India, under the new political leadership, seeks to rapidly build upon her strategic dialogue with the US and give much greater content and depth to her economic relations, making them self-sustaining and stand alone. Both China and India are considering their respective options and are yet to take a view on TPP which will, no doubt, depend upon fast moving regional dynamics and bi-lateral considerations. Meanwhile, sub-regional cooperation arrangements like BIMSTEC will need to be pro-actively pursued and every option explored.

XVII

As an emerging pillar of Asia-Pacific security, stability and prosperity, India will need to engage the other major regional powers (China, Japan, South Korea, Australia and ASEAN) to evolve and ensure a regional architecture that will safeguard our collective political, security, strategic and economic interests. We will also need to engage major extra-regional powers and explore new options (e.g. BRICS, India-China-Russia triangle, etc.) as a part of our strategic dialogue with them to ensure that our legitimate interests, concerns, role and responsibility are fully taken on board. We have to be an equal and integral stakeholder in shaping and managing the emerging strategic and economic architecture of the Indo-Pacific.

XVIII

This volume, essentially, is a somewhat delayed sequel to the ICWA's earlier book *Two Decades of India's Look East Policy: Partnership for Peace, Progress and Prosperity* (2012) which included essays, mostly by practitioners who had provided policy inputs from the headquarters of the Ministry of External Affairs, in the initial phase of our engagement with the Asia-Pacific. The present volume carries forward and updates the discussion of India's engagement and seeks to provide a somewhat different or additional perspective of the evolving story, mostly from the practitioners who had helped shape and provide inputs for the policy at the field level (our Missions in the region). It contains twenty essays from practitioners and experts, narrating with candour their own accounts, insights, contributions and perceptions of the evolving policy up to the present day and, in some cases, also peeping into the future and suggesting the possible next steps in this partnership. Like in the earlier volume, the essays in this collection have neither been 'edited' nor abridged; the contributors, hopefully, enjoyed full liberty to articulate their thoughts, criticize the constraints of working in the field and express frustrations at the inability of the system to always absorb and incorporate their well-considered suggestions and policy inputs. It is hoped that these essays will complement and supplement the material in the earlier volume and give the reader a fuller and a more complete up to date picture of this extraordinary policy and its evolution. Any failings or shortcomings in this compilation, however, are mine alone; I am conscious that any volume of this nature will understandably invite criticism and comments for what was not included or analysed. I hope that someday, a more complete and revealing story of India's engagement with the Indo-Pacific will be written. If this – and the earlier volume – succeed in creating a better awareness of the policy, the constraints, the missed opportunities and mistakes and generate a healthy discussion on the subject, the purpose, in large measure, would have been served.

PART I

India-ASEAN Partnership: Impulses and Imperatives for Integration

CHAPTER 1

India-ASEAN Summit Level Partnership and its Salience in the Evolving Architecture of the Region

SANJAY SINGH*

ASEAN-India Commemorative Summit held in New Delhi on 20 December 2012 was not only a celebration of twenty years of Dialogue Partnership and ten years of annual summits between ASEAN and India but also of our centuries-old civilizational links reflected today in our culture and custom, art and architecture and indeed in our way of life. This was the first time that leaders from all ten ASEAN countries were together with us in Delhi and this was indicative of the coming of age of a major component of our Look East Policy. The Vision Statement adopted by the Heads of State/Government at the commemorative summit declared that the partnership stands elevated to a *strategic partnership*.

Closer relations with countries of Association of South East Asian Nations (ASEAN), given their centrality in the evolving economic and political architecture of the region, was at the core of India's Look East Policy. Initiated in the early 1990s, this policy was a natural corollary to the economic reform agenda launched in 1991 and of Indian efforts towards globalization. It underlines the process of India reaching out and participating in the Asian resurgence, which is propelled by rapid economic growth.

Starting from a dialogue partnership initiated in 1992, ASEAN-India (A-I) relations have traversed a long distance and marked today by regular official, ministerial and summit level interactions. ASEAN and India have established a comprehensive agenda of cooperation

* Amb. Sanjay Singh, Former Secretary, Ministry of External Affairs and Ambassador of India to Vietnam.

and a wide-ranging framework to pursue it. The ASEAN-India Action Plan for 2010-15 lays priority on capacity building, sharing of expertise and bridging of institutions between ASEAN and India. Many of the cooperative projects under it are coming to fruition. We have 26 mechanisms for dialogue and cooperation, some at ministerial level, covering virtually every field of human endeavour. We have developed cooperative programmes to address common challenges of energy and food security, health, urbanization, environment, climate change and natural disasters, education and capacity building, S&T, etc., through support of mechanisms like the ASEAN-India Fund, the ASEAN-India Green Fund and the ASEAN-India S&T Fund. India is to soon set up a separate Mission to the ASEAN in Jakarta with a full-time resident Ambassador.

An important pillar of ASEAN-India Partnership is people-to-people engagement. The creation of a regime that facilitates our professionals and entrepreneurs to travel and work across our region is a work-in-progress. We have established exchange programmes for students, farmers, diplomats, media and parliamentarians. Our strategic communities interact through the annual Delhi Dialogue and the ASEAN India Network of Think Tanks. There is considerable support for the revival of the Nalanda University, a common heritage of India and Southeast Asia. India has also set up an ASEAN-India Centre in New Delhi to supplement these efforts towards cooperation. ASEAN-India trade has grown over ten times in the decade since 2002. This was given new impetus by the implementation of A-I FTA in Goods in 2011. ASEAN-India trade stood at 76 billion US dollars in 2012 and the target is 100 billion US dollars by 2015 and double that volume by 2022. Bilateral investments have also grown rapidly over the past decade and amount to more than 45 billion US dollars. A trade and investment partnership is being forged between Indian and ASEAN companies. The Federation of Indian Chambers of Commerce and Industry (FICCI) has revitalized the ASEAN-India Business Fair and Conclave, the ASEAN-India Business Council and is to set up an ASEAN-India Trade and Investment Centre. The signature of the ASEAN-India Free Trade Agreement on Services and Investments and its early implementation will complement the Agreement on Goods and bolster our economic partnership.

In this context, connectivity – physical, institutional, people-to-people, digital and by sea and air – will be vital in promoting a closer partnership between India and ASEAN. The ASEAN-India Car Rally symbolized how connectivity can link people, stimulate trade and generate prosperity across the region. The implementation of the India-Myanmar-Thailand Trilateral Highway would be an important step in this direction. In a later phase this highway is to be extended to Cambodia and Vietnam and also to branch out at Mandalay directly into Laos PDR and Vietnam. Further linkage of these highways with ports in ASEAN countries and their integration with models like Special Economic Zones is also envisaged. In particular the Mekong-India Economic Corridor study conducted by the Economic Research Institute for ASEAN and East Asia proposes the linking of corridors in the peninsular, and possibly the northeast regions of India with the East Asian region. Innovative ways of financing and executing these projects are required, which would also draw upon the expertise and resources of the private sector.

The Vision Statement adopted by the heads of state/government at the ASEAN-India Commemorative Summit held in Delhi in December 2012 derives from the comprehensive report of the 'eminent persons' group. This underlined that ASEAN and India share the vision of a peaceful, prosperous and resurgent Asia, contributing to global peace and security. ASEAN and India together create a region bound by age-old civilizational ties of around 1.8 billion people with a GDP of over US $3.8 trillion.

The success of the Commemorative Summit and the adoption of the Vision Statement was the result of strengthening engagement which has created a critical mass in ASEAN-India relations. In the two years that led up to this event there was increasing awareness of its importance and this gave the relationship significant impetus as it began to be increasingly factored into A-I interactions and bilateral ones with individual ASEAN countries.

The 13th AI-SOM held in New Delhi in March 2011 with Cambodia, the ASEAN coordinator, as co-chair concentrated on giving a push to various flagship projects. These are contained in the 82-point A-I Plan of Action for the period 2010-15 adopted in the Hanoi Summit in 2010 and financed by the 50 million US dollar ASEAN-India Cooperation Fund. A-I SOM's recommendations were endorsed in the A-I ministerial meeting held in Bali in July 2011.

The ASEAN-India Free Trade Agreement for Trade in Goods came into effect in all ASEAN member-states and India following its ratification by Cambodia on 1 August 2011 and trade grew by 41 per cent in 2011-12. At the 9th ASEAN-India Economic Ministers

Consultations held in August 2011 in Manado the ministers agreed to a structured private sector engagement in the five areas of pharmaceuticals, innovation and skills training, information technology, manufacturing and infrastructure. We also began direct consultations on deepening our linkages in the sector of medium- and small-scale industries.

The first ASEAN-India Meeting on Agriculture was held in October 2011, and the first meeting of the ASEAN-India Green Fund was held in Cambodia in October 2011. Implementation of several projects under the ASEAN-India Science and Technology Fund was initiated.

India expanded its programme of hosting students from ASEAN countries to 100 per annum in September 2011 and further to 250 per annum in 2012. The ASEAN-India Media Exchange Programme was institutionalized for a period of three years. Indian parliamentary delegation started participating as Observer in the ASEAN Inter-Parliamentary Assembly (AIPA) from 2010 and AIPA delegates visited India for the first time in 2012.

The 9th AI summit-level interaction that took place in Bali in November 2011 took stock of A-I interactions and provided guidance for the future. At this meeting the then Prime Minister Manmohan Singh invited the ASEAN leaders to the Commemorative Summit and their countries to participate in the intensive programme for the commemorative year in 2012, marking 20 years of the relationship.

The A-I Eminent Persons Group (AIEPG) which had been tasked to draft recommendations towards an ASEAN-India Vision 2020 document finalized its report in 2012 after holding the last two meeting in May 2012 and September 2012 in Kuala Lumpur and Kochi. The AIEPG had held its first meeting in Phnom Penh in August 2011 and the second in New Delhi in October the same year. The Delhi Dialogue in February 2012 had ministerial participation from most countries and began emerging as a major Track 1.5 dialogue focusing on regional issues. An ICCR-sponsored meeting on A-I civilizational contacts was held in Patna and an A-I artists camp in Darjeeling. ASEAN and India signed a unique MoU on Strengthening Tourism Cooperation in early 2012 and India has since notified the visa-on-arrival facility for seven ASEAN countries.

The 14th A-I SOM was held in Phnom Penh in May 2012 at which the elements of the Vision Statement were discussed. This was further discussed at the A-I Ministerial Meeting in July 2012. The task of drafting was then taken on in earnest to have it ready by the Commemorative Summit.

In 2012 discussions were initiated with ASEAN in the Land Transport Working Group and the Maritime Transport Working Group. The Trilateral Highway Task Force met in New Delhi and resolved to establish connectivity from Moreh in India to Mae Sot in Thailand by 2016. The first meeting between the ASEAN Connectivity Coordinating Committee and India took place in 2013. It has since been decided to establish a Working Group on Soft Infrastructure along the corridors of connectivity and discussions are to begin on an ASEAN-India Transit Transport Agreement with a view to completing it by 2015. A Maritime Transport Working Group is to be set up soon.

The meetings between our Ministers of Environment, New and Renewable Energy, Agriculture and Telecommunications were initiated during 2012, the commemorative year, taking the ministerial-level consultations between ASEAN and India to seven per year. The ASEAN-India Newsletter on Agriculture and Forestry was launched at the first A-I Agri-Expo in October 2012 and a meeting was organized between agricultural universities in the region.

The first meeting between the heads of space agencies of ASEAN and India held in Bengaluru in June 2012 agreed to enhance cooperation in application of space assets and science for mutual benefit. The project to establish a Satellite Tracking and Data Reception Station and Data Processing Facility in Vietnam and the upgrading of a Telemetry Tracking and Command Station in Indonesia will begin to see implementation in 2014.

At the 10th A-I Summit Meeting, which took place in Phnom Penh in November 2012 the leaders were handed over the AIEPG report. They also took cognizance of the strengthening of the partnership.

The two years preceding the Commemorative Summit were marked by heightened high-level bilateral interactions with ASEAN countries. The President of Indonesia Susilo Bambang Yudhoyono was the Chief Guest at the Republic Day celebrations in January 2011. We hosted two Thai prime ministers, Abhisit Vejjajiva in April 2011 and Yingluck Shinawatra as the Chief Guest at the Republic Day celebrations in January 2012. The Vietnamese President Truong Tan Sang visited India in October 2011. Prime Minister Manmohan Singh had earlier visited Hanoi in October 2010 for the Hanoi ASEAN

Summit. Prime Minister Manmohan Singh held bilateral meetings with the President of Indonesia Susilo Bambang Yudhoyono and the prime minister of Cambodia Hun Sen at the sides of the Bali Summit in November 2011. Prime Minister Manmohan Singh paid an official visit to Singapore on his way back from Bali. In May 2012 he made the first official visit to Myanmar by an Indian prime minister since 1987. We hosted the prime minister of Singapore Lee Hsien Loong in July 2012. At the Phnom Penh Summit in November 2012, Prime Minister Manmohan Singh held bilateral meetings with prime minister of Singapore Lee Hsien Loong, the president of Philippines Benigno Aquino and the Thai prime minister Yingluck Shinawatra. Prime Minister Najib Razak of Malaysia and Prime Minister Manmohan Singh had exchanged bilateral visits in 2010 in January and October respectively. At each meeting the ASEAN leaders invited India to enhance its engagement with ASEAN, describing India as a force for stability and progress and also sought greater bilateral engagement. The details are contained in the detailed joint statements issued after each high level bilateral engagement.

We held Joint Commission meetings with Malaysia (Kuala Lumpur, May 2011), Vietnam (Hanoi, September 2011), Thailand (New Delhi, December 2011), Singapore (New Delhi, May 2012) and Indonesia (New Delhi, July 2012) and held Foreign Office consultations with Vietnam (Hanoi, August 2012), Cambodia (Phnom Penh, November 2011), Brunei (Brunei, December 2011), Singapore (Singapore, March 2012), Malaysia (Kuala Lumpur, March 2012), and Laos (Vientiane, May 2012). At these meetings we gave concrete shape in terms of programmes to the vision of our leadership. Our ties with each of our ASEAN neighbours are multifaceted, marked by expanding trade and economic cooperation.

We also hosted the ministerial meeting of Mekong-Ganga Cooperation in September 2012 in Delhi marked by the completion of the building for the MGC Museum of Traditional Asian Textiles in Siem Reap. EAM participated in the ASEM (Asia Europe Meeting) Summit in Vientiane in November 2012. The institutionalization of the BIMSTEC mechanism was strengthened and work was completed towards finalizing the structure and set up of the BIMSTEC Secretariat in Dhaka.

ASEAN-India Commemorative Summit held in New Delhi on 20 December 2012 elevated the ASEAN-India relationship to a *strategic partnership*. It was a joyous event marked by a presidential banquet and a remarkable A-I fusion cultural performance involving troupes from all the 10 ASEAN countries and India. It was preceded a day earlier by the meeting of economic ministers held against the backdrop of a business conclave and A-I trade fair. At the meeting agreement was reached on the FTA on investment and services. The summit was also marked by the ceremonial flag down of the AI Car Rally in New Delhi at which besides the ASEAN leaders a large number of ASEAN students, senior editors, diplomats and farmers were also present emphasizing people-to-people connectivity. Earlier the A-I economic ministers along with leaders of our north-eastern states had welcomed the car rally at Guwahati underlining that ASEAN and India were geographically contiguous. The Indian naval ship *INS Sudarshini*, marked the commemorative year through a six-month expedition to nine ASEAN countries, drawing attention not only to our maritime links, but also to the economic potential of sea-based connectivity and contributed to strengthening naval links.

It was a natural corollary, therefore, for the Vision Statement adopted at the Commemorative Summit declared that the partnership stands elevated to a *strategic partnership*. In order to implement the Vision Statement adopted by the heads of state/government at the Commemorative Summit, ASEAN and India would need to:

1. Further strengthen relevant institutional mechanisms and broaden the network between government institutions, parliamentarians, business, scientists, think-tanks, media, youth and other stakeholders. These linkages exist but we need to make their interactions generate a self-driven momentum regarding frequency and regularity.
2. Promote defence and military exchanges and cooperation, and foster constructive dialogue and consultation on political and security issues.
3. Foster greater security cooperation and information sharing to address traditional and non-traditional security challenges, including transnational crimes, terrorism and drug trafficking.
4. Cooperate to promote maritime security and freedom of navigation, and the safety of sea lanes of communication for unfettered movement of trade. This would be furthered by the institution of a Track 1.5 dialogue.
5. Advance regional economic cooperation and engage in constructing the emerging regional economic architecture. Exchange

of views on the progress of RCEP on a regular basis would be mutually beneficial.

6. Early signature to the FTA on services and investments to realize fully the ASEAN-India Free Trade Area (FTA), will encourage business relations and achieve a target of $100 billion for ASEAN-India trade by 2015. To achieve this we need to encourage the setting up of regional value chains and promote PPP model and innovative financial mechanisms for infrastructural development.
7. Strengthen cooperation in the agriculture and energy sectors and the use of appropriate technologies towards ensuring long-term food and energy security. There should be special emphasis on rice production, a staple of the region, and on malaria eradication.
8. Work together towards overcoming challenges from climate change and natural disasters. India was among the first few countries to respond to the region's requirement after the Asian tsunami in 2004 as well as after the cyclone in Philippines in 2013.
9. Encourage the study, documentation and dissemination of knowledge about the civilizational links between ASEAN and India and preserve, protect and restore symbols and structures representing civilizational bonds between ASEAN and India.
10. Continue the special focus on the CLMV countries (Cambodia, Laos, Myanmar, Vietnam), especially through capacity building. A project to set up four IT centres in CLMV countries, supported by a resource centre located in India, has been finalized for implementation.
11. Enhance air, sea and land connectivity between ASEAN and India through ASEAN-India connectivity projects. The promotion of tourism to places of civilizational interest such as places associated with Lord Buddha's life is especially important.

This vision of multifaceted strengthening of the relationship derives from the trend of the last two decades and the potential that exists but its realization will require political will, resources, time and effort.

The ASEAN-India partnership subserves the basic objectives of the nations of the region: peace and stability, progress and prosperity. Naturally, this partnership is important because our histories are intertwined. Equally, our future is interlinked and a stable, secure and prosperous Indo-Pacific region is crucial for our own progress and prosperity. There is, therefore, mutual benefit in these aspects of our engagement.

With the accumulation of economic power in the region the global centre of gravity is shifting towards Asia. As a natural consequence of the redistribution of political and military power and of a major build up of arms and increasing military expenditures, friction between the rising powers of the region is likely to grow. The US-sponsored Asia-Pacific security order of the last three decades is coming under strain from the rise of China with a concomitant shock to the Asian order. This is manifested in boundary tensions, and disputes in the East and South China seas (SCS). It is therefore essential that the countries of the region come together to devise a regional architecture that promotes peace and stability and assists in the peaceful resolution of disputes. This path to regional peace and stability will require greater coordination, cooperation and integration among the nations of the region and their economies. ASEAN has shown the way for the entire region, building a regional mechanism of cooperation and consensus that has become a great force for peace and prosperity. It is also the glue for the economic and security structures and institutions that are emerging in the region. India fully supports ASEAN centrality and leadership as essential elements for the success of these forums.

The ASEAN-India engagement began with a strong economic emphasis, but it has also become increasingly strategic in its content given that they share values, have convergent world-views and similarities in approaches to the region. This engagement responds to our shared security challenges and supplements India's deepening bilateral security cooperation with ASEAN countries. As maritime nations, India and ASEAN nations are intensifying their engagement for maritime security and safety, for freedom of navigation and promotion of peaceful settlement of maritime disputes in accordance with international law. We are fostering regional cooperation in ensuring the security of the SLOCs and addressing non-traditional threats from piracy, terrorism, extremism, and narcotics. The growth of our political dialogue, the intensification of our consultations in regional forums, and the expansion of our defence and counter-terrorism cooperation has had a salutary effect on regional peace and stability.

The year 2011 was marked by the US pivot to Asia-Pacific

underlined by its joining the EAS mechanism and the participation of President Obama in the 6th EAS Summit in Bali in November 2011. Russia too became a member of the EAS mechanism. This mechanism was conceived to enhance regional understanding through engagement in the areas of education, health and pandemic issues, energy and environment, finance, disaster management, connectivity, economic integration – CEPEA (now RCEP, or Regional Comprehensive Economic Partnership). The developments in 2011 shifted the primary focus of the EAS process to issues of peace and stability. It brought to the fore divisive issues with the dispute in the SCS acquiring particular attention. In May 2012 for the first time, owing to differing perceptions on the SCS issue, the ASEAN ministerial meeting in Phnom Penh could not agree on a common statement and none was issued. The issue was larger than that of just the SCS but of how to deal with the 'rise of China' and its possible domination of the region. China, the largest economic partner of nearly all countries in the region, poses both a challenge and an opportunity. Leading ASEAN countries began an exercise in damage control and by the time of the 7th EAS Summit in November 2012 their differences were broadly papered over.

In this context the role of India which is perceived in the region as a benign power culturally linked to the region increases in import. There is no major issue between the ASEAN countries and India and we are not in competition. We add value to each other. While our emphasis is on economic development and connectivity the strategic dimension of the relationship is growing in importance. The strengthening A-I relationship, therefore, assumes greater salience in the region. ASEAN and India cooperate closely under the aegis of the ASEAN-centred political structures such as the EAS, the ARF, the ASEAN Defence Ministers Meeting ++ (ADMM++) and in the negotiations for the creation of a region wide free economic space through RCEP.

In the broader Asian region India has developed close economic partnership with Japan, Korea, China, Australia and New Zealand – countries with which we also cooperate under the aegis of the ASEAN-centred political structures such as the EAS, ARF and ADMM++. We have separately put in place institutional mechanisms for dialogue on political and strategic issues with each of these dialogue partners of ASEAN. We have entered into comprehensive economic partnerships with both Japan and the Republic of Korea. Both are important trade and investment partners. Japan is a major source of capital and technology for infrastructural development in India. Korean companies are today household names in India. China, our neighbour to the north, is our major trading partner. Our bilateral relationship with China includes elements of both cooperation and competition. India's ties with Australia today are strengthened by people-to-people contacts and expanding trade and cooperation in fields of energy and natural resources. The two countries share a similarity of views on the future direction of IORA. India is negotiating FTAs with both Australia and New Zealand. India has a multifaceted partnership with the US which has a major presence in the region. India and the US share a commitment to democratic values and the rule of law, and have become strong and durable partners.

In the region our emphasis has been on economic integration and connectivity and bringing to the table our considerable expertise on areas covered by the EAS. We have also worked to promote regional cooperation to meet non-traditional threats. India's role has been welcomed as a factor of peace and stability. At the 6th EAS Summit Prime Minister Manmohan Singh emphasized the need to work for the evolution of an open, balanced, inclusive and transparent regional architecture, which found a welcome echo from ASEAN countries and our other partners. India's counsel is welcomed and its voice is strengthened through its partnership with ASEAN countries.

ACKNOWLEDGEMENTS

1. Opening statement by prime minister at 11th ASEAN-India Summit in Brunei Darussalam, 10 October 2013.
2. Opening statement by prime minister at Plenary Session of India-ASEAN Commemorative Summit, 20 December 2012.
3. Opening remarks by prime minister at 10th India-ASEAN Summit, 19 November 2012.
4. Statement by prime minister at the 9th ASEAN-India Summit, 19 November 2011.
4. Vision statement – ASEAN-India Commemorative Summit, 20 December 2012.
5. Realizing the ASEAN-India Vision for Partnership and Prosperity – Translating the Vision Statement. Abstract of the presentation of Sanjay Singh at DDVI – IDSA, February 2014.

CHAPTER 2

Engaging East: A Personal Experience

LATHA REDDY*

While India's Look East Policy (LEP) existed from the early 1990s onwards, my own exposure to the intricate web of relationships between India and Southeast Asia, and with ASEAN and ASEAN-led mechanisms, began only in early 2007, when I was posted as India's Ambassador to Thailand.

Apart from the fact that I was physically in the heart of Southeast Asia, with Thailand being a key player in ASEAN, there were some interesting and fortuitous links to our LEP which immediately struck me. Firstly, Thailand was to take over as the rotating Chair of ASEAN from July 2008 to December 2009, as part of the switch-over to a calendar-year term for the chairmanship. This 18-month chairmanship was a key one and Thailand and its government remained focused on meetings and its role as Chair, both in preparations from early 2008 onwards, and during the actual chairmanship after July 2008.

Unfortunately for Thailand, 2008 and 2009 were years of great political turmoil. While in 2007 there was a period of relative stability under the military-led government established after the October 2006 coup which ousted the Thaksin-led government, after elections were held in early 2008, the situation became extremely volatile. There were four prime ministers within the space of a year, and with frequent 'yellow shirt' and 'red shirt' demonstrations taking over the streets of Bangkok and paralysing the functioning of the government, foreign policy implementation and the ASEAN agenda were among the casualties which resulted.

* Amb. Latha Reddy, Former Secretary, Ministry of External Affairs, Former Deputy National Security Adviser and Ambassador of India to Thailand.

While the intention of the Thai government and the ASEAN Secretariat was to hold two ASEAN/ASEAN+3/EAS Summits – one in late 2008 and one in late 2009 – this volatile environment led to many postponements, one violently aborted summit in April 2009, and only one ASEAN/ASEAN+3/EAS Summit being held in October 2009.

The remarkable thing was, however, the importance attached by Thailand to the success of their chairmanship of ASEAN and the related meetings. Even under siege, the Thai Foreign Ministry did do their utmost to hold the meetings on schedule, although the violence that disrupted the April 2009 summit was a huge disappointment and humiliation for the government.

We, at the Embassy, were deeply involved in all ASEAN matters. One of the reasons was that the Deputy Chief of Mission, Bhagwant Bishnoi, had just completed his tenure as JS (MER), dealing with all ASEAN matters, in the Ministry of External Affairs in Delhi before taking up his assignment in Bangkok in January 2007. The then Secretary (East), N. Ravi, continued to rely on his expertise, and, at his request, Bhagwant Bishnoi crafted many of the documents, and attended the January 2007 ASEAN and EAS summits in the Philippines. The Mission also benefitted greatly from Bhagwant Bishnoi's expertise, and he added real substance to our preparations for the subsequent ASEAN preparatory meetings at the senior officials levels in 2008 and 2009, as well as for the incomplete summit in April 2009, and the final successful summit chaired by Thailand in October 2009 at Hua Hin.

Another interesting area of India-ASEAN interaction was our relationship on trade and investment. The figures speak for themselves. In 1993 India's trade with ASEAN countries stood at just under US $3 billion, and by 2013 it had risen to US $70 billion. Much of the growth in the last few years has happened due to the conclusion of the India-ASEAN FTA in goods. Negotiations, which were highly technical, complex and protracted, had gone on for years, and we, at the Bangkok Embassy were involved in many of the discussions held in Thailand. The then Commerce Secretary G.K. Pillai, and his able team led by P.K. Dash, were frequent visitors. The team was joined by our Counsellor Tanmaya Lal, and at times by the DCM and myself, at the negotiating table. As G.K. Pillai observed on one occasion, we were really trying to negotiate 10 separate agreements as each ASEAN country had its own sensitivities and demands, and we were then trying to amalgamate them into one comprehensive agreement.

While the August 2009 signing of the India-ASEAN FTA in goods was trumpeted as a major milestone in India-ASEAN relations, in hindsight, the de-linking of the India-ASEAN FTA in trade and investment from the FTA in goods was perhaps not the best decision. For various reasons, negotiations on the trade and investment FTA have dragged on for years, and the process has been unduly delayed. Many analysts feel, and perhaps rightly so, that since the FTA in goods mainly benefited the ASEAN countries, once this was achieved, their interest in concluding the trade and investment FTA was lukewarm, as this latter agreement was seen as of greater benefit to India.

The unique experience we had at Pattaya when the ASEAN-India Summit and the East Asia Summit meetings were to be held in April 2009 is worth recounting. The Thais began by planning that the summit meetings would be held in Bangkok in October 2008 and we had made all the logistical arrangements.

These were, of course, hugely cumbersome arrangements as there were 16 HOS/HOG-led delegations attending, and a perpetual shortage of good hotel rooms and meeting venues. The Bangkok meetings were then cancelled due to the widespread protests in the city.

Fresh arrangements were then set up for holding the summits in December 2008 in Chiang Mai in northern Thailand. When the advance team from Delhi was actually in Bangkok, and preparing to depart for Chiang Mai the next day, we received the news on the night of 25 November, while at a dinner at the Embassy Residence, that Bangkok's Suvarnabhumi Airport had been shut down indefinitely by the 'yellow shirts'! The team, accompanied by the DCM and other officers, set off by train to Chiang Mai. The very next day, 26 November 2008, we received news of the massive terrorist attacks in Mumbai at the Taj and Oberoi hotels and the Chhatrapati Shivaji Railway Terminal.

The Embassy had to swing into action on both fronts and simultaneously deal with the fallout of the closure of the airport for eight days, which left over 10,000 Indians stranded in Thailand, and also run a 24/7 information service on the Mumbai attacks for panic-stricken Thais and local Indians who had family members and others in Mumbai. We were able to handle both situations successfully, and our Counsellor Tanmaya Lal received the S.K. Singh Award for his sterling work during this period.

But, to get back to the saga of the ASEAN summits in Thailand, once again the Chiang Mai Summit was cancelled, and the decision was then taken to hold the summits in April 2009 in Pattaya. Our prime minister was unable to attend the meetings for health reasons, and deputed the Commerce and Industry Minister, Shri Kamal Nath to attend the summit meetings in his place. The protestors – the 'red shirts' (pro-Thaksin) this time – were present around the venues in large numbers but the Thai government was confident they would not disrupt the proceedings. Most of the 16 HOS/HOG leaders had arrived in Pattaya and we, with some difficulty in negotiating our way through large crowds of protestors, received our minister who had arrived by a special flight at Uthapao Military Airport. We managed to bring him into the complex of hotels where most of the delegations were staying and where the meetings would be held.

The night before the summit meetings was relatively quiet and everything seemed to be on track. However, the morning TV news had reports of more massing of the red shirt protestors, and a group of rival protestors joining them, outside the entrances to the summit venue. I then received an urgent phone call from a journalist friend (Nirmal Ghosh of the *Straits Times*) who was at the site of the protests, warning me that things were getting out of control and that I should not allow Indian delegates and colleagues to move outside the hotel complex.

We had planned a briefing meeting with our minister and senior officers at 10 a.m., followed by the India-ASEAN Summit meeting to be co-chaired by the Thai prime minister Abhisit Vejjajiva and our minister. Later in the day the EAS Summit was to be held with all 16 leaders (the ASEAN 10, plus China, Japan, South Korea, India Australia, and New Zealand) participating.

We received an alert from the Thai protocol that there were likely to be some delays in our meetings and we continued with our internal meeting. Meanwhile, I was called by the Australian Ambassador who needed inputs on whether to advise his prime minister, who was in mid-flight over the Pacific, to turn back or to reach Pattaya as scheduled. I also heard from my New Zealand counterpart who was with his prime minister at Bangkok Airport, and wondering whether to bring him to Pattaya or hold him at Bangkok till the situation became clearer. It turned out that the UN Secretary General was also waiting at the Bangkok Airport, and so the two leaders finally held an impromptu bilateral meeting while waiting for news!

Meanwhile, the delays were becoming worrisome, when the minister was suddenly called to an urgent meeting with the Thai prime minister. All the leaders present, 11 in all, were there except for the Chinese, Japanese, Indonesian, Australian and New Zealand leaders who had not reached the venue. The Thai prime minister announced that as the protestors had entered the hotel compound, and in the interests of safety, the summit was being cancelled. He invited the leaders to join him at lunch while plans were put into place to evacuate them from the venue by helicopters and boats.

However, while the leaders were proceeding for lunch, the protestors actually broke into the hotel lobbies, and we were forced to secure our minister in his hotel suite and to await news for the evacuation drill to be followed. Eventually, leaders were evacuated by helicopters from the hotel rooftop. As the Thai prime minister and the foreign minister were speedily evacuated, the protestors quickly and peacefully dispersed, but the situation could have turned ugly as the protestors were baying for their blood.

We saw many of the Southeast Asian delegates visibly alarmed, with some women even weeping, as they had probably never been exposed to such scenes and protests. We Indians, being relatively hardened to chaos, were rather more philosophical in our reactions. In fact, our minister consoled the Thai prime minister by saying that 'we understand that in a democracy we have to sometimes bow to the will of the people'. The Thai prime minister told me at a subsequent meeting that these words of solidarity from an Indian leader had been a great comfort to him at a difficult time.

It took some time for the Thai government to recover from this catastrophe, and there was even talk of shifting the chairmanship and the venue of the Summit to another ASEAN country. But Thailand persisted and finally succeeded in hosting the summits in Hua Hin in October 2009. Our prime minister and delegation attended the summits. The meetings went off smoothly with the signing of the India-ASEAN FTA in goods coming for special mention and praise as an important forward step. The EAS had also endorsed the setting up of the Nalanda University in India, which enabled its subsequent creation as an international university.

The preceding section has largely dealt with India and ASEAN and the LEP in a regional context. But there were important lessons to be learnt from our bilateral interactions with Thailand as well. During my three years in Thailand, I received a remarkably consistent message from the Thai government, through the many changes in leadership with four prime ministers and six foreign ministers during this period. Whether it was the People's Power/Peu Thai (pro-Thaksin) party, the democrats, or even the military government which was in power, the message was the same – that Thailand valued its relationship with India and wanted to enhance our bilateral ties.

When our external affairs minister came to Thailand on a bilateral visit in September 2008, he met not only with the foreign minister and prime minister, but also had a rare audience with HM King Bhumibol Adulyadej, and a personal dinner was hosted in his honour by the Crown Princess Mahachakri Sirindhorn.

Prime Minister Surayud, heading the military government, paid a state visit to India in 2007, and Prime Minister Somchai attended the BIMSTEC Summit in India in 2008. Princess Mahachakri also paid five visits to India during the period 2007-9.

The Thai government very proudly organized and participated in several events in 2007 commemorating the 60th Anniversary of the establishment of bilateral relations between India and Thailand. They provided us with copies of the original letters exchanged between our governments even slightly prior to 15 August 1947, which formally established our diplomatic relationship. The Thai foreign ministry mounted a historic exhibition of rare photographs of dignitaries of both countries interacting during bilateral visits in both countries.

For the first time I understood how important India and Southeast Asian countries were to each other and how much value we should attach to these relationships. Not only the potential for trade and investment, but fundamental issues emerged – such as the need for India to project itself as a major Asian power; to engage more actively in this region; to use regional groupings strategically to position itself as a credible alternate power centre; and, finally, to act as a counter-balance to China's rising influence and assertiveness. We needed to build even stronger, lasting bilateral ties with countries in this region to reinforce our regional structures and to say that we were indeed 'Engaging East'.

It was this knowledge and conviction that I took back with me to India in December 2009 when I went back to take over as Secretary (East) in the MEA. While my brief included Central Asia and West Asia, the Southeast and East Asia regions, as well as the Pacific, remained a key interest area for me as I was a firm convert by then to our LEP and in fact to the need to truly engage in a more substantive manner with this region.

As Secretary (East) in the foreign ministry in Delhi, I was involved in two key decisions which I believed did strengthen our involvement with the region. The first was to create the post of JS(MER-ASEAN) so that there would be an officer at a senior level exclusively dealing with ASEAN, EAS, ASEM, ARF, BIMSTEC, MGC and other regional groupings. The second was to designate our Ambassador in Jakarta, Biren Nanda (an acknowledged expert on ASEAN and Southeast Asia), as our permanent representative to ASEAN. I am happy to see that this second step has been taken to its logical conclusion by creating a new and separate post of an Indian permanent representative (PR) to ASEAN, who will work exclusively on ASEAN and related groups and issues. And, by a happy coincidence, the new PR to ASEAN is the first JS(MER- ASEAN) to hold that post – Ambassador Suresh Reddy.

Simultaneously I concentrated on strengthening our bilateral relations with all the countries in the region by encouraging regular visits at all levels and strengthening institutional mechanisms, and initiatives such as the Delhi Dialogue (a Track 1.5 ASEAN annual conference supported by MEA, the Singapore government, and think tanks in India and ASEAN countries). The many high-level and other visits to and from Malaysia, Singapore, Indonesia, Australia, South Korea, Vietnam, Laos, Cambodia, and Thailand, have, I believe done a great deal to boost our bilateral and regional relationships.

Once again, where ASEAN was concerned, I was actively involved in the preparations for the next India-ASEAN Summit and the East Asia Summit to be held in October 2010 in Hanoi. Prime Minister Manmohan Singh led the delegation and I had the privilege of accompanying him as the Sherpa to both summits. One of the important announcements made by the prime minister at Hanoi was the invitation to all the assembled ASEAN leaders to attend a Special Commemorative ASEAN-India Summit to be held in India in 2012 to mark the 20th Anniversary of the ASEAN-India dialogue. The theme of this Commemorative Summit, which was held as planned in December 2012, was 'ASEAN-India Partnership for Peace and Shared Prosperity', and I believe this summit was the successful culmination of a long and sustained engagement with this region and this dynamic grouping over the last two decades.

At the Hanoi Summit, the whole character of the East Asia Summit, which till then was a leader-led and more informal grouping (compared to ASEAN itself and the ASEAN+3), suddenly began to be seen as an important potential security architecture mechanism in the region.

The catalyst in the process was the entry of US and Russia into the East Asia Summit. At Hanoi, Hillary Clinton, the then US Secretary of State made a bold and assertive statement formally announcing the US acceptance of the invitation to join the EAS, and its intention to make this forum a key player in regional security issues. The Russian foreign minister, Lavrov, made a more subtle but equally strong statement of Russia's intention to play a major role in Asia. With the entry of these two major powers, a tectonic shift in the EAS dynamic was visible. The introduction of regular ADMM+Defence Ministers Meetings, and the scrapping of the ASEAN+3 and the CEPEA (ASEAN+6) trade pacts and the adoption of the much broader RCEP, were clear indicators that the new and revitalized EAS grouping, with its new entrants, will play a different role in the future. In some ways, this benefits India, as now China will no longer be an unchallenged, privileged, and dominant partner in the ASEAN equations.

With a flexible approach and a long-term vision, and using its strategic ties with the US, Russia, Japan, Korea, and Australia, India can craft a new role for itself in this important region.

This does not purport to be a comprehensive history of the LEP or of India's role in this region. This is simply a recounting of some of the highlights of my own discovery of India's role in Asia over the period 2007 to 2012, and the potential benefits for India in Engaging East.

CHAPTER 3

Bridging the Hiatus of History: India's Look East Policy

PINAK RANJAN CHAKRAVARTY*

At a lecture in Singapore in September 1994, then Indian Prime Minister Narasimha Rao adumbrated a vision of building closer relations with the countries of the Association of Southeast Asian Nations or ASEAN. He did not call it India's Look East Policy (LEP), a name that was tagged on later as that vision was translated into action.

Prime Minister Rao's appeal for closer relations with ASEAN nations was not the first time that India had reached out to East and Southeast Asia in India's long history. India's historical tryst with East and Southeast Asia was via maritime routes. Over a thousand years, before the Muslim Sultanates were established in Delhi, Indian ports along the Coromandal Coast and the coast of Orissa and Bengal were trading with East and Southeast Asian ports in Malaya, Sumatra, Java, Borneo, the Maluccus (Moluku) and China. Cultural and religious influence went along with trade. India's Look East began, most likely, in ancient Kalinga (modern Odisha) which pioneered maritime exchanges to lands east of India before the beginning of the Christian era. Odisha's folklore has plenty of references to merchants sailing to this region, the most famous of which is the annual festival of *Bali jatra* or Voyage to Bali, the Indonesian island that is still predominantly (95 per cent) Hindu, in the largest Muslim country in the world. The powerful Chola Empire in southern India in the eleventh and twelfth centuries inherited this strong maritime

*Amb. Pinak Ranjan Chakravarty, Former Secretary, Ministry of External Affairs, Former High Commissioner of India to Bangladesh and Ambassador to Thailand.

tradition and legacy of the Kalingas. Over several centuries on interaction with India, much of Asia had embraced Sanatana Dharma and Buddhism. Indelible remains of Indian culture remain to this day. Hinduism, Buddhism, Sanskrit, Pali, the *Ramayana* and the *Mahabharata* are living examples of this influence. Angkor Wat in the Cambodian town of Siem Riep; Borobudur and Prambanen in Jog Jakarta, Indonesia; the temples of the Champa Kingdom in Vietnam are world heritage sites, inspired by the philosophy, art, architecture and sculpture that flourished since the pre-Christian era and peaking during the Gupta empire in northern India. Even in Catholic Philippines, there is a version of the *Ramayana* which is performed as a ballet. The King of Thailand Bhumibol Adulyadej or in Sanskrit 'Bhoomi Bal Atulya Tej' is also known as King Rama XI. Bangkok's international airport is called Suvarnabhumi (Golden land). This harks back to a Buddhist legend in the Sri Lankan *Theraveda* (*Sthaviravada* in Sanskrit) chronicles. The national airline of Indonesia is called Garuda, the mythical bird from the *Ramayana*. The establishment of the Muslim Sultanates in Delhi did not cut off Indian influence which continued in Southeast Asia even after the Cholas. Muslim merchants, Islamic scholars and Sufi mystics, travelling from India, continued the maritime trade and helped spread Islam in the Malayan peninsula, Sumatra and Java. India's strategic outreach into East and Southeast Asia is unique in world history, though some Western scholars claim that India did not have a tradition of coherent strategic thinking.

Western imperialism and colonial rule in Asia undermined India's intimate links with East and Southeast Asia as Europeans took over the maritime trading routes by force. The advent of indentured Indian labour into Malaya, Singapore and Indonesia, working on rubber and sugar plantations of the British and the Dutch colonizers, began with British colonial rule in India. This also left its mark on the image of India in these countries, different from what Southeast Asia had seen more than a millennium before. The Indians who went as indentured labourers were escaping abject poverty. India by then was a subject nation, suffering under debilitating colonial British rule that had impoverished and devastated India's economy. The indentured Indian labourers were not from the India, the peoples and kingdoms in these countries had known in the past, whose religion, art, sculpture and architecture once inspired them. Consequently, their impact on the societies in which they were supplanted was largely negative, since they came to seen as instruments of their exploitative colonial rulers.

The post-Second World War era and the beginning of the Cold War placed independent India at odds with countries of Southeast Asia who also became independent of colonial rule in the late 1940s, 1950s and 1960s. India's multifarious challenges of governance and a policy of economic insularity distanced her from the countries of the Southeast Asia. British colonial rule had linked India's economy to the West and India's economic engagement with the Southeast Asian nations decayed over time. The policy of non-alignment led India to look at the Southeast Asian countries increasingly through the prism of the Cold War. As allies of the USA, India viewed them as Western lackeys. Prime Minister Nehru's efforts at the Asian Relations and the Bandung conferences for an Asian consensus were dealt a grievous blow by the 1962 India-China war. India's image plummeted. The historical hiatus and the Cold War led to cool relations between India and countries of this region. This situation continued for almost four decades till the beginning of the 1990s.

Prime Minister Rao's statement in 1994 in Singapore is justifiably regarded as a breakout moment and as a tectonic shift in Indian diplomacy, comparable to the significance of non-alignment in the Cold War era. It was India's response to a unipolar world, marked by the end of the Cold War and the demise of the USSR. The economic reforms, initiated in 1991, started the process of integration of the Indian economy with the global economy. India's search for expanding global markets for Indian products, services and investments had begun. The LEP was a logical outcome of India's search for expanding trade and investment with the dynamic ASEAN economies, as well as the pessimistic outlook for regional integration of South Asia through SAARC.

In the backdrop of the rise of China as a booming economy and a manufacturing superpower, there were also compelling factors that made ASEAN reach out to India. The need to balance China's rapid rise by inviting and facilitating a stronger engagement of India and others with the region was a strong motivation. Also, two years before the Singapore lecture, India had shed her old Myanmar policy and started to engage pragmatically with the military junta. Moreover, since 1992, India had joined a limited Sectoral Dialogue with ASEAN. Thus Narasimha Rao's course correction in India's foreign policy was visionary but also a cautious move, consistent with incremental moves after ensuring that some building blocks were in place.

Though the immediate focus was on Southeast Asia, specifically the ASEAN, over time, the scope of LEP has come to encompass a much wider and interlinked region: Southeast, East and South Asia. At the sub-ASEAN level, there are institutions such as the Bay of Bengal Initiative for Multi-Sectoral Technological and Economic Cooperation (BIMSTEC) and Mekong-Ganga Cooperation (MGC). They link select countries of South Asia with select countries of Southeast Asia, with India enjoying an important position in both. Whether these institutions can optimize their potential is doubtful.

The LEP operates at the bilateral, sub-regional, regional and extra-regional levels. The core of India-Southeast/East Asia relationship is the India-ASEAN equation. A variety of institutions are now operational for holding regular dialogue. The annual summit is the highest body. Separately, India is also a member of ASEAN Regional Forum (ARF) and ASEAN Defence Ministers Meeting (ADMM)+8 where the focus is on security, defence and strategic issues.

The LEP's journey has been somewhat slow, but the following milestones have been reached:

- Full Dialogue partnership with ASEAN, India-ASEAN Summit mechanism, founder membership in the East Asia Summit (EAS), Free Trade Area (FTA) in goods, etc., all happening over 20 years. One reason for this gradual progress is that ASEAN itself has been in an evolutionary mode, triggering and reacting to movements towards an even larger Asian community, the first step of which was the EAS.
- India can justifiably claim that 'visible progress' has been achieved in attaining this goal.
- Similarly, on the foreign policy front, while LEP has delivered substantially and its success has raised expectations or highlighted problems which were earlier suppressed. India's trade with ASEAN has galloped ahead, air connectivity to Southeast Asia has exploded with growth of tourism especially between Singapore, Thailand and Malaysia and investment has made impressive strides in construction and infrastructure, coal, palm oil and automotives.

Over the years, India-ASEAN dialogue and cooperation have transcended functional areas, extending quite deeply into areas of political, security and defence cooperation. This has resulted in the two sides working closely on a range of international and regional issues including UN reforms, global economic crisis, climate change, maritime security and future of community-building in Asia as well as on issues of national concern such as terrorism. This is a wide area covering cooperation in diverse fields such as civil aviation, transport and infrastructure, small and medium enterprises (SMEs), science and technology, human resource development and people-to-people contacts. This cooperation has been developing quite well through the implementation of the Plan of Action for the Partnership for Peace, Progress and Prosperity adopted in 2004. The historical maritime connection with Southeast Asia reminds us today that a major share of world trade goes through the straits of Malacca. With the rise of piracy on the high seas, security concerns are naturally high on the agenda. Rampant piracy has been controlled and the India Navy has played an important role in this endeavour. For many years we have been conducting regular maritime exercises known as 'Milan', with Thailand, Singapore, Malaysia and Indonesia. India's strategic interest in the Indian Ocean and the Indo-Pacific arena is to keep trade and commerce open, safe and inclusive. The security dimension of the LEP developed in tandem with economic engagement and was a logical corollary of this growing engagement.

Within economic cooperation, trade and investment are two important pillars. Trade has shown a steady growth, going up from $2.9 billion in 1993 to $12 billion in 2003, at an annual growth rate of 11 per cent. In 2008, the value of bilateral trade was over $47 billion. Of this, ASEAN's imports from India amounted to $17.4 billion and exports to India were valued at $30 billion. In 2010, India signed the FTA with ASEAN; the value of two-way trade was about $50 billion. Trade has increased from $4 billion in the early 1990s to nearly $70 billion in 2013. The goal is to boost trade to US $100 billion. When eventually a full-fledged FTA is established with ASEAN, it will be one of the world's largest markets, of 1.8 billion consumers with a combined GDP of $2.8 trillion. At present, the two sides are engaged in negotiations of agreements for trade in services and investment. Our LEP, moving ahead on the two pillars of India's relations with ASEAN and with the larger community EAS, needs to be put on a path characterized by increased stress on implementation. Unfortunately popular perception seems to be strengthening that top leaders, meeting every year amidst drama and diplomatic glamour, end up making lofty declarations and signing new agreements which, however, do not really mean much to ordinary people. Overall, there is growing debate about FTAs, generated by the fact that India's exports have not grown to the extent its imports have grown from ASEAN and other LEP focus countries.

India's LEP has, thus, been consistent and bipartisan, though many would argue that implementation has been slow. While the LEP started by addressing only the 10 ASEAN member-countries, after we joined the EAS in 2005, the nomenclature was used to cover relations with China, Japan, Korea, Australia and New Zealand, i.e. East Asia beyond ASEAN. Last year, the USA and Russia joined the EAS. But to allay apprehensions among the smaller ASEAN countries of being overtaken by China (or India or any other big country), India has assured ASEAN that it will remain in the 'driver's seat' of EAS. Next only to the G-20 (and of course the UNSC), EAS is the most important forum for deliberation on development and security issues in the world's most dynamic region, the Indo-Pacific.

Beyond ASEAN, the EAS has emerged as the larger institution, with ASEAN as its driver and hub. It includes not only ASEAN member-states but also China, Japan, and South Korea as well as India, Australia and New Zealand. This institution now includes the USA and Russia as well. Thus India has to nurture bilateral relations with ASEAN countries and others, deepen cooperation with institutions such as BIMSTEC, ASEAN and EAS and to craft strategic understandings with major powers such as China, Russia and the USA on the future of Asia. The architecture of Southeast and East Asian relationships has become complex and so has the evolving architecture of relations between India and countries in these regions. Whether EAS will someday pave the way for the formation of East Asian Community (EAC) or Asian Economic Community (AEC) or eventually even to Asian Community (AC) remains to be seen. Besides, India is a member of Asia-Europe Meeting (ASEM) and is also interested in joining Asia-Pacific Economic Cooperation (APEC).

The LEP has domestic implications on the development of India's northeast region and the Indian economy in general. In the context of cross-border transformation in the northeastern region of India physical connectivity is a very important component of the LEP. The India-Myanmar-Thailand trilateral highway is a game-changer to connect India's northeast with East Asia. This 1,360-km long highway would establish seamless territorial connectivity when it is completed by 2016. It is a challenging task which requires substantial financial outlays with matching political commitment from all stakeholders. India is a party to the ambitious trans-Asian railway project. Myanmar is not yet linked by railway to India or Thailand. The difficult hilly terrain would require major investments. A 180-km segment from Assam to Moreh via Imphal is under construction and the pace of work needs to be speeded up. Without adequate cross-border connectivity, it would be very difficult for our northeastern states to reap the benefit of LEP.

Because of security concerns, the only infrastructure projects in the northeast so far have been undertaken by government's own agencies. While the Moreh-Tamu-Kalemayo road has been completed, other projects like the India-Myanmar-Thailand trilateral highway, Kaladan multi-modal project, Tamanthi hydroelectric project, etc., are facing delays due to political, security and financial problems. Some projects, such as the Stilwell Road to Kunming, China, are stuck in controversy as no clear policy line exists about whether a road to China will be helpful for India's trade or harmful for India's security. Partnerships with the Southeast Asian countries such as Thailand, Indonesia, Malaysia and Singapore can generate healthy competitive impulses to get some of these projects moving. In this task governments of the northeastern states could consider formation of a special council to speed up implementation of infrastructure projects and other related issues that have direct bearing on the economies of the northeastern region as a whole. A laser-like focus on implementation will be the key to the future success of the LEP and the northeastern states reaping the benefit of its success.

The BCIM project, which has been the subject of discussions and debates for more than a decade among scholars from the four countries, finally received official support earlier this year when India and China agreed to push it forward. Representatives from the four nations met in Kunming to draw up a specific timetable on taking forward the need to quickly improve physical connectivity in the region. It was agreed that the BCIM connectivity corridor will run from Kunming to Kolkata, linking Mandalay in Myanmar as well as Dhaka and Chittagong in Bangladesh. The plan would 'advance multi-modal connectivity, harness the economic complementarities, promote investment and trade and facilitate people-to-people contacts', the four nations said in a statement, after a meeting of the Joint Study Group. The Chinese have appeared to take the lead in pushing forward the corridor which they want to promote as a platform to not only boost strategic ties with India, but also as a means to inject vitality into its landlocked southwestern provinces. As a first step, the four countries have agreed to identify realistic and achievable infrastructure projects to boost physical connectivity. Each country will come up with a joint study report proposing concrete projects and financing modalities. Ambitious proposals that include developing multi-modal transport such as road, rail, waterways and airways, joint power projects and telecommunication networks have been mooted. A first ever BCIM car rally between Kolkata and Kunming took place successfully in early 2013. The corridor is likely to follow the rough route of the rally, which served to highlight the inconsistent road conditions, especially in parts of Myanmar. Security concerns in parts of Myanmar remain an obstacle.

The investment climate in Myanmar seems to have improved with a more democratic regime in that country. Trade at the border town of Moreh is opening up and smuggling may soon come down, improving revenue and living conditions in our northeastern states. Myanmar is already India's chief source of imported pulses. The country is today rethinking its policy towards ethnic groups and a second Panglong Conference has been proposed by Aung San Suu kyi. This could be a very important development for peace and to help it along we should stay closely engaged with Myanmar. The Rohingya issue is a problem that Mynamar has to deal with pragmatically and find practical solutions.

There are some imponderables impacting on the future of the LEP. China's assertive behaviour in the South China Sea, where it is embroiled in disputes with almost all littoral nations, has peaked recently, with the stand-off between China and Vietnam over oil exploration attempts by China at a site which is claimed by Vietnam as falling within its Exclusive Economic Zone (EEZ). Chinese moves have raised the ante and disputes and conflict brewing in the South China Sea are worrying for all countries. India is encouraging all claimants to the disputed islands to maintain peace and find a solution within the UN's Law of the Seas and ASEAN's Code of Conduct.

With the historic visit of the Emperor and Empress of Japan to India, our LEP has to move into overdrive with respect to Japan, the third largest economy and a technological power which is already playing a transformational role in building infrastructure in India (Delhi Metro and the Delhi-Mumbai industrial corridor). Security relations are also growing and India and Japan are on the verge of reaching an agreement on a civil nuclear agreement. Prime Minister Abe of Japan was the Chief Guest for the Republic Day celebrations in January 2014. Undeniably, Japan is moving centre stage in our LEP and with Prime Minister Narendra Modi leading a new government in India, Japan is likely to become a key partner in India's

LEP. Defence cooperation with Japan is likely to receive a boost after Japan has decided to tweak its pacifist constitution and set the legal framework for security cooperation with other countries.

The Republic of Korea (ROK) has also acquired a crucial profile in our LEP. ROK has steadily invested in sectors like automobiles, white goods, electronics and mining, making a mark in the manufacturing sector. From the geo-strategic point of view, Vietnam is another pivot in India's LEP. India will have to nurture these three crucial relationships because of the added dimension of security while building a web of relationships with major countries, including China which is increasingly taking the lead in initiating moves for a larger economic and security architecture in Asia. China's holding the 60th anniversary of the Panchsheel, its proposal to set up an Asian Investment and Infrastructure Bank and its initiative in BRICS, all point towards a long-term approach towards an architecture in the Indo-Pacific region, crafted with China's desire to play the hegemon in Asia. For India different strands of the web of relationships and the strength of each strand will define India-China interaction.

It took a crisis to create the opportunity for India to embark on the LEP. Faced with multiple problems, economic and political, India adopted two parallel new paths – a domestic policy path of economic liberalization and the external policy path of LEP. These two choices have transformed India's economy and foreign policy in the past 20 years. LEP had a strategic objective and an economic one. With the passing of the 'unipolar' moment and the gradual shift to a multi-polar world, when shifting and short-term cooperation rather than long-term alliances have become the norm, the LEP has acquired great relevance. It has acquired a profile that makes it a pillar of India's foreign policy, competing with our South Asia policy and our policy towards the USA, Russia, China, Japan, the European Union and other emerging economies. The LEP is now firmly embedded in India's foreign policy and provides the necessary space for India to play its legitimate role as an emerging power.

As the new government settles in, a top foreign policy priority will be for India to further consolidate its LEP. Prime Minister Modi will look towards Asia first, having visited several Asian countries as chief minister of Gujarat. This will give greater heft to India's Look East Policy.

PART II

Strategic and Political Relations: Prospects and Limitations

CHAPTER 4

Unfolding of the Look East Policy: A Personal Memoir from Field Outposts

RANJIT GUPTA*

This is not a treatise about the Look East Policy (LEP) or a paper about how the policy was formulated. It is not about India's relations with ASEAN and countries of the Asia-Pacific. An earlier book, *Two Decades of India's Look East Policy*, edited by Ambassador A.N. Ram and other chapters in this book cover all this brilliantly. This essay is a factual account of my experiences and perceptions in the context of the title, which is what Ambassador Ram asked me to write about.

INTRODUCTION

By the end of the Cold War India was politically isolated, on the verge of economic collapse and had reached the lowest point in terms of influence and standing in global affairs since its independence. On 21 June 1991 P.V. Narasimha Rao became India's prime minister and with his stewardship of the nation and in particular of its foreign policy began the process of India's recovery and India has been on the ascendant ever since. With the initiation of economic liberalization and reforms, India began its transition from the earlier national consensus on building a socialist society towards a new consensus on building a modern, free market one. This heralded the era of seeking to integrate the Indian economy with the global economy. This also resulted in a new emphasis on economic issues in the making of foreign policy. Another important transition was the shift from according priority to supporting 'Third World' causes to the

* Amb. Ranjit Gupta, Former Ambassador of India to Thailand.

promotion of its own national interest; from abstract idealism to national interest oriented pragmatism. Anti-imperialism had been at the heart of India's struggle for decolonization which had led to anti-Westernism becoming ingrained in the national political psyche; a significant dilution of this traditional anti-Western mode of thinking as a natural reaction to events was the third important transition. I had been witness to these changes vis-à-vis West Asia too, in Oman. India's conscious and deliberate high profile post-Cold War re-engagement with Southeast Asia – dubbed the 'LEP' – was one of the most significant manifestations of this reorientation. I feel highly privileged to have been a participant in and witness to, at very close quarters, the unfolding of the LEP as India's Ambassador to Thailand from January 1994 to November 1997.

This was not only my first posting east of India but the first time that I was even travelling east of India. I had very superficial knowledge of India's relationships in and with the region and the nature of regional politics. Since I had only two weeks or so in Delhi between handing over charge in Muscat where I had been India's Ambassador to Oman and taking over charge of my post in Bangkok I did not have the advantage of the guidance of the prime minister or the minister for external affairs as meetings with them were not arranged; nor with the then vice-president, who had been a former Ambassador to Thailand. Mani Dixit was retiring as Foreign Secretary at the end of January and Kris Srinivisan was going to take over and therefore neither had time for any detailed briefing; the prospective Secretary East felt that he was not in a position to provide any meaningful briefing. The Joint Secretary of the Southern Division did his best but the briefing was related primarily to bilateral relations, with India's Sectoral Partnership with ASEAN only tangentially mentioned, presumably because I was going to Bangkok and not Jakarta, where ASEAN headquarters were located. The really meaningful briefing was in the Ministry of Commerce about trade matters of course but particularly relating to ESCAP – I was to be Permanent Representative.

I hold Mani Dixit in high esteem and he treated me as a good friend. He was the Foreign Service's first strategic thinker. Two of Mani's comments have stayed vividly in my memory. He told me that India will not get Full Dialogue Partner status with ASEAN 'anytime soon'. To my suggestion of the desirability of a sub-regional economic cooperation group linking Thailand, Bangladesh, Myanmar and India he responded that given the difficult if not adversarial nature of the bilateral relationships between the countries involved 'this simply will not happen'. I recall this not as criticism – factually his views were based on the then existing ground realities – but since these things actually happened just a few years later, to emphasize and underline the outstanding success of the LEP even in its relative infancy.

A LEARNING CURVE

After arrival at a new station it is normal to pay courtesy calls on diplomatic colleagues. I concentrated on ASEAN Ambassadors and went out of my way to develop personal friendships with them. The Philippines, Myanmar, Laos and Malaysian Ambassadors had become good friends and the Singapore Ambassador a particularly close friend. They all talked fondly of Dr. Thanat Khoman, a respected former foreign minister of Thailand, dubbed the 'Father of ASEAN' – he was the leading light in the internal deliberations during the period leading up to the formation of ASEAN. He was a permanent presence on the very hectic Bangkok social scene. I got to know him very well and had extensive and frequent discussions with him on many subjects but particularly about ASEAN and ASEAN related interactions with India from the mid-1960s to the present. He was by now very anti-American. He was very fond of India – his first posting as a Thai diplomat had been Delhi. He was a great admirer of Nehru and cherished memories of seeing him at close quarters even as a junior diplomat – in the first few years after independence this happened often. Amongst his many visits to India, he specially recalled those in 1966/7 as foreign minister, specifically in an effort to persuade India to become actively associated with the yet to be formed ASEAN, the creation of which was then under discussion between five Southeast Asian countries.

He also told me about the visit of Lee Kuan Yew, the prime minister of Singapore, to India in 1966 or 1967 for the same purpose. He recalled with palpable sadness not only the failure of his mission but the lectures he was subjected to about Thailand's 'misconceived' foreign policy; Thailand and the other Southeast Asian countries were accused of being pawns and client states of the West. He volunteered the comment more than once that Lee Kuan Yew, whom I have never met, had specially looked up to India and had felt strongly that everything that the new state of Singapore needed and wanted he had hoped to get from India but did not. Khoman often added that over these past decades nobody has felt more let down by India than Lee Kuan Yew. He also mentioned a visit of the Indian foreign minister to some Southeast Asian countries in May 1967 before the formal setting up of ASEAN in August 1967, during which despite efforts from both sides the gulf between Southeast Asian countries and India could not be bridged, which prevented any Indian association with the envisaged entity, with whose ideological moorings India remained uncomfortable.

In these contexts, I recall, in particular, one, amongst several, conversations with Anand Panyarachun, a highly-respected non-politician former prime minister of Thailand, who told me that the entire world had grown tired of listening to lectures from India telling everybody what was good for them; he also said wounds from hurtful actions can be healed but harsh words get ensconced in the heart and are difficult to eradicate or forget, specifically referring to alleged remarks by Pandit Nehru and later Indira Gandhi about Thailand being 'a Coca-Cola Kingdom'; anybody who knows anything about Thailand knows just how much His Majesty the King is revered and therefore it can be imagined how this alleged remark from somebody of Nehru's stature would hurt particularly badly. Considering that the king is Rama IX and a very devout Buddhist, India is a particularly conspicuous absentee from the long list of countries that the Thai monarch has visited officially and privately. He had of course been invited, but the Thai establishment, unreasonably I believe, did not feel confident of the reception he would receive.

I was also told that apparently India had made a formal approach under Morarji Desai's Janata Party government in late 1978 for association with ASEAN. This was welcomed and led ultimately to a meeting of Indian and ASEAN officials in early 1980 as a result of which India was invited to participate in an ASEAN meeting in July 1980. However, under the new Congress government India recognized the Vietnamese-installed regime in Kampuchea, greatly angering ASEAN members, in particular Singapore and Thailand, while the Indian foreign minister excused himself from attending the July meeting for 'personal reasons'. This put paid to any further consideration of a formal association between ASEAN and India.

Never having dealt even remotely with the region, I was completely unaware of all this background. As a result of my intensive interaction and background reading I also became aware of the enormous visionary statesmanship displayed by the five countries in establishing ASEAN despite intense bilateral rivalries and serious disputes between them at that time, and the success they have made of it since then – an object lesson for other Asian regions. I became aware of something unique – 'the ASEAN way' of doing things. I will confess to having become an admirer of ASEAN by the time I left Thailand and remain so.

In response to my queries as to why ASEAN was so anxious to involve a clearly reluctant and unenthusiastic India, responses from all my interlocutors were consistent and straightforward – notwithstanding foreign policy differences, India was highly respected; was the source of their religion and culture;[1] of whom they had no fear as India did not interfere in the internal affairs of countries of the region and had no ambitions in the region in strong contrast to China – a point strongly emphasized; is potentially a very large market and economic partner; and finally, most relevant to their then current major concern, because *they wanted a viable, geographically close Asian counterbalance to China*.[2] I felt then and, have continued to do since, that India is not adequately cognizant of the weightage that the more important ASEAN countries have attached and continue to attach to the China factor in ASEAN's India calculus. In contrast, from the Indian perspective the economic factor was the overridingly important motivation particularly in the beginning and still remains perhaps the single most important factor. LEP-2, to which I will come later, has evolved to include, very rightly, a significant and increasing strategic component.

INDIA AND ASEAN

A great deal of what I had heard had been discouraging. On the other hand, I now knew what I was up against and what I would be expected to counter or build up as the case may be. I was conscious that ASEAN then had seven members but each had to be worked on – so I had my work in Thailand cut out. From the very first week I brought up the subject of the desirability of India being given Full Dialogue Partner status in every conversation with every influential or prominent Thai. I spoke of a new post-Cold War India consciously reaching out to Southeast Asia and East Asia exemplified by an absolutely unprecedented torrent of visits of India's prime minister, foreign minister, finance minister, commerce minister, etc., to countries of the Asia-Pacific. I discovered that this conscious wooing had been and was being very favourably noticed. I commended ASEAN countries' statesmanship in embracing their erstwhile most bitter enemy Vietnam as a member of ASEAN and congratulated them in quickly and innovatively creating and granting a new category of association with ASEAN to accommodate India – Sectoral Dialogue Partner. I emphasized that we should not dwell on the past but focus on the future. In these one-to-one conversations I will confess I also did my bit in adding to their mounting fears from a strong and expansionist China – particularly as the soil for doing so was fertile.

My activism was noticed and led to a particularly satisfying personal outcome for me – I was invited by Dr. Krasae Chanawongse, the chairman of the Foreign Relations Committee of the House of Representatives, who at that time was the front runner to become the new Thai foreign minister, to address the committee, becoming the first and perhaps only Indian Ambassador ever to do so, on 28 September 1994. I spoke about India's new approach to the region. The speech was particularly well received and later circulated by the chairman to all members of parliament. He also sent it to many other institutions such as universities, think tanks, selected government ministries and departments, etc.

It is particularly noteworthy that ASEAN's decision to accord Full Dialogue Partner status to India in December 1995 at the ASEAN Summit in Thailand was made without India being given any prior indication whatsoever. It was an absolute and utter surprise, coming completely out of the blue. I knew Dato Ajit Singh, the Secretary General of ASEAN.[3] He had come home for drinks – by this date the SOM had taken place and the foreign ministers' meeting was due to start the next morning. Singh told me categorically that there was absolutely nothing on the agenda that was of any special interest to India – upgrading of India's status vis-à-vis ASEAN was certainly not up for even informal consideration; interaction with India as Sectoral Dialogue Partner is not a subject at summit level. On the afternoon of the second and final day of the summit I managed to speak to him on the telephone to specifically enquire whether I should come for the end-of-summit press conference; he could not conceal a hint of exasperation when he replied that he had already told me very clearly there was nothing of interest for India – coming or not coming was my call.

Around midnight I received a telephone call from my close friend, the Singapore Ambassador, who was extremely excited to inform me that the summit had decided to accord India Full Dialogue Partner status. Prime Minister Goh Tok Chong had told the press about it as he emerged from the conference hall. Before thanking him, I jokingly chided him saying that he must have known that this was going to happen and yet he (and Ajit Singh), had deliberately kept me in the dark despite being a particularly close friend. He repeatedly assured me that neither he nor anybody that he knew had the slightest inkling that anything like this was even remotely possible let alone going to happen.

The next morning the Permanent Secretary of the Thai foreign ministry, who had become a good friend, granted my request for an immediate meeting. After arrival at his office I was kept waiting for almost half an hour – this was highly unusual as this sort of thing had never happened even when I had gone to meet the highest dignitaries such as His Majesty the King, the Crown Prince, Princess Mahachakri, the prime minister, etc. The Thais are just so well organized and extraordinarily courteous! The reason soon became abundantly apparent – his door had been flung open and out marched a lobster red, very agitated Chinese Ambassador, still virtually frothing at the mouth; the Permanent Secretary had been at the receiving end of a particularly angry tirade – how did ASEAN have the temerity to grant India Full Dialogue Partner status ahead of China. That too at a meeting chaired by a friendly country like Thailand – this was simply incomprehensible and unacceptable; appropriate amends will have to be made and made very quickly! Apparently the Chinese vented their ire in all the ASEAN capitals and most of my ASEAN diplomatic colleagues in Bangkok regaled me with accounts of their lively personal encounters with their Chinese colleague! China (and Russia) – heretofore Consultative Partners – was thereafter informed through diplomatic channels that they will be accorded Full Dialogue Partner status soon – the relevant procedures were fast tracked and expeditiously processed and all the three new Full Dialogue Partners attended the ASEAN PMC together for the first time under their new status in June 1996.

The Permanent Secretary first spoke to me about China's unhappiness, while volunteering the interesting and noteworthy information that the Chinese Ambassador had come without an appointment, apologizing for but thus making clear the reason for my having to wait. Thereafter, the Permanent Secretary said that he was availing of this opportunity to formally and officially inform me about the summit's decision to upgrade India's status. In response to my query about the lack of any official announcement on behalf of ASEAN he said that I need not worry because the decision had been recorded in the minutes of the summit and, in any case, all heads of government/state were personally involved in and witness to the decision. All this came as an enormous relief because though the morning newspapers had carried this news, the text of the official summit communiqué that all newspapers also carried did not have any such provision. He offered his personal congratulations to India and graciously said very kind words about my own personal efforts. He added that in due course India will be receiving an official written communication from the new ASEAN chair – Indonesia – and from the ASEAN Secretariat. He then said that as very good friends personally he would take the liberty of being candid and frank with me. With this introduction he told me that ASEAN countries were very unhappy about India's past attitude towards ASEAN and about India's past policies towards Southeast Asia. He added that ASEAN was disappointed at the tardy pace of substantive interaction and lack of focused interest even after ASEAN had made a special gesture in making India a Sectoral Dialogue Partner by creating a new category. ASEAN had nevertheless decided to upgrade India's status in the expectation that she will be much more proactive in the future. Finally, he made another important substantive point – ASEAN has taken considerable risk in deliberately granting India this status ahead of China, knowing full well that China would be very angry; he added this greatly increased India's responsibilities as a Full Dialogue Partner. However, he also emphasized ASEAN's happiness in that its long quest for having India as a close associate had finally been fulfilled.

The following week was frenetic as I tried to find out exactly what had happened that last evening of the summit that had resulted in such a wonderful outcome for India. After all that I heard, learnt and read during my almost four years in Thailand, it was clear that from the very beginning (and that holds good even now), of all the members of ASEAN, Singapore has been and remains by far the most enthusiastic about India's involvement, except episodically whenever Lee Kuan Yew became particularly disenchanted with India. Prime Minister Goh Tok Chong of Singapore paid his first official visit to India in 1994 – he was the Chief Guest at India's Republic Day – and on his return said, 'I recognized the potential of the country; I returned to Singapore determined to spark off an India Fever. Although many doubted India's commitment to economic openness I never lost faith in India.' It seems he had confided to one or two senior members of the Singapore delegation, who in turn had kept the ASEAN Secretary General in the loop but sworn to secrecy, that agenda-dictated discussions for India's Full Dialogue Partner status would mean endless delay – and their very discreet soundings during the SOM seem to have confirmed this conclusion – and since the overall environment was propitious due to growing anger against China, a surprise ambush was the need of the hour. Accordingly, in the last half hour of the summit, Goh Tok Chong made a short but very passionate speech that they should decide now, at this summit itself, to make India a Full Dialogue Partner. Other delegation heads were caught completely unawares, apparently nobody objected (there were some discrepancies amongst my interlocutors' recollections as to whether there were brief statements of support from the Philippines and Vietnam). All participants felt that Prime Minister Banharn Silpa-archa of Thailand had been a cooperative, particularly efficient and effective chairman. Apparently Goh Tok Chong had taken the Thai prime minister into confidence minutes before he made the proposal and after Goh Tok Chong's speech, the chairman quickly brought down the gavel saying it has been so decided. As the chairman, the Thai prime minister could very well and easily have stymied the whole idea and would have been well within his rights to do so but he displayed enormous friendship for India and true statesmanship! The mystery about the decision not being mentioned in the joint communiqué was also resolved – such documents are agreed to well in advance and since the India decision took place at the eleventh and a half hour it had not occurred to anybody to revise the draft communiqué before it was released for issue.

Continuing to exhibit its very strong commitment to the relationship with India, ASEAN countries succeeded in ensuring that India became a member of ARF at the first available opportunity, summer of 1996, despite the particularly ferocious opposition of Australia, China, Japan and New Zealand and, surprisingly, even of Russia.

INDIA AND APEC

India was not considered for membership when APEC was formed in 1989 and in the first round of induction of new members in 1991 for obvious reasons. However, with its opening to the East, India wanted to become a member. With countries such as the US, Australia, Japan, etc., then inimically inclined towards India and being particularly influential in APEC, it was clearly very difficult for India to become a member. An entirely unrelated and unexpected possible pathway for a serious attempt opened up through a Thai initiative. Thais are deeply devoted Buddhists. Within months of assuming office in July 1995, Prime Minister Banharn Silpa-archa had approached me with a request that an exhibition of Buddhist relics be organized in Thailand. Banharn was naturally exceedingly keen that the exhibition be held while he was prime minister and as an incentive to India he held out the assurance that as the leader of the Thai delegation to the next APEC Summit, he would propose India's name for membership and work hard with ASEAN partners to achieve that objective. He had been in the chair and had played an important role at the summit when India was given Full Dialogue Partner status with ASEAN. After much effort on my part, the Government of India finally agreed to the exhibition proposal but unfortunately a last minute sticking point emerged – relating to dates.

We have been witnessing for the past many months that Thai politics is notoriously unstable. Thailand has had more prime ministers since Second World War than any other country – during my tenure there were three and the fourth was due to be sworn in three days after my departure on transfer. Due to domestic political considerations parliament was dissolved at the end of September 1996 and elections were slated for mid-November 1996. For reasons best known to our Ministry of Culture they took the line that the exhibition cannot be held while the country was in election campaign mode. Even if such a rationale had the slightest validity – in my view there was absolutely no connection between the two issues – this was a decision for the Ministry of External Affairs to take. It saddened me that despite my intensive personal efforts and plaintive pleading with the powers that be, my own MEA chose not to support a proposal – so self-evidently in national interest – made by one of their own but took the side of the Ministry of Culture. Whether Thailand would have succeeded in its endeavour is another matter but a potentially golden opportunity presented to us on a platter was spurned – at least the issue of India's membership would have been on the agenda formally. The exhibition was held from 30 December 1996 to 7 March 1997 but after a new government was in office. The new government took the line that

Thailand will support India's candidature but by itself it could do little.

A NEW IDEA: BIMSTEC

Thinking of what I could contribute in the new optimistic milieu created by the LEP, I felt that the LEP was the ideal vehicle for the economic development of India's isolated, remote, insurgency-wracked, underdeveloped northeastern states. Contiguous areas of India, Bangladesh, Myanmar and Thailand had over centuries traditionally constituted a natural economic, geographic and socio-cultural unit. This concept needed to be revived. The best way to do this was to establish physical connectivity between India and ASEAN countries, which was only possible through Thailand. In turn, physical connectivity to Thailand was only possible through Bangladesh and Myanmar. The creation of a sub-regional group involving these four countries would enable bilateral differences between India on the one hand and Bangladesh and Myanmar on the other, as well as some problems between Thailand and Myanmar to be overcome in the shared common interests of all.

During my courtesy call on Dr. Supachai Panitchpakdi, on 31 May 1994, then Thailand's deputy prime minister (later Secretary-General of UNCTAD and Director General of WTO) he raised the issue himself – though obviously his motivation was not the development of India's northeast. It did not matter – his putative proposal was immediately conveyed to the ministry and further details were sent soon thereafter. There was no response from Delhi. On 5 July 1994 Thailand publicly announced a proposal for an Economic Cooperation Group which also included Sri Lanka. Thailand had decided to add Sri Lanka on its own and there was a straightforward rationale that all these five countries constituted the rim of the Bay of Bengal segment of the Indian Ocean. Frankly, I was delighted because if a proposal came from a high dignitary of a foreign government there were much better prospects of acceptance than if it had come from an Indian functionary in a field office. Thereafter there was much correspondence – MEA seeking many clarifications.

However, when the formal proposal for a sub-regional group came from the Thai side officially addressed to India at the end of April 1995, it mentioned only India, Sri Lanka and Thailand; Bangladesh and Myanmar were omitted. They had probably concluded that given the less than satisfactory nature of India's relations at that time with Bangladesh and Myanmar, India may not be very favourably inclined to have them in, at least at the outset. Their assessment was not wrong. The ministry seemed adamantly opposed to the idea of involving Bangladesh; and, it was only after some time that they had started viewing the idea of Myanmar's involvement more positively. But forward movement remained at a snail's pace. On a recent visit to the ministry I came across a file where I found something relevant – an extract from a fax that I had sent to MEA dated 10 January 1996:

> This proposal was originally made on May 31st 1994. . . Frankly, I find it very difficult to understand that after almost one year and nine months we are still examining/studying the proposal. The issue is not at all complicated. . . . The Sri Lankan Foreign Minister visited Thailand last week and has publicly supported the Thai proposal.

Yet another reminder was needed – my letter had requested that all papers be put up to EAM which was done and we finally entered the last lap.

After intensive Bangladesh lobbying in all capitals but particularly with Sri Lanka and Thailand, it was finally settled that Bangladesh would be involved virtually from the beginning and that Myanmar too would soon be taken on board. On 4 and 5 June 1997, the preparatory meeting for the launching of BISTEC was held involving the visiting JS (MER) and Secretary (ER) from India's Ministry of External Affairs, the Sri Lankan Ambassador and the Thai Permanent Secretary; on 4 June I waited outside the main hall with the Bangladesh Ambassador for a few minutes after the meeting began when he was invited in and thereafter participated in the discussions as a full participant. On 6 June the declaration launching BISTEC was formally signed by Abul Hasan Chowdhury, MOS for Foreign Affairs of Bangladesh, Shri Saleem Iqbal Shervani, MOS for External Affairs of India, D.P. Wickremasinghe, Deputy Minister of Foreign Affairs of Sri Lanka, and Pitak Intravityanunt, Deputy Minister of Foreign Affairs of Thailand.

Feeling somewhat paternal and possessive about this issue, I was very keen to ensure that it was fully launched during my tenure in Bangkok. Therefore, as a result of a personal initiative, the Myanmar Ambassador was present as an Observer on 5 June and at the ministerial meeting on 6 June. A note from a ministry file is relevant:

> Our Ambassador in Bangkok, Shri Ranjit Gupta, has just informed me that

he has approached the Ambassador of Myanmar in Bangkok with a view to seeking Myanmar's participation as an Observer in the inaugural meeting of the Bangladesh-India-Sri Lanka-Thailand Economic Cooperation (BISTEC) arrangement from June 4 to 6, 1997, in Bangkok. While the Ambassador did act without specific instructions from Delhi, the fact that Myanmar has agreed to participate as an Observer in this important meeting should be welcomed. I have informed our Ambassador in Myanmar who also welcomes this development. The Thais also, according to Ambassador Gupta, are pleased with this development. I have further advised Ambassador Gupta not to take any further initiatives and let the Thais, as hosts, do the needful in extending an invitation to Myanmar. Sd/- AN Ram, Secretary ER, 4 June 1997, marked to Foreign Secretary.

At the first BISTEC Working Group meeting on 10 July 1997 chaired by Thailand, the Thai representative told the other delegates that Myanmar had informed Thailand that it was ready to join BISTEC in June itself but could not send a written communication in time due to its extremely heavy preoccupations with joining ASEAN as a member, which happened on 7 July 1997. He added that Thailand has since then received a written request from Myanmar for joining BISTEC. Delegates from all four countries supported Myanmar's membership without the need for any further formalities. In an innovative display of constructive pragmatism displayed by all four BISTEC member countries, Myanmar participated in all BISTEC meetings from 10 July onwards until it formally joined on 27 December 1997at a ministerial meeting.

BIMSTEC had finally come into existence. At that time the alphabets of the acronym BIMSTEC referred to the first letter of the countries that were members; it is only much later that that the entity acquired its present name. This, in short, is the story of the formation of BIMSTEC.

THE NAGA PEACE PROCESS

In the context of the imperative need to establish peace in the insurgency-wracked northeast, I take very great satisfaction in having taken the initiative personally and playing a pivotal role[4] in the establishment of contacts between senior officials of India's Home Ministry and the two pre-eminent Naga leaders – T. Muivah and Isaac Swu, who had been living in Thailand for some years, operating with impunity. Two home secretaries came and MHA delegations visited several times. A ceasefire agreement was signed in Bangkok in August 1997 and this was the beginning of the Naga Peace Process, which I understand is still continuing. All this was very greatly facilitated by the unstinted cooperation extended by Gen. Charan Kullavanijya, the Secretary General of Thailand's National Security Council, partly because he had become a particularly close friend.

EXPOSURE TO LEP AGAIN

On a cold January morning 10 days into the new millennium I got a call from Additional Secretary (AD) inquiring whether I would be interested in going on a posting to Taiwan. This was so totally and completely unexpected that I had to ask more than once whether what I was hearing was right; this was the best New Year gift I ever got. I had heard that there was some kind of Indian representation in Taiwan which I had assumed to be an office of FICCI or a similar organization. Indeed, the then Minister for External Affairs apparently also only became aware of the existence of this office when the file relating to my appointment went up to him for approval. Not having been a 'China hand' my appointment was very strongly resisted by the East Asia Division, with the consequence that I got no briefing and was not given access to any classified files. There was no answer to my repeated queries as to why the office was established despite my going to MEA every single working day for almost two months. However, JS (AMS) gave me very useful perspectives. Whatever I learnt about the relevance of Taiwan was due to personal reading. On the final afternoon before my departure I managed to persuade the Director of EAM's office to give me a few minutes with the minister. I told the minister that amongst strategic circles Taiwan is conventionally regarded as the world's best place for 'China watching' and yet, despite being lucky enough to have an office in Taipei, there was no diplomatic bag facility. The minister was aghast and he personally dictated a note instructing that this should be instituted – this was in May 2000 but the bag system was implemented only from March 2001 due to my relentlessly pursuing the matter through more sympathetic colleagues in MEA. I had to go every two months to Bangkok on bag duty. Throughout the remaining two years and two months of my tenure the incoming bag only contained circulars relating to administrative and consular matters whereas I used to send copious and lengthy dispatches and reports, the receipt of not one of which was ever even acknowledged.

I was posted in Taiwan from May 2000 to May 2003. This was

the last of my 12 foreign postings and turned out to be the most intellectually stimulating and satisfying, opening up a vast new world for me – studying China, Japan, the Far East and observing how India's LEP was acquiring new and strategically very important Asia-Pacific dimensions. Importantly, speaking and writing about these subjects, apart from the Persian Gulf region where I spent the maximum time of my career, is what has sustained me in post-retirement life.

Everything that I know about India-Taiwan interaction prior to 15 May 2000, when I arrived in Taipei, I discovered in Taiwan itself through conversations and interaction with Taiwanese officials and academics – there is an excellent network of think tanks and universities and a lot of lateral movement between government and academia, who are very well informed and really clued in – and a few other interesting things from serving career diplomats from other countries who were posted in Taipei. One conclusion that I drew was that India's opening up to Taiwan was also a conscious part of the LEP.

In 1991 when India had to physically pawn its gold reserves, so precarious were its financial straits that in sheer desperation India even decided to dispatch an official, and that too from the Prime Minister's Office, to Taiwan to explore possibilities of a loan; if this were not a fact it would be completely and absolutely unbelievable, a completely unthinkable idea – a figment of somebody's fertile imagination. Given that India was perhaps the most vociferous supporter of the 'One China Policy', obviously the question of Taiwan extending a loan to India simply did not arise. However, this foray opened up the process which ultimately led to India and Taiwan establishing 'informal' relations and the opening of mutual offices in each other's capitals in 1995. The Narasimha Rao government sent a very high level but strictly unofficial delegation for discussions with Taiwan where they met senior dignitaries from the president downwards. The delegation was led by I.K. Gujral and included, amongst others, former Foreign Secretary A.P. Venkateshwaran, former RBI Governor R.N. Malhotra, and former Finance Secretary Venkataraman. The delegation had strongly recommended establishment of relations similar to those that some 40 other countries, including most from the Asia-Pacific region, had done. There was no intention whatsoever on India's part to establish relations stealthily; negotiations were held with China before the offices were finally opened in 1995. Needless to say Taiwan was delighted.

Taiwan's office in New Delhi is called the Taipei Economic and Cultural Centre and the Indian office in Taipei has an innovatively conceived name – the India-Taipei Association and the head of the office is designated as Director General.

Ambassador Vinod Khanna opened the Indian office in Taiwan and I was the third Indian Representative. I arrived in Taiwan five days before the swearing in of Chen Shui bian of the Democratic Progressive Party as the president of the Republic of China, but commonly referred to as Taiwan. The DPP's charter states independence of Taiwan is the party's objective. Political differences between China and Taiwan notwithstanding, since 98 per cent of the population of Taiwan is Han Chinese, Taiwan is clearly a Chinese civilizational entity. This was going to be the first ever peaceful transfer of power in the over 5,000-year old history of Chinese civilization. The atmosphere was absolutely electric. There were rumours of a possible coup. There was much speculation about what China might do; it is probably unprecedented in diplomatic history but the invitation card to the presidential inauguration ceremony had a printed notice attached entitled 'Instructions in the event of an air raid'!

The DPP and government viewed the Indian Representative very differently from the way earlier KMT governments did. DG Asia – after the minister and the deputy minister, the number three ranked person in the Foreign Ministry, along with the Chief of Protocol, were at the airport to receive me – a deliberately huge gesture in the context of so many functions being planned and held in the shadow of the imminent inauguration of a new president. That evening the incoming foreign minister hosted a dinner for representatives of all countries which did not have diplomatic relations with Taiwan but only 'unofficial' offices. I discovered later that the Taiwanese were great sticklers for protocol. Therefore, they were sending a clear message in seating me on the left hand side of the new foreign minister though I had arrived in Taipei less than three hours earlier; the seating arrangement was noted by and remarked upon by my surprised new 'diplomatic' colleagues. Throughout my tenure there I was granted easy, even privileged, access to Taiwanese dignitaries.

I developed an excellent relationship with the vast majority of fellow foreign representatives but the Singapore, Japanese, Australian and the Thai – he was the main dealing officer for India when I was posted in Bangkok – representatives became particularly close friends. While the American representative was publicly seen as the 'Pro

Consul' and was one, there was another 'Pro Consul' – the Japanese representative; though extremely low key and hardly visible in public, he commanded enormous influence. The Singapore representative, a former head of their intelligence agency, and given the special relationship between Taiwan and Singapore – Singapore's army trains in Taiwan – was particularly well informed. The Australian representative, ethnically a White Russian born in Harbin and posted throughout his career in Chinese speaking posts – Beijing, Shanghai, Hong Kong, Singapore – was another well-informed diplomat. For me they were a gold mine of information relating to Taiwan, to Taiwan-China relations and indeed in relation to China's activities and intentions in the Asia-Pacific.

But I was even more interested in their assessments of how they saw India in relation to the Asia-Pacific region. The Japanese representative repeatedly said that Prime Minister Yoshiro Mori believed that the India-Japan relationship would be the key to stability in the Asia-Pacific, adding that the LDP leadership in Japan had taken a substantive policy decision that India was going to be its key global partner in the decades ahead. He spoke of the singular importance of the signal conveyed through Defence Minister George Fernandes' visit to Japan in August 2000. He said the Japanese leadership believed firmly that a strong defence relationship between India and Japan was absolutely necessary. He was very pleased that India's LEP was now consciously being extended to embrace strong relationships beyond ASEAN and was acquiring strategic content. The Australian Representative often said that there were compulsions for a strong economic relationship with China but looking ahead India had to be the strategic partner of choice for Australia in the Asia-Pacific. The Singapore representative always emphasized that his country would continue to spearhead India's deeper involvement with ASEAN, ASEAN-related entities and East Asian countries. Later, Singapore and Japan played very significant roles in ensuring India's membership of the East Asia Summit.

An Investment Promotion and Protection Agreement and a Civil Aviation Agreement were signed during my tenure. Direct flights between Delhi and Taipei were started on 1 April 2002; this led directly to the starting of direct flights between China and India – with the Chinese insisting that it be done one day before the flight from Taiwan! An extremely successful four-month exhibition on Indian civilization was held in Taipei. Trade, visits of business and investment delegations and the number of tourists from Taiwan continued to increase year by year. Till my time the three persons posted in Taipei had to be retired officials but one recommendation that I made week after week was that we should have serving persons as the vast majority of other countries' offices had. From my successor onwards in 2003 serving officers are being posted. What was particularly satisfying was the initiation of visits of the delegations from Taiwanese think tanks to India, overcoming strong resistance from headquarters; today we have at least one such delegation each month. This is very valuable.

However, I found an absolutely huge contrast in the manner in which all other countries interacted with Taiwan and how India interacted – severely hampered by a very large number of entirely unnecessary self-imposed restrictions needlessly depriving ourselves of the possibility of significant economic and technological advantages if we had had a more open mindset. My 'diplomatic' colleagues had not only noticed this but questioned it often. It has to be said that particularly in the past four years the MEA has commendably displayed much greater and welcome creativity.

Having said all this, I do not subscribe to the view that in the context of Sino-Indian relations there is a 'Taiwan card' that India can use – such suggestions are not only immature but dangerous.

CONCLUSION

To conclude, India's relationship with China, complex and difficult as it is, is going to be increasingly India's most important relationship in the twenty-first century. India's LEP, now extended to cover countries of the entire Asia-Pacific region, is going to be of immense importance in how we handle the challenge that China poses. Given that China has always had an unmistakably India-centric relationship with a perpetually hostile Pakistan; has consistently done its utmost to undermine India's relations with its direct South Asian neighbours; tried its best to impede India's relationship with ASEAN and in the Asia-Pacific region; and opposed India's aspirations on the global stage I cannot understand why India should have hesitations in evolving multilateral strategic partnerships with countries such as Australia, Japan, Singapore, Vietnam and as well as the United States in the Asia-Pacific region along with an increasing emphasis on a strategic component in India's relationships with ASEAN countries. India's navy is in bad shape and needs to be proactively upgraded and naval diplomacy given high priority. Defence-related infrastructure development all along the Sino-Indian border but particularly in the northeast, must be given top priority. Our participation in BIMSTEC needs proactive leadership. BIMSTEC should be accorded priority over BCIM, which is a Chinese idea pre-eminently in China's interest and which largely bypasses the northeast and thus would only marginally contribute to the development of the northeast – the main motivation behind BIMSTEC. All this should become an integral part of the evolving LEP-2 and constitute entirely legitimate activity and necessary to ensuring that we build capability and relationships to protect our national interests in this vitally important part of the world.

NOTES

1. Throughout my tenure I never ever told a Thai that they got Buddhism and Hindu culture from India knowing that they will do it themselves and with a feeling of genuine affection. Indians, particularly official visitors, even academics and leading businessmen had this propensity to do so, which goes down poorly. MEA/Embassies must brief all important visitors to Southeast Asia suitably.
2. Evolving Chinese policy helped. Its rising and unabashed assertiveness in the context of the South China Sea issue (occupation of Mischief Reef in 1995), and Taiwan (lobbing missiles off the coast of Taiwan in July and August 1995 and conducting large amphibious exercises), was creating increasing anxieties throughout the region. On 18 August 1995 the Chinese conducted a nuclear test also. As early as February 1994 in a gesture deliberately designed to assert policy independence Thailand had invited President Lee Teng Hui of Taiwan for a visit – he was received by the king in a private audience and a lunch meeting and golf game was hosted by the deputy prime minister and foreign minister. Lee also visited Indonesia and the Phillipines where the reception was even more official and elaborate.
3. When I was Ambassador to Venezuela Ajit Singh was the Malaysian Ambassador in Brazil, concurrently accredited to Venezuela. Even though I had had no exposure to Southeast Asia, whenever he visited Caracas I used to invite him for a meal and try to be of help in any way I could.
4. For some inexplicable reason MEA was very unhappy with this intensive direct interaction between MHA and me. MHA's request for me to be called to India for Gen. Charan's visit was not agreed to. I was told that I must not communicate directly with the MHA; apparently the Home Secretary was advised along the same lines. Both disregarded the advice/instructions – otherwise the happy outcome would not have been possible.

CHAPTER 5

India-ASEAN: Thirsting for a New Thrust in Relationship

PARAMJIT S. SAHAI*

SYNOPSIS

I have decided to write on this topic, as I was directly involved with India-ASEAN relationship in the initial stages, during my posting as Indian High Commissioner to Malaysia during 1996-2000. It was in 1995 that India had graduated from a Sectoral Partner to a Dialogue Partner of ASEAN. Indian prime minister Narasimha Rao had just concluded a highly successful visit to Malaysia, resulting in the signing of around ten agreements and Memorandum of Understandings. Hopes were high on India's increasing involvement with the Southeast Asian countries, both at the regional and bilateral levels. This has come to be known as 'Look East Policy' (LEP) in the present-day context. Prime Minister P.V. Narasimha Rao was its architect and this was later vigorously pursued by I.K. Gujral, in his capacity as EAM and later PM. Along with the hopes were concerns over Indian commitment to take this relationship to a higher level. Such concerns were borne out of fears, arising from the slow implementation of signed agreements, raising questions of credibility, capabilities or constraints. Was it a case of lack of commitment or was sheer procedural hurdle coming in the way? None the less, there was a desire and commitment to raise India-ASEAN relationship to a higher plateau. How has this 'Thirst' translated into a 'Thrust' over the two decades? Has it further ignited an urge for a 'New Thrust', to go beyond 2015?

* Amb. P.S. Sahai, Former High Commissioner of India to Malaysia and currently Principal Advisor, CRRID, Chandigarh.

INTRODUCTION

An attempt is made in this paper to look at the trajectory of India-ASEAN relationship as it has unfolded over the years. What have been the milestones covered and where are we headed for? What were the areas of achievement and where were the pitfalls or shortcomings? Was it a story of gradual growth or did it witness periods of high and low tides? Was this inherent or inbuilt in the ASEAN process, requiring consultation and consensus, or were external factors dictating the pace of relationship? The overall picture that, however, emerges is a positive one, beckoning us to explore new openings and hence to give a 'New Thrust' to this relationship. Does the old 'Thirst' still continue on both the sides? We would gradually discover this, as we move along, in a calm and placid way, looking at this India-ASEAN story of a multifaceted relationship.

BEGINNING OF THE ENGAGEMENT PROCESS

It was the joint 'Thirst' that led to India's engagement with ASEAN, as the same was considered to be mutually beneficial. This was a positive augury as in the past one-sided approach, earlier by ASEAN and later by India, did not yield any results.

Singapore, on behalf of ASEAN, led the charge as it had clearly seen the advantages of an economic engagement with India. It was a sea-change on the part of Singapore, as during the 1970s, it had viewed India as inconsequential. It was, therefore, not surprising, when on a later occasion, Singapore's prime minister Goh described India and China as the two wings of the Boeing airplane, both seen as essential for the upliftment of ASEAN, which had already taken off. The initial 'Thrust' for the relationship was the upliftment of economic relationship, which still remains centred to connectivity. India had the advantage as it did not carry a hostile baggage, unlike China; yet India had to prove that it possessed the 3Cs-'Capability, Capacity and Competitiveness'. It had already demonstrated its willingness, through other 4-Cs, by expressing its 'Commitment' to 'Cooperate' by choosing the path of 'Coexistence' on the road that ensured 'Co-Prosperity'.

India-ASEAN engagement process starts in 1992, when India became its sectoral partner in three areas, namely trade and investment, tourism and science and technology. In 1995, it was accepted as full dialogue partner; a status it achieved before China's admission. India attended the first Post-Ministerial Conference (PMC) in 1996 in Jakarta, when it also became a member of ASEAN Regional Forum (ARF). It was the urge for 'co-prosperity' that gave a push to this relationship, as neither India nor ASEAN members wanted to be left out of the economic opportunities that would become available to one another (Sahai 2008). It was also seen 'as a step forward and as a move from a derivative to a direct relationship' (Gujral 1996). Following the first PMC, an India-ASEAN framework for cooperation was designed, called 'Vistas of Cooperation'. India-ASEAN cooperation was also viewed by Gujral as a conduit to Indian participation in other Asia-Pacific structures in the future, as he saw it 'as a window to a progressive participation in other ASEAN-related fora such as the Asia-Pacific Economic Cooperation (APEC) and Asia Europe Meeting (ASEM)'. It was during 1996-2000 that they discovered a new level of comfort in their relationship, as India slowly and steadily got the feel of ASEAN and gradually integrated into the ASEAN stream.

What are the pull and push factors that guided India's increasing engagement with ASEAN, besides the primary pull of the economic engagement? These are as follows:

- Growing perception among ASEAN members about India's importance in the world arena, not only as an 'economic storehouse', but also as an emerging political power;
- Subterranean feeling that India's involvement would act as a checkmate and balancing factor against China;
- Desire for renewal of old and traditional cultural bonds;
- Acceptance of India's 'soft power' and its IT 'capacities' in building multifaceted linkages at the bilateral and regional levels;
- Emergence of diaspora as a bridge builder, as it had passed the loyalty test.

India was thus eminently qualified as a suitable partner or 'Suitable Boy' of Vikram Seth's vintage, for ASEAN in its three pillars – political and strategic, economic and socio-cultural.

FACILITATING INDIA'S CONNECTIVITY WITH ASEAN

As a new member to the ASEAN club, India, being a non-voting member, had to understand the rules of the game in this ASEAN-centric club. Our biggest supporter was Singapore, which shepherded Indian entry as a dialogue partner. After Singapore, this mantle had passed into the hands of Malaysia, making it incumbent on us to deal with Malaysia, both in the bilateral and regional contexts. Our stock was rather low for poor delivery on bilateral agreements. This was not only in the present-day context, but we carried the historical tag of a 'non-serious partner' in the region (Malik 2012). How does India then ingratiate itself with ASEAN and this was the challenge for me.

A multipronged approach, therefore, had to be developed in these formative years of India's membership as a dialogue partner. Apart from learning the ropes, it was also about generating awareness on India and India's interest in Malaysia and ASEAN. The ASEAN process, built on the twin principles of consultation and consensus made way for smooth discussion, even though individual countries had harboured different approaches on certain issues. In the initial stages, Singapore and Malaysia were the two main interlocutors for India. With the entry of CLMV countries, India's role and involvement increased as these countries had greater cultural and political affinities with India.

India's integration had to be both at the symbolic and substantive levels. Symbolically, India tried to imbibe the SAARC-friendly spirit at the 1997 ASEAN Ministerial Meeting at Kuala Lumpur. We demonstrated ala Bollywood style, how ASEAN mattered to India through rending of a song 'Made in India'. At the substantive level, exchange of high-level visits helped in spurring up bilateral relations. Prime Minister Mahathir's visit to India in December 1996 helped in showcasing the economic strength of India and possibilities of cooperation in the areas of ICT and infrastructure development. Mahathir's visit was also significant from ASEAN perspective, as he delivered the first lecture under the ASEAN Eminent Persons Series.

Visits by Indian VIPs, like the Vice-President of India Krishan Kant and other leaders were helpful. At our request, Malaysia was prepared to accord special place of honour to Prime Minister I.K. Gujral at the 1997 ASEAN Ministerial Meeting. This opportunity, however, was lost as he changed his plans at the last minute. Instead, Finance Minister Chidambaram deputized for the EAM. At a dinner hosted by me, Chidambaram had good interaction with CEOs of leading Malaysian companies who were enthused to look at India. We started issuing liberalized visas to the business community. India, however, failed to offer any meaningful bilateral programme, to meet the challenges arising out of the Asian economic crisis, apart from offering advisory opinion on the likely causes of the crisis.

A unique development in this regard was the visit by four chief ministers from India in 1997 and 1998. The most successful visit was that by Chandrababu Naidu, chief minister of Andhra Pradesh who on his return, set up an IT city in Hyderabad called 'Cyberabad', modeled on 'Cyberjaya' in Malaysia. Two lessons learnt from Malaysia were the need to take policy decisions expeditiously and thereafter implement the same, without dithering on one or other ground. The message was on 'governance', which was the main plank of the election campaign of Modi in 2014.

Malaysia had made great strides in infrastructure development, be it ports, roads and airports. There was a spurt of visits by Indian minister of surface transport and other officials. Given India's interest in building roads on BOT (Build, Operate and Transfer) basis, an infrastructure conference was organized with CII in Delhi in 2000, with Malaysia as country partner. This became the starting point for Malaysian involvement in building roads with a Malaysian company getting its first contract to build part of the Mumbai-Pune highway, which was the first highway project open to international participation. Earlier, Malaysia had offered to build 'road corridors', like the Japanese now, and had conducted feasibility studies for the same, but we were not ready to accept that concept then, as it was ahead of its time.

We, however, failed to provide relief by way of reduction in import duties of palm oil, as unlike soybean, it was not GATT-bound. Innovative arrangements like linking import of palm oil by India with the award of railway projects by Malaysia were worked out. Malaysia-India relations now had got economic content. Mahathir participated at the First India-ASEAN Business Summit held in New Delhi and Hyderabad in October 2000. There was now a change in Malaysia's perceptions, as pointed out by Mahathir that 'India should prove a good partner both in terms of sourcing various requirements and essentials as well as exports (Barua 2001).

As Malaysia was the shepherd for India, it was necessary to have direct working relationship with ASEAN. Luckily, for us, Tan Sri Ajit Singh, a Malaysian diplomat of Sikh origin, was its Secretary General. It was, therefore, easier to interact with him, whenever he visited Kuala Lumpur, which was quite frequent. He remained a good contact, even after he handed over the post of Secretary General. He became a good channel in facilitating India's linkages with ASEAN and he was awarded Padma Shri in recognition of his contribution.

Malaysia was emerging as an important hub for international strategic conferences, necessitating contacts with think tanks. Institute of Strategic and International Studies (ISIS) had emerged as an important international think tank, which hosted prestigious conferences annually on Southeast Asia called, 'Asia-Pacific Roundtable'. At the governmental level, Institute for Diplomacy and Foreign Relations (IDFR) was another important institute that focused on foreign policy-related issues. Malaysian leaders also had set up their own think tanks, such as Asian Strategy and Leadership Institute (ASLI), which had the support of Prime Minister Mahathir. Malaysian Resource Centre (MRC) was another think tank promoted by the then Defence Minister Najib, who is presently the prime minister. We also established connectivity with the newly set up, Institute of Islamic Understanding, Malaysia (IKIM) and this helped in projecting secular India. We regularly participated in their activities and facilitated participation by Indian experts.

With IDFR, we took the initiative to organize two conferences on India and ASEAN relations and India's nuclear policy. India-ASEAN Conference was held on 12 November 1997 and deliberations were published by IDFR in a book titled *India and ASEAN: The Growing Partnership for the 21st Century*. Former Foreign Secretary Salman Haidar attended the seminar on nuclear issues. Another seminar was organized on Indo-Malaysian relations by MRC in 2000 and the inaugural address was given by Najib, the present prime minister. From India, N.N. Vohra, late Air Cdr. Jasjit Singh and other academics attended.

Contacts were also established with the universities. Some of the universities had Indian Studies Department but the focus was on Tamil Studies. They were encouraged to branch out to the study of modern India. Steps were taken to facilitate entry of Indian institutes, such as the National Institute of Information Technology (NIIT) for IT education and Manipal University for setting up a medical university. Exchange of academia was promoted. A number of Indians got teaching assignments at the universities.

In the area of non-military security threats, India was able to demonstrate its capabilities and interest as the Indian Coast Guard successfully intercepted the *MV Alondra* (*Rainbow*) in November 1999 in the Malacca Straits. This resulted in Malaysia and other countries accepting the positive role that India could play in ensuring safe passage through the sea lanes contiguous to the Straits of Malacca.

India hosted an ARF workshop on anti-piracy in Mumbai in October 2000. Four navies from ASEAN countries – Singapore, Thailand, Indonesia and Malaysia – participated at the first international fleet review in Mumbai in February 2000. India started participating annually at the Langkawi International Maritime and Air Show (LIMA) exhibitions. India naval ships made frequent visits, with *INS Delhi* making its maiden visit to Penang in 1998. The Chief of the Naval Staff visited Malaysia in 1999, while the Director General of Coast Guards and the Chief of the Army Staff made visits in 2000.

In June 2000, India became a full member of Track II security forum, Council for Security Cooperation in the Asia-Pacific (CSCAP). We were not at the core of the CSCAP and ARF processes in the early years (Ram 2012). Malaysia, as co-chairman facilitated India's admission. Earlier IDSA was a member as an institute. In the initial stages, our involvement was limited as we were hesitant. Regional fora like ARF and ASEAN 'gave us a voice, though not always commensurate with our size and influence in the Asia-Pacific' (Ram 2012).

ASEAN understood India's genuine security concerns following India's nuclear test at Pokhran in June. The air was further cleared by me at the Asia-Pacific Roundtable organized by ISIS in July 1998, where a special session was organized. Steps were taken to promote understanding of our security concerns – the Chief of Indian Naval Staff Admiral Bhagwat delivered the keynote address at the prestigious Malaysian Institute of Maritime Affairs (MIMA) in 1999, which was the first by a serving chief. Later in 2000, the Director-General of Indian Coast Guards had good interaction with official and non-official groups, which was well appreciated. India, therefore, was making a niche for itself in the area of maritime security.

Malaysia decided to set up its Coast Guard Organisation based on the Indian model. It also showed interest in establishing links with India in the maintenance of Mig-21 aircrafts and training of air force personnel. Malaysia actively supported the 'Milan' exercise to promote linkages between India and other ASEAN countries. Professor Jayakumar, Singapore's foreign minister, did not fail to notice this in July 2000, when he stated that whatever 'the new equilibrium on security architecture or geo-political balance that eventually emerges; India will be a part of it'.

Cultural connectivity was helpful in facilitating commercial links.

Indian Bollywood music had captivated the Malaysians. Even the king would listen to the song '*Kuchh Kucch Hota Hai*', while Prime Minister Mahathir was fond of '*Dost Dost Na Raha*'. Malaysia had developed its tourism logo, 'Malaysia, Truly Asia'. It used Bollywood to promote tourism by allowing shooting of films in Malaysia and thus get free publicity. Frequent visits by film stars and musicians were also used to promote the country. Malaysia thus became an important tourist destination for Indians and an 'Incentive Destination' for Indian companies; however, we failed to attract tourists from Malaysia and could not generate an image of tourist-friendly India.

Under Malaysia's political dispensation, an Indian political party, Malaysian Indian Congress (MIC), was a coalition partner of the ruling party, the United Malay National Organisation (UMNO). MIC was thus a part of the government and had a minister and a few deputy ministers. Samy Velly, the minister, became the unofficial envoy for India. As minister of works, he was directly involved in road building projects. Other members of the community held prominent positions in Malaysia and helped in providing connectivity. At present, Samy Velly is Malaysia's Special Envoy for India.

INDIAN CONNECTIVITY WITH SOUTHEAST ASIA

How does India now connect with Southeast Asia through its 'Look East Policy'? It connects at different levels and forums. At the regional level, it connects through ASEAN and other ASEAN forums that have evolved over the years. At the sub-regional level, it connects through groupings like Mekong-Ganga Cooperation (MGC), Bangladesh-China-India-Myanmar (BCIM) and Bay of Bengal Initiative Multi Sectoral Technical and Economic Cooperation (BIMSTEC). Bilaterally, it connects with individual countries as it forges relationships. Connectivity at the regional level results in the creation of a broad framework for cooperation. At the sub-regional level connectivity helps in focusing on areas of culture and commerce that provide geographical contiguity and promote people-to-people connectivity. The real connectivity, however, still remains at the bilateral level, where the action takes place. These processes operate, jointly and vicariously at different levels and times.

At the regional level, the core of the relationship is India's status of dialogue partnership with ASEAN. It is here that India interacts with ASEAN in chartering a broad framework for cooperation. This is usually done in the context of ASEAN+1 meetings, where India-specific agenda and policies take shape. Indian engagement with ASEAN is at various forums, as in a concentric circle. Dialogue partnership is in the centre; India attended the first meeting in 1996. India acquired the status for enhanced dialogue partnership at ASEAN+1 in 2002, with India-ASEAN ties upgraded to summit level, with focus on India-specific linkages.

In 2005, India was admitted to the East Asia Summit Process, what was called the ASEAN+3+3 process. It was recognition of 'India's potential role and contribution to the Asia-Pacific security architecture and economic integration' (Devare 2012). The relationship was raised to the level of strategic partnership in 2012 at the Indian-ASEAN Commemorative Summit, New Delhi. India also participates in other allied forums like ARF, ADMM+ and ASEM. India is also specially focusing on CLMV countries through its involvement at sub-regional level arrangements like MGC, BIMSTEC and BCIM.

India engages with ASEAN through the Asian Regional Forum (ARF) and ASEAN Defence Minister's Meeting Plus (ADMM+) in defence and security related issues. ARF was set up in 1993 as a regional security cooperation and dialogue platform. ADMM's inaugural meeting was held in Kuala Lumpur on 9 May 2006. An offshoot of ADMM is ADMM+, which was established in 2010 and the inaugural meeting was convened in Hanoi on 12 October 2010. The second meeting was held at Brunei Darussalam on 29 August 2013.

ARF aims at fostering dialogue on political and security issues 'of common interest and concern', aimed at confidence building and preventive diplomacy in the Asia-Pacific region. ADMM+ serves as a platform for 18 defence ministers (10 ASEAN members and 8 dialogue partners), aimed at strengthening security and defence cooperation towards peace, stability and development. ADMM supplements ARF in promoting practical cooperation in designated areas, while ARF helps in sharing of knowledge and practices. The focus of both is on preventive and not coercive diplomacy in the Asia-Pacific region. ARF has 27 member states, 10 ASEAN members, 10 dialogue partners and 7 other countries (Bangladesh, DPRK, Mongolia, Pakistan, Papua New Guinea, Timor Lestz and Sri Lanka). It is adopting a three-stage evolutionary approach to security related issues, namely Confidence Building Measures, Development of Preventive Diplomacy and Elaboration of Approaches to Conflicts. So far, it has embraced the first two.

ARF's uniqueness lies in connecting defence officials and diplomats at one forum. India became an ARF member in 1996. It has organized several seminars, workshops/training programmes for ARF members in the areas of anti-piracy, cyber-security, maritime security and peacekeeping. India also co-chaired an Inter Sessional Meeting (ISM) on counter-terrorism and transnational crimes, which was held in February 2008 in Indonesia. India has voiced concerns over terrorism and stressed the need for 'a stable maritime system and unimpeded right of passage and other maritime rights' (ARF Meeting, 2013).

As far as ADMM+ is concerned, five areas for practical cooperation were identified initially. These included maritime security, counter-terrorism, disaster management, peace keeping operations and military medicine. The year 2013 was a milestone as defence forces of ADMM+ members joined in exercises in the areas of Humanitarian Assistance and Disaster Relief (HADR) in Brunei Darussalam on 17-20 June; Counter-terrorism Exercises (CTX) in Sentul (Indonesia) on 9-13 September and training exercise in Sydney (Australia) on 28 September-1 October. India has offered to participate in a new area, 'Humanitarian Mine Action', in partnership with Vietnam (ADMM+ Meeting, 2013).

ASEAN-India strategic partnership presently involves multifaceted cooperation in 26 inter-governmental mechanisms at various levels. These include annual meetings among ministers of agriculture, tourism, foreign affairs, commerce and telecommunications. Ministerial level meetings are also held in the areas of global energy and environment. There are Working Groups for SMEs, heads of space agencies, etc. ASEAN-India Joint Cooperation Committee (JCC) meetings and Senior Official Meetings (SOM) are held regularly. India maintains regular connectivity with the ASEAN Connectivity Coordination Committee (ACCC).

ASEAN-India Plan of Action (2010-15), which delineates various activities, is at the heart of cooperation. At the 7th ASEAN-India Summit in 2009, India committed US $50 million for its implementation. There is good progress in the implementation of various programmes and activities. India extends 'visa on arrival' facility to seven ASEAN countries on a reciprocal basis. The other focused areas for cooperation include agriculture and forestry; small and medium enterprises; trade and commerce. A notable feature was the organization of adjunct promotional activities along with the ASEAN-India Commemorative Summit, like ASEAN-India Business Fair in December 2012 and Agro Expo in October 2012 in New Delhi.

Connectivity remains a strategic priority between India and ASEAN. It is both physical and human connectivity. India is for timely implementation of the India-Myanmar-Thailand Trilateral Highway and the Kaladan Multimodal Transit Transport Project. The importance of road connectivity was symbolically highlighted through the ASEAN-India Car Rally, covering 8,000 km in 22 days during November-December 2012, with the prime minister receiving rallyists in Delhi on 21 December on the completion of journey. The rally 'symbolizes the vision of an ASEAN-India community where people, goods, services and ideas travel freely between us'. The maritime connectivity was underscored through the shipping expedition of *INS Sudarshini* to ASEAN countries during September 2012 and March 2013. A special feature was the holding of 'Marker' events at various places en route, to connect people culturally and commercially.

India is also actively involved in human resource development as it supports the ASEAN Community Building (ACB) process. A key component is the setting up of Centres for English Language Training (CELT) and Entrepreneurship Development Centres (EDC) in CLMV countries. Other programmes include participation of school students in the National Science Congress, Farmers' Exchange Programme and training of ASEAN diplomats at the Foreign Service Institute (FSI), New Delhi.

Certain other steps have also been taken to enhance connectivity at the people-to-people level. Some of the measures include the setting up of the ASEAN-India Network of Think Tanks (AINTT) and ASEAN-India Centre (AIS) at the Research and Information Systems (RIS), New Delhi in July 2013. These are aimed at connecting the academics and the academic institutes, as so far the engagement has been largely government-centric. Media exchange programme for journalists and interface between parliamentarians are the other new additions to widen cooperation among different interest groups.

INDIA AND ASEAN: SUB-REGIONAL COOPERATION AND BEYOND ASEAN

At the sub-regional level, India connects with some ASEAN members through three arrangements, called the BIMSTEC; MGC Programme and BCIM Corridor. Primary focus of the sub-regional groups is to connect northeast India with the Southeast Asian countries. BIMSTEC is more important from the Indian perspective as it provides a 'unique link between South and Southeast Asia' (EAM 2014), connecting five South Asian countries (Bangladesh, Bhutan, Nepal, Sri Lanka and India) with two countries in Southeast Asia (Myanmar and Thailand). BIMSTEC, which 'lies at the crossroads between SAARC and ASEAN' (PM, 2014: 1), facilitates cooperation in five areas – connectivity, economic cooperation, energy, security and people-to-people links. India attaches importance to promotion of parliamentary youth and sporting and cultural exchanges and has started organizing 'an annual BIMSTEC Seminar to increase awareness of our grouping (PM, 2014: 2).

India is shepherd in four areas, namely, transport and communication; tourism; environment and disaster management; and counter-terrorism and transnational crime. Prime Minister Manmohan Singh attended the third BIMSTEC Summit at Nay Pie Taw in Myanmar on 4 March 2014. He stressed the need for connectivity in trade, energy and tourism, urging the declaration of 2015 'as a year of BIMSTEC Tourism'. He also sought early ratification of the Convention on Cooperation in Combating International Terrorism, Trans-National Organized Crime and Illicit Drug Trafficking and early signing of the BIMSTEC Convention on Mutual Legal Assistance in Criminal Matter and early commencement of negotiations on a BIMSTEC Convention on Extradition (PM, 2014: 2). India also offered to establish BIMSTEC Centre for Weather and Climate in Bengaluru. India has also agreed to provide 31 per cent of the budgetary support to the BIMSTEC Secretariat to be set up at Dhaka.

On the other hand, the MGC Programme connects India with five ASEAN countries (Cambodia, Laos, Myanmar, Thailand and Vietnam). This aims at renewing civilizational links, as we connect people inhabiting two major river banks. The focus of cooperation is in the areas of education, tourism, culture, transport and communications. Under this programme, India provides 50 MGC scholarships for the study of culture, Buddhism, IT and vocational training. India hosted 100 Buddhist pilgrims during 5-12 September 2007. An important milestone for cooperation was the establishment of the MGC Museum of Asian Traditional Textiles in Siem Reap, adjacent to Angkor Wat, Cambodia. This museum was inaugurated on 7 April 2014, and is expected to develop into a 'live' museum that symbolizes not only 'cultural and institutional linkages between us but also of our commercial trade over centuries' (Secretary East 2014: 1).

The third sub-regional grouping, BCIM, providing an economic corridor among the four countries, however, has been slow in taking off even though it was mooted a decade ago. This obviously got a push during the visit of Chinese prime minister Li Keqiang to India in May 2013. At a meeting of officials from the four countries in January 2014 in Delhi, it was agreed to come up with a joint study report by June, providing concrete proposals and financing modalities. The ultimate aim is to identify 'achievable infrastructure projects to boost physical connectivity' (Tuteja 2014).

India also connects beyond ASEAN through other ASEAN-centred forums such as the Asia Europe Meet (ASEM) and the East Asia Summit (EAS). ASEM, a dialogue forum between Asian and European countries was created in 1996. I recall that our initial efforts in getting admission were not successful, as Europe would toss it to ASEAN and ASEAN would stall on account of its then concerns in accepting Australia as an Asian country. India was finally admitted in 2007. ASEM summits are held biannually and the then Prime Minister Manmohan Singh attended the 7th ASEM Summit in Beijing on 24-5 October 2008. ASEM serves as 'a bridge between Asia and Europe and as a platform for dialogue to promote stability, peace and development (ASEM 2013:1). The Asia-Europe Foundation (ASEF) was created in 1997, as ASEM's permanent institution, to facilitate cultural, academic and people-to-people exchanges.

The EAS group is the result of an initiative taken by the then prime minister of Malaysia Mahathir Mohammad in 1991. The first EAS was held in Kuala Lumpur in 2006. The membership then included ASEAN+3 (China, Japan, Republic of Korea)+3 (Australia, India and New Zealand). Russia and USA were included as members at the 6th Summit held in Bali (Indonesia) on 19 November 2011. The primary focus of EAS has been on energy and environment; finance; education; natural disaster management and pandemics. Later, two more areas, Connectivity and Comprehensive Economic Partnership in East Asia (CEPEA) were included. A major initiative of the EAS was the launching of the negotiations on the Regional Comprehensive Economic Partnership (RCEP) in 2012 and these are expected to be completed by 2015.

India is actively associated with ASEM and EAS. It is involved in the current negotiations leading towards RCEP. It was at the 4th EAS in Thailand on 24-5 October 2009 that India received the endorsement for the setting up of the Nalanda University as a 'non-state, non-profit, secular and self-governing international institution'. The university has become partially functional from the academic year 2014-15 and is located at Rajgir, Bihar. Amartya Sen, Nobel Laureate, is the Chancellor of the university and expects it to 'provide high quality education relevant to India and the region' (Guha 2014). India is also involved with other EAS activities and it hosted the 'EAS-India Workshop 2012: Building a Regional Framework for Earthquake Risk Management' in New Delhi in November 2012.

India is also participating in various activities of the ASEM and has made an annual contribution of US $100,000 to ASEF since 2007, which was enhanced to US $120,000 in 2011. ASEF projects in India have focused on art and education. India also hosted two important meetings – ASEF Board of Governors (BoG) meeting on 9-13 October 2012 and the 11th ASEM Foreign Ministers Meeting held on 11 November 2013 in New Delhi. Indian focus at ASEM, as conveyed by the external affairs minister at that meeting, was to promote 'tangible cooperation' through 'result-oriented initiatives' and move ASEM 'beyond a declaratory political dialogue, towards tangible deliverables and concrete action in a more predetermined manner' (ASEM 2013: 3). It is also to make it move beyond 'a forum for political dialogue' by reaching out to people by involving 'civil society, industry and media' (ASEM 2013: 2). There was none the less recognition of the need to create public awareness on ASEM, given the lack of knowledge about this organization.

CHANGING WORLD ARCHITECTURE

What is the changing world architecture, which has a bearing on India's LEP? Asia is emerging on the world scene with two countries, India and China, leading the way. Japan is regaining its importance, while South Korea and Vietnam have also appeared on the horizon. Would it usher in an era of cooperative peace, development and prosperity – the core goals of ASEAN? Would China force its own way, as it struts on the global stage, with India remaining on the margins at the regional level? How would the United States place itself, as a 'pivot' in Asia as earlier stated; or would it adopt a modified posture, playing the 'rebalancing' role? How would it strike a balance between 'its security commitments to Japan and South Korea and its economic engagement with China' (Raja Mohan 2014:1)?

What role does Japan see for itself as a new spirit of 'nationalism' engulfs it under Prime Minister Shinzo Abe, forcing it to come out of its 'self-defence security shell'? How would a confident Vietnam stake its claims in this new emerging 'Asia'? How would an unpredictable nuclearized North Korea behave? This raises the question as to how these Asian powers would engage with one another, either in partnership or in competition, as they try to enhance their spheres of influence, while pursuing ASEAN's stated goals.

While there is a climate for cooperation, yet there are conflicts that are visible; some others are still latent or dormant. Conflict and cooperation go hand-in-hand. Territorial jurisdictions over the islands in the South and East China Sea have emerged as flash points from time to time. It is the desire to control the sea-bed resources, which is at the root of this, as each country would like to plunder the 'Sea Commons', giving go bye to cooperative endeavours.

It is China which emerges as the main adversary on the one side, while Japan, Vietnam, Malaysia or the Philippines find themselves placed on the other side. So far, no compromise appears to be in sight. This is the factual position as it stands today and we are not going into the rights or wrongs of the claims or counter-claims of the respective parties. India had a taste of Chinese power and its confrontationist approach when it tried to assert its right of passage through the South China Sea, in compliance with UNCLOS, in pursuit of its commercial interests for offshore drilling.

The four-nation trip of President Obama of the United States to Japan, South Korea, Malaysia and the Philippines in April 2014 stayed focus on the concerns in the region over the rising Chinese power. A deft balance between geopolitical interests in the region with the geo-economic necessities was worked out. The US-Japan joint statement expressed its opposition to China for 'any attempt to assert territorial or maritime claims, through the use of intimidation, coercion or force'; simultaneously it recognized the important role of China by reaffirming 'their interest in building a productive and constructive relationship'. In the Philippines, Obama assured its security through a defence pact, but was careful to point out to China that it was not to 'counter' or 'contain' it, as it celebrated its progress. The United States is thus playing 'hide and seek' with China.

The 2014 USA-Japan joint statement also imparted an element of trilateralism, as it sought cooperation 'with like-minded partners, including the Republic of Korea, Australia and India' in 'promoting peace and security in the Asia-Pacific and around the globe' (US-Japan Joint Statement, 2014). Is India willing to be drawn into such an arrangement and play this role?

Seeds for latent conflict are also visible as China expands its power beyond its natural sphere of influence. China's commitment to Pakistan, which is its 'all-weather friend' (Krishnan 2013: 1), is well known, as it tries to reach the Indian Ocean through the Gwadar Port by constructing the Karakoram Highway (Joshua 2013: 1). Its efforts in making inroads into Maldives, Nepal and Sri Lanka through establishing strong economic and strategic links are also a pointer in this regard (Krishnan 2014: 2).

In its approach, China has made a tactical change by sugar-coating its interests, as it diplomatically gives a civilizational slant. It would not like to be seen decorated by the so-called 'String of Pearls', as it acquires rights over seaports. Rather, it would like to be seen as a partner in the 'Maritime Silk Road (MSR)' and has committed US $500 million (Krishnan 2014: 1) to MSR by projecting its strength as a force 'for peace and the positive energy for friendship', as it would result in strengthening 'maritime, economic, environment, technical and scientific cooperation' (Chaturvedy 2014).

China's claims over airspace in East China Sea through the declaration of Air Defence Identification Zone (ADIZ) have added another flashpoint, as the same is being challenged by the USA and Japan (BBC 2014). China has won the first game of chess, as USA-Japan failed to effectively checkmate it.

The world attention is focused on post-2014 Afghanistan. The US departure from the front positions would create vacuum. Pakistan would like to increase its profile in this area which it considers to be of strategic depth to itself. Would it join hands with the Taliban, making it a hotbed for future terrorist acts? Would India, on the other hand, like to move beyond its present developmental role as a soft power in Afghanistan? Would it consider entering the field of military hardware? Would India be prepared to undertake this high risk route as the two Super Powers had to bite the dust in this process? It is not in India's ethos to embroil itself in a war zone or theatre. Nor is it prepared to receive body bags.

The world is also witnessing a complex phenomenon where there is a confluence of economic interests, while leaders cry themselves hoarse as they harp on their sovereign rights. This results in creating a delicate balance between 'geo-politics' and 'geo-economics'; it is precariously held and is always under pressure. A diplomatic game is in constant play, in forging relationships between the United States and China, or China and Japan or the two Koreas or even China and Taiwan or Hong Kong.

The world financial architecture has not changed, apart from cosmetic references on the need to bring about greater equity in its functioning. At the global trade front, regional trade agreements are vitiating the atmosphere. Protectionist forces are reappearing, be it the EU banning the import of mangoes (*The Hindu*, 2014: 2) or the looming conflict on IPRs with the USA (Sharma 2014), the decision on which was postponed, given the diplomatic sensitivity in India at the time of elections (Chaudhuri 2014).

Some silver linings are, however, appearing on the horizon as countries start reposing their faith in the World Trade Organization in pursuing the Doha Development Agenda. Hopefully, this would put on hold the worldwide trend towards signing Regional Free Trade Agreements as leaders reaffirm their faith in a non-discriminatory world trade regime. This is bound to have its impact on regional arrangements like ASEAN. There are some other positive developments as congruity of views emerges on the environment and other areas. Terrorism is another area where leaders share their concerns at the global level but leave the individual countries to find their own solutions.

Post-Cold War era has seen the emergence of new arrangements like IBSA, BRICS and ASEM, which cut across continents and ideological divides. New strategic partnerships are emerging and reemerging as the countries look to protect their economic and political interests by forging various pluralistic arrangements, rendering the concept of sovereignty amorphous. Regimes are changed in the name of safeguarding human rights and promoting democracy. The United States is working on an ambitious arrangement, the Trans-Pacific Partnership (TPP), even though there are concerns over certain issues in Japan and other likely partners.

We are now again seeing the return of the Cold War days, with Russia incorporating Crimea into its territory, justifying the same on the grounds of it having acceded though a referendum. The heart of the problem is the country's sovereignty. Could one country acquire another sovereign territory to protect its sovereignty? It is simply a game of 'real-politik'. It is now no more 'resetting' of relationship between Russia and USA, but preventing the 'refreezing' of the same, as they re-enter the Cold War days. India's response is calibrated as it abstained from vote on Crimea at the UN General Assembly Resolution, reiterating its known position against individual sanctions, while extending its support to the principle on respecting and preserving the territorial integrity and sovereignty of nations (Dikshit 2014).

INDIA'S RESPONSE TO THE CHANGING WORLD ARCHITECTURE

How does India view its role in this emerging political, security and economic architecture? India has adopted the strategic partnership route. It established such arrangement with France in 1998; with Russia and Germany in 2000; with the UK in 2004 and China in 2005; with Australia and USA in 2009; with Saudi Arabia in 2010 and with ASEAN in 2012. These relationships exist with over 30 countries; with the USA it is known as Global Strategic Partnership, as the focus is on bilateral and global issues.

India's pluralistic approach in entering into strategic partnership with big and small powers has resulted in fuzzing the line between strategic and non-strategic content of its relationship. The driving force at one end has been the need to have access to nuclear power and dual-use technology while on the other hand, it is to procure critical and strategic raw materials. From the other side, it is their desire for share in the Indian economic pie, through the setting up of nuclear power plants and supply of defence equipment, be it through direct sales or joint-manufacturing facilities.

Such relationships have been dubbed differently, inviting some catchy phrases like 'natural allies' (*Indian Express*, 2000) or 'one of the defining relationships in the 21st century' as later stated by President Obama. Please note that the word 'allies' does not mean 'Allies' as comrades-in-arms and does not take away independence from India's foreign policy. India-Russia Strategic Partnership was announced during the visit of Putin to India in October 2000, focusing on 'enhanced cooperation in political, trade and other fields' (Declaration 2000).

Does the above approach dent India's so-called 'Nonaligned Policy'? Is this policy still alive or is it already debunked? Has it emerged in its new 'Avatar', called 'Nonalignment 2.0' as stated by a group of former diplomats and academicians? The report stated that India's 'strategic objectives' had to be against the backdrop of its 'development needs' and 'constitutional provisions'. It further opines that India would have to stand for 'the highest human and universal values'; while aiming at 'being powerful', it must set 'new standards for what the powerful must do' (Nonalignment 2.0 Report, 2012). Would such high sounding and laudable objectives, mixing power with morality, work?

To put it simply, would this mean 'Non-alignment with a strategic tilt towards the West', unlike 'Non-alignment 1.0', which was perceived to have a tilt towards the East? Could this be called the vintage 'Genuine Non-alignment', a formulation adopted by the former Prime Minister Vajpayee? How would national interest be determined? Would it be dictated by universal values or pragmatism or an alloy of the two, as India steers its way through international minefield? India is likely to adopt the 'Golden mean' of Buddha, between morality and real-politik

How should India respond to China? Should it be through the usual cliché, 'there is enough space for both'? Should we go ahead with the Track-2 approach of cooperation in economic and other areas, while letting the issue of territorial dispute move at its own pace? While doing so, we have to be alert to the Chinese global and strategic interests as we safeguard our security concerns. We should, however, avoid offering alibi, on behalf of China, on ticklish border or territorial issues.

India has to simultaneously ensure that Chinese penetration in the power, telecommunication and infrastructure (roads) sectors does not impinge on its security interests. We need to safeguard against a scenario where increased Chinese economic power would result in enhancing its negotiating power. India its part has to increase its economic profile in China and hence create a dependency situation for China also. With China, India has moved from a *Bhai-Bhai* to a 'Buy-Buy' relationship where we are becoming dependant, even for our religious figures (*The Hindu*, 2014: 4). It should not be allowed to lead to confrontation and reach a 'Bye-Bye' stage.

How would India like to fit 'Cherry Blossoming' of its relationship with Japan in the context of 'USA-China-Japan triangle? How do we factor in Chinese hostility, while honestly saying that 'we are not building relations in hostility against China?' (Shankar K. Bajpai). Japan would like to see increasing involvement with India in maritime exercises (Patranobis 2014: 2). Simultaneously, we have to build enough mutual stakes to ensure its longevity, as cherry blossoms have a short life. This would need to be nurtured carefully given lingering differences on nuclear policy-related issues. Japan would like India to become its trilateral partner with the United States. So far, it has been ambivalent and has responded in a halting and hesitating manner.

After the holding of the first phase of presidential elections in Afghanistan on 5 April 2014, the media message for the new government in India was the need 'to demonstrate much stronger commitment to the unity, stability and security of Afghanistan amid the continuing threats from Pakistan and declining western support to Kabul' (*Indian Express*, 2014). India's development assistance was to build 'infrastructure, aid capacity building and support social empowerment'. Some experts suggest that this 'may now be expanded to incorporate military cooperation', as without 'backing it with a display of intention to protect Indian interests would be a waste of strategic effort and investments' (Afghanistan Task Force Report, 2014). They further suggest that this could be carried through 'non-interference in Afghanistan's internal affairs through regional compacts guaranteed by the State'. Are we thinking to go beyond our original mandate, limited to protecting our interests? India has reportedly adopted a median path in channelizing its assistance for military hardware through the intermediation of other countries. Are we on the right track? Not necessarily.

India would also like to see a greater role for itself in the international and regional organizations. It would like to see the principle of equity prevail, whether it is a question of a seat in the UN Security Council or the question of greater weightage at the International Monetary Fund or the World Bank. Similarly, it would like to ensure that the rights of have-nots are protected, whether it is in the arena of environment (climate change) or global trade [agriculture in the World Trade Organization (WTO)]. India would like to see a role for itself in the governance of the cyber world, in the direction of 'Internet' becoming 'Equinet', providing for say for all nations (Joshi 2014).

India definitely sees a larger role for itself, even though not inspired by erstwhile slogans like 'India Shining' or 'India Awakening'. Modi's election victory has given a new slogan, 'India reinvigorated'. To do so, is it prepared to go beyond the use of 'soft power'? India is perceived to be a 'benign power', and it has held steadfastly to this. Is it willing to use a mix of hard and soft power? So far, it has avoided the hard power option; it even failed to follow through in executing its own threat of use of right of 'hot pursuit' against Pakistan.

This raises another issue. Does India have 'strategic culture', as this question is often asked by experts? Views among the experts are divided, depending upon how the term 'strategic' is defined. Let us grant that India has strategic culture, as it is strategically prepared to meet global challenges, even though it has not been spelt out in a White Paper or enunciated as a policy. Shivshankar Menon, former National Security Advisor, said that India needed its own 'strategic vocabulary and doctrines, as it engaged the world, while avoiding entanglement', keeping in view 'the extent and limits of India's power and its potential uses, and a clear prioritization between our interests and our goals' (NSA 2013: 1).

While geo-economics had been the driving force, yet this cannot be at the cost of geopolitics. The Russian incorporation of Crimea fully demonstrates this. In the Indian subcontinent we see a constant interplay of geopolitics vs. geo-economics, as for Pakistan geopolitics acquires primacy over geo-economics, as seen from the delay in the grant of MFN to India and instead negotiate a new arrangement called Non-Discriminatory Market Access (NDMA). Therefore, geopolitics cannot be wished away as physical boundaries do matter.

Some doubts have been raised by the strategic community over India's capabilities. The current debate on civilian-military relationship (Malik 2014) creating the office of the Chief of Defence Forces and streamlining procedures for defence procurement, only shows chinks in India's defence armoury and hence its likely constraints on the use of 'hard power'. India has the world's third largest army which is highly professional but is deficient in modern equipment. Indian Navy, which had earlier caused concern to Australia, as a 'Blue Navy' is still not adequately equipped to play the role of a maritime power and the likelihood of its edge over China eroding, even in the Indian Ocean looms large (Saran 2014: 1).

India would like to enhance cooperation with ASEAN countries in meeting security challenges from terrorism and other non-traditional areas. This was reiterated at the BIMSTEC Summit by the Indian prime minister by stating, 'Like our prosperity, our security too is indivisible – whether it is the security of sea lanes of communications in our region or the persisting challenges of terrorism and transnational crimes (PM, 2014: 2).

India also recently demonstrated that it could play a global role when it joined other countries in April 2014 in looking for debris of the Malaysian Airways Flight MH 730. India, however, excels itself at another level – placing itself in the role of a 'friendly navy', whether playing host to a group of navies in an annual exercise called 'Milan' (Togetherness) or conducting naval exercises with other countries or undertaking goodwill visits by its naval fleet, from time to time. While doing so, it has to be mindful of the sensitivities of certain powers.

India, however, is not alone in this respect. An interesting phenomenon is developing where navies from countries belonging to different defence arrangements and subscribing to different ideologies, criss-cross one other in naval meets and naval exercises. At a recent naval exercise in April 2014, marking the 65th anniversary of the founding of the Chinese People's Liberation Navy (CPLN), held in Qingdao (East China), naval ships from India and Pakistan participated, even though they were involved in different sets of exercises. On the other hand, the Japanese Navy was not invited for the exercise, although the Japanese naval chief participated at the Western Pacific Naval Symposium (WPNS). The US reportedly refused to participate in the exercise.

An interesting side development at Qingdao was the interest shown by Admiral Kawano from Japan to rejoin the Indo-US Malabar Exercise (Patranobis 2014: 3), while the Indian Naval Commander made a diplomatic excuse not to show the Operation Control Room of *INS Shivalik* to the Chinese Admiral Wu Shangli, when he visited the ship (Krishnan 2014: 4). Pakistan Navy on its part also held its 'Aman 13 Exercise' with the Chinese and other navies in the Arabian Sea in February 2013 (Krishnan 2013: 2).

Could India play the role of a global power if it finds its hands shackled in its neighbourhood? Pakistan had literally tied down India in a Hamletian dilemma, 'To be or not to be', on the commencement of dialogue by cleverly skirting India's concerns on terrorism-related issues. India's domestic compulsions had also stood in the way of improvement of relationship with Bangladesh. Domestic pressures and politics had also been responsible for creating concerns in Sri Lanka, as India shifted its stand at UNHCR during 2012-14. A clash of economic interests has dented relationship with Maldives on the management of an airport by GMR. Problems have also arisen with its closest neighbour, Bhutan, on the issue of gas price. Nepal feels itself distanced as no Indian prime minister has graced it with a bilateral visit to that country since 1997. This concern has been mitigated with Prime Minister Modi's visit soon after his swearing in.

Would success in India's 'Extended Neighbourhood' mitigate its failure in its neighbourhood policy? Or would India have to tend its relationship with neighbours if it has to reach its 'Extended Neighbourhood'? India took a 'political decision' to abstain from voting at the UNHRC resolution against Sri Lanka, as stated by Foreign Secretary Sujatha Singh (*The Hindu*, 2014: 3). Media greeted this with positive headlines, 'Abstention Louder than vote' (Haidar 2014) and 'Diplomatic Gains from a Strategic Abstention' (Srinivasan 2014). India's approach was hailed as 'excellent diplomacy', with the Sri Lankan foreign minister Peiris calling it 'a significant development' and President Rajapaksa announcing the release of Indian fishermen, as a gesture of goodwill.

There is hope that the 'seemingly strategic abstention in Geneva could potentially turn into actual gain' and we see similar other positive attitudes in the neighbourhood. Pakistani prime minister Nawaz Sharif's message to build a 'peaceful neighbourhood' based on 'cooperation' and not 'confrontation' is a good augury. Is he prepared to 'walk the talk', as in the past he has often stumbled, as India-Pakistan relations are accident prone.

How would Modi's masterly diplomatic stroke of inviting SAARC leaders to the swearing-in-ceremony, akin to coronation, on 26 May ultimately play out? Would he succeed in injecting the spirit of *Sab ka Saath, Sab ka Haath* (With everyone, holding everyone's hand), a la ASEAN spirit? The main focus, however, remains on India-Pakistan relations, diminishing the SAARC character. How would these play out in the future; 'more of same or making a fresh start' (*The Tribune* 2014: 3).

India recognizes that it has to win the hearts in its neighbourhood if it wants to play a major role in the world. What we need is a change of mindset in the neighbourhood, as a realization emerges that peace, cooperation and development in South Asia are interlinked and are in our mutual interest.

PERCEPTIONS IN ASEAN ON ENGAGING INDIA

What are the messages that echo from leaders in ASEAN countries on engaging India? Delhi Dialogue VI held on 8-9 March 2014 provided an ideal opportunity to feel the ASEAN pulse. There was a certain amount of congruity of views among leaders, even though it is customary to make positive statements on such occasions. A common refrain was that ASEAN-India Strategic Partnership was 'benign'. This relationship was among 'natural partners' thrust together, who had 'mutual affinity' and thirst for 'mutual prosperity' (Singapore). India is viewed as 'a key regional and global player' (Thailand) and is perceived to have become 'a big stakeholder in the security and geopolitical architecture of the region' (Philippines).

Given this mutuality of interests, what really mattered was 'where to go' and 'how to go' (Philippines). The focus had to be on 'concrete action and not on statements' (Laos). The key to success lay in ensuring the delivery of the Action Plan of 2011-15 and the joint statement issued at the ASEAN-India Commemorative Summit of 2012.

India-ASEAN relationship was anchored in trade, and it had to be taken to higher levels of US $100 billion in 2015 from the current level of US $72 billion. A target of US $200 billion was set for 2022 (AIEPG 2012). India needed to give a new 'Thrust' by adopting 'Go East' motto, as it went for increased investments in ASEAN countries.

There was also a need for providing greater thrust to ongoing activities in the areas of infrastructural linkages – physical and human. Similarly, cooperation needed to be accelerated in non-traditional security areas like food and water management; anti-piracy; terrorism and disaster management, as the countries cooperated in defence and security-related areas under the auspices of forums like ASEAN Regional Forum (ARF) and ASEAN Defence Ministers Meeting (ADMM)+.

While the above was the broad thrust as seen by ASEAN members, yet there were other areas where country-specific thrust was given by some. Some of these are given below, as these would need to be factored into future action programme for 2016-20.

- To establish a 'code of conduct governing the countries in East Asia', in response to changing 'geopolitical, geo-strategic and geo-economic developments' (Vietnam).
- To develop a legally binding instrument on the lines of the Treaty of Amity and Cooperation (TAC) for a wider region, covering countries around the Pacific and Indian Oceans, which could be called 'Indo-Pacific Treaty of Friendship and Cooperation' (Indonesia).
- To consider facilitating greater involvement of northeast India

in the context of India's Look East Policy, resulting in economic benefits to the northwestern part of Myanmar (Myanmar). The Seven Sisters of the northeast had to become an integral part of the 'Look East Policy' (Thailand).

- To facilitate implementation of the Master Plan on ASEAN Connectivity, with India taking initiative by inviting members of the ASEAN Connectivity Coordination Committee (AICC), who visited India in February 2014 (Myanmar and Thailand)?
- To provide connectivity between Southeast Asia and South Asia, as India developed the Mekong-India Economic Corridor (MIEC) (Myanmar).
- To promote maritime security by addressing piracy and other threats to maritime connectivity (Thailand and Indonesia).
- To reach out to 'wider public on both sides' and jointly addressing 'threats to human security, such as climate change, natural disasters and food and energy security' (Thailand).
- To involve other stakeholders, including civil societies (Thailand).
- To promote the 'core principles of democracy and economics' (Philippines).
- To put in place 'transparent economic and regulatory rules' by upholding and promoting 'the Panchsheel principles and the rule of law, in accordance with international laws, including UNCLOS (Philippines).

CONCLUDING OBSERVATIONS

India-ASEAN relations were catapulted to strategic level in 2012 from what started as a baby step in 1992. It has followed a positive trajectory in attaining present heights. What is the strategic content in the relationship? How does this relate to India's strategic partnership with other countries? What are the pillars on which this strategic partnership rests? Do we need to go beyond ASEAN and inlet into Indo-Pacific Partnership structures?

We have seen a strategic shift in India's approach to ASEAN over the years. While Narasimha Rao was writing 'a new chapter in India's relations with ASEAN', he simultaneously stressed the importance of giving 'mutually beneficial content' to bilateral relations (Ram 2012). Gujral on the other hand was keen to build 'permanent institutional linkages with ASEAN'.

Since 2010, we have given a new dimension to the relationship, where India-ASEAN relations at the regional level are giving a push to bilateral relations, as seen through India-ASEAN FTA and India-ASEAN Commemorative Summit. India has entered a proactive phase in implementing the ASEAN-India Action Plan (2010-15).

The Look East Policy has come to 'occupy a pivotal place in India's foreign policy concerns' (Haidar 2012). The policy, however, has enjoyed national consensus and the new Modi government stands committed to the same as affirmed in the BJP's manifesto to strengthen forums like SAARC and ASEAN.

Let us first look at the guiding principles that govern India's strategic partnership with other countries. India entered into its first strategic partnership with France in 1998. The push came from a desire for cooperation in the defence and nuclear fields. This was also the moving force that guided other strategic partnerships that followed, with Russia, Germany, UK and the United States. The list of strategic partners is growing. It was the same omnibus thrust that pushed India into this partnership. India now has strategic partnership with over 30 countries. Were there any distinguishing features or were these fashioned in the same mould? Was India entering into strategic partnership on the lines of MFN clause in international trade agreements, which implied equal treatment?

Seen in this context, the advantages that come out of any special relationship or strategic partnership tend to get lost. The strategic partnership was, therefore, not aimed at any other force or to serve any specific interests. There was no punch and the beef was missing. Do we need to adopt a selective approach?

Where does India-ASEAN Strategic Partnership fit into this overall scheme? Is it a statement of intent and meant to act as a guidepost in giving a new thrust to the development of multi-faceted India-ASEAN relationship? The three broad pillars of ASEAN are: political and security, commerce and socio-cultural. India is for 'open, balanced, inclusive security architecture', given its shared interest with ASEAN in 'maritime security, counter-terrorism, anti-piracy and disaster management' (ASEAN-India Summit, 2012).

India-ASEAN Strategic Partnership Statement contains everything under the sun. There is, therefore, a genuine concern over implementation, as it is not possible to implement everything in a short timeframe. It is, therefore, not surprising that the theme of the Delhi Dialogue VI, which is a Track 1.5 process, was the implementation of the vision statement of the ASEAN-India Commemorative Summit

2012. What is, therefore, required is to identify areas and programmes to which thrust could be given in strengthening our relationship. This could be done by developing a new Plan of Action, 2016-20, as the present action plan comes to an end in 2015.

How would this work out in the area of maritime security, which would be the lynchpin of security relationship? India cannot remain a bystander after having flagged its commercial interests in the South China Sea. This would, therefore, necessitate our developing congruity of views, to ensure the safety of sea lanes and respect for international rules facilitating commerce, ensuring unhindered flow of goods. India would be willy-nilly drawn into the vortex if it wants to protect its commercial interests in the contested spaces in the South China Sea. For China, maritime security is showing its flag in the Indian Ocean, while for India it is still grappling with building adequate port infrastructure. China is committing US $500 million for developments of ports in the Indian Ocean (Krishnan 2014: 2). India would have to increase its capabilities as it tries to cooperate with other navies.

How do we evolve our strategic relationship with Russia and USA in this emerging security architecture, based on our experiences? In the case of Russia, I saw them honouring their commitments during 1991-2; while in the case of the USA, we continued facing problems in the implementation of the 1984 India-USA MoU on Technology Transfer, which dealt with dual-use technology.

How does India deal with a trusted friend, Russia, which stood by it and delivered, even when the Soviet Union withered away? Should India recognize 'Russia's legitimate interests in Ukraine' (Sibal 2014). How would India like to be seen as a trusted friend by Russia?

On the other hand, how can we place trust in the United States, where national interests are dictated by domestic compulsions that overtake international commitments? How could India also sustain strategic partnership with the USA without ensuring it economic returns through projects? Would democratic norms and practices stand in the way of awarding contracts? These relations are likely to remain transactional and not become transformational? If so, would it then result in India and the USA returning to the old era of 'estranged democracies'?

In the case of Russia, India has to ensure that it does not result in dilution of its principles, while in the case of the USA, it has to be ensured that there is 'strategic depth' in the relationship and the same is not destabilized by individual cases like the Khobragade visa issue or India being declared a priority country under Section 301 of the 1984 Trade and Tariff Act. While protecting trees we have to ensure that we do not destroy the woods.

How do we ensure strategic partnership, if it is not value but interest-based, as the same keep shifting? It is likely that a new architecture would be issue-based, where there would be shifting alliances, where countries holding similar interests would join hands to push a particular agenda. We may see more of 'coalition politics' in the international arena, as we are seeing in the domestic arena. We may see an era of pluralistic strategic partnerships like regional trade agreements.

How would India see the implementation of India's 'Nationalist Agenda' in foreign policy, as per BJP's manifesto to 'build a strong, self-reliant and self-confident India, regaining its rightful place in the comity of nations', as it builds 'Brand India' through '5T's – Tradition, Talent, Tourism, Trade and Technology' (BJP, 2014). Do we see a good mix of *Shanti* and *Shakti*? (Patranobis 2014: 1).

Is India getting ready to go beyond a *status quo* power as a call for review of its nuclear policy has been voiced? In any such review, jingoism should not be allowed to prevail and sobriety should rule in defining national interests in foreign policy.

Ultimately, national interests would govern the pursuit of foreign policy interests. Who will decide or arbitrate as to what is national interest? Would it be based on values or pragmatism? Would the pursuit of economic interests overtake other interests as stated by Prime Minister Narendra Modi? Would it be a new ball game or only a nuanced difference in approach from that of the UPA government?

States would have to find a place in the formulation/implementation of foreign policy. We are already moving in this direction. It would be more so in the context of LEP where northeast India has to be woven into this framework. While facilitating participation, it has to be ensured that they do not hold 'veto' over foreign policy, which should remain the preserve of the central government.

India-ASEAN relationship rests on the premise that India's interests in the region are benign and the same has stood the test of time. This strength, however, also becomes a constraining factor. This amounts to India restraining its role, taking recourse to use of 'soft' and not 'hard' power. The thrust of 'Strategic Partnership' would, therefore, be in pursuing a 'Developmental Agenda', by acquiring a 'Cooperative Character'.

THE WAY AHEAD

What is the way ahead? First and foremost, we have to evaluate the ASEAN-India Action Plan 2010-15, as we consider launching a new five-year Action Plan for 2016-20. This would need to reflect the continuity and the change in ASEAN-India relationship, while reaffirming ASEAN centrality. ASEAN-India connectivity process has to move to 'how' and we need to focus on a limited number of priority areas (EAM 2014: 1).

For India, the challenge would be how to collaborate with its ASEAN partners in creating 'an inclusive, pluralistic and balanced regime architecture', which genuinely represents 'multi-polar Asia' with no single power getting to set the agenda (Secretary East, 2014: 2). Our thrust has to be in this direction.

We, however, have to bear in mind that India-ASEAN relationship at the multilateral level would essentially be ASEAN-driven and ASEAN-centric. How could India provide greater thrust by being more proactive in realizing the unfinished goals of the 2010-15 Action Plan? At the sub-regional level it could be the product of a joint push and India could play a proactive role. At the bilateral level, India could play a greater proactive role.

We have also adopted the ASEAN-India Strategic Partnership route. This would need to be strengthened. While we pursue our engagement regionally, we have to strengthen our relationship bilaterally, recognizing its inevitability and diversity of relationship, as earlier noted by ASEAN-India Eminent Persons Group (AIEPG 2012).

India-ASEAN cultural relationship has taken a positive turn and thrust. It has shed its one-dimensional character. It is now viewed as a two-dimensional phenomenon where both gain from such cultural connectivity with each playing its role (Sahai 2013).

The existing exchange programme needs to be activated. There is also a need to promote regular and frequent exchanges of media personnel between India and ASEAN member countries and accelerate the existing programme on media exchanges. Recommendations of the ASEAN-India Eminent Persons Group need to be implemented on a priority basis (AIEPG 2012).

Eminent Persons Lecture Series, with which I was involved, commenced in 1997 with the Malaysian prime minister Mahathir delivering the first lecture. This has been lost in the sands of history.

It needs to be revived even though RIS has initiated a modified version.

India has taken some laudable initiatives, facilitating student exchanges, farmers' delegations, children's participation at the National Science Congress and training of diplomats at the Foreign Service Institute (FSI). Here again, there is a need to provide greater focus on the youth, be these academicians, parliamentarians or sports persons. The response from ASEAN countries is rather inadequate.

We need to extend visa facilities on arrival to the other three ASEAN member countries – Brunei, Malaysia and Thailand – hoping that they would reciprocate. In fact, Malaysia and Thailand had earlier granted visa on arrival facilities to Indians. We cannot talk of connectivity without free flow of persons.

We need greater collaborative arrangements between academic institutes. A prerequisite of this would be to determine equivalence of degrees, which is still not in place in many of the countries. The setting up of the India-ASEAN Centre in June 2013 at the Research and Information Systems (RIS), New Delhi, is a step in the right direction.

Hopefully, RIS would help in giving a push to promote academic linkages and provide the necessary thrust. It has taken India over a decade to set up such a centre. Therefore, energetic steps are called for to compensate for the lost time as well as clarify its mandate, whether it would be a promotional body facilitating linkages at the practical or academic levels.

India would have also to give a new thrust to its LEP. I would like to call it 'Act East Policy', while some of our friends from ASEAN would like to call it 'Go East Policy'. The emphasis would have to be on 'delivery' on the 'Actionable Points'. This is the message that echoed from ASEM Ministerial Meeting in November 2013 (ASEM 2013: 1) and Delhi Dialogue VI in March 2014. We need to take a leaf from the 2008 report of the ASEAN-Japan Eminent Persons Group (AJEPG 2008). India's involvement in 'Tangible Initiatives' in ASEM-related programmes is a welcome approach.

There is, therefore, a need for greater involvement in investment-related projects, as we have inherent advantages in establishing a sound and competitive supply chain system by capitalizing on our Free Trade Agreements in Goods, Services and Investments (AINTT 2012). Such an involvement would also take us a step further as we move towards building equities societies and world.

Discussion on social agenda issues like food security, poverty alleviation, corporate social responsibility (CSR) and other related themes would help us in learning from one another and adopting relevant policies. There would be a need to build synergies in the education sector through exchange of students and facilitating workable agreements on the equivalence of degrees.

Here it would be important for us to see how India regains what I would call 'Advantage Education', as the same has now passed on to some countries in Southeast Asia. India needs to turn its eyes on skill-based education if it has to reap the benefit of its demographic advantage. Could Nalanda University become the model for educational connectivity? We need to aim in this direction, given its global mandate and multi-country support.

India-ASEAN connectivity story would remain incomplete unless northeast India becomes an integral part of this process. Redoubled efforts would need to be made in this direction. This would lead to connectivity between South and Southeast Asia. This is, in particular, relevant for the success of sub-regional arrangements like BIMSTEC and Mekong-Ganga Cooperation (MGC). MEA has to play not only a coordinating role but also that of a catalyst, to give a push to connectivity-related issues.

Joint naval exercises with friendly countries and goodwill visits by naval ships could help in promoting understanding. India has such arrangements with a number of countries. While doing so, India would have to ensure that it takes into account the sensitivities of other countries. We see India even participating with China in both naval (Krishnan 2014: 5) and army exercises (Banerjee 2014).

The moot question would be how to turn this in to a Confidence Building Measure (CBM) and thus generate goodwill, even among competing countries with a history of conflict. A *modus operandi* has to be found where these do not result in enhancing security concerns of the partners or those who are excluded from the process.

Simultaneously, India should expand the 'Milan Exercise', which started as a goodwill programme, connecting naval officers from a few countries in Southeast Asia. In October 2011, it entered into a Trilateral Maritime Security Arrangement with Sri Lanka and Maldives. On the other hand, defence ties would have to be built on a bilateral basis, as it is being done with some countries.

How far are we prepared to go beyond the existing matrix of 'benign' relationship? Does India have the capacity and the capability to emerge into a 'hard' power by crossing the dashes and the dots in the political and security arena? Basically, we would have to see how we could expand relationship under the 'benign' matrix.

Should we go for India's inlet into the existing or new structures, embracing the Asia-Pacific region? We have no choice but to pursue this path. India cannot be seen to remain outside, when in these days, the trend is towards 'inclusive membership'. We have to be a part of that inclusivity and flow with the tide. Along with the above, it would be necessary to look at the larger picture and see how India and ASEAN could respond to the changing world architecture.

It would be necessary to see how India's passage is facilitated into Asia-Pacific architecture, be it the existing one like APEC or a new emerging Indo-Pacific group whose contours have still to be developed. This issue has still not been formally discussed among ASEAN members. It would, therefore, be in India's interest to engage ASEAN members and evolve an approach. Delhi Dialogue VII in 2015 could be the appropriate forum to discuss this, as some contours would have emerged by then.

How can we do that? Should we go with a begging bowl or place ourselves in a position where we are invited? Our experience in seeking membership of ASEM is a pointer in that direction; India would be welcome if it is perceived to be a strong power.

Therefore, in the final analysis, India has to emerge as a credible world power, going beyond a regional power. It need not stake such claims, but would get automatic acceptance if it emerges as an economic power by 2025, as predicted by experts. India is now recognized as the third largest economy in the world by experts from the World Bank. The high target of US $200 billion, as set for ASEAN-India trade by 2020, therefore, rests on these premises.

The story, however, would be incomplete if India is not able to tend its neighbourhood. Extended Neighbourhood policy has to be built on that edifice. Could India learn from the ASEAN experience of building cooperation by following the principles of consensus and consultation? Could we successfully apply this approach in changing the mindset of some of our partners in SAARC? A sincere effort would be required, hoping that this would get reciprocated under the dynamism of developmental compulsions.

India, therefore, has to impart greater thrust to India-ASEAN strategic partnership by making full use of its soft power. This could be achieved through building joint programmes in the education sector, like the Nalanda University. A greater thrust would need to be given to Knowledge Initiative towards Innovation by enhancing the existing programme by earmarking larger funds for the ASEAN-India Science and Technology Fund and ASEAN-India Green Fund. We need to take an initiative on the lines of India-USA Technology and Knowledge Initiative.

Indian diaspora has also failed to connect and become a bridge builder, as it has largely played a role for the host country. It has to connect with the home country also. India diaspora that is highly professional is imparting new dynamism to the relationship. How does it gel with the old diaspora? How could this diaspora play a meaningful role in the emerging world architecture?

Indian diaspora is eminently suited to play the role of a bridge builder as ASEAN countries have recognized its positive role, with some countries like Malaysia having an 'India Envoy' at the ministerial level. A focused discussion on 'India Diaspora in Southeast Asia' could be the theme for the Pravasi Bharatiya Divas (PBD) 2015.

India-ASEAN relationship, however, lacks visibility. It has still not enthused the media; even if it is accepted, the general preference of media is for coverage of domestic over international news (Panneerselvan 2014: 1). Steps have to be taken to bridge this gap. May be members of the Eminent Persons Group could write columns on a monthly basis in the media of different countries.

Finally, we have to impart greater visibility to the ASEAN-India growth story as we take it to peoples' doorsteps and should not allow it to remain anchored at the level of governments. The Delhi Dialogue Process should become the test of this trend, as and when it moves from Track 1.5 to Track 2. A people-driven and not government-driven programme would impart the necessary width and depth to ASEAN-India relationship.

We are 'Thirsting' for this new 'Thrust' in our relationship, as we recognize the strength of 'co-existence' through 'cooperation' in our march towards 'co-prosperity' in the twenty-first century. Let us, therefore, strive to strengthen 'regional institutional capability and capacity and investment in connectivity', thereby also fulfilling the 3Cs of Prime Minister Manmohan Singh's directive to Indian Heads of Missions (HOM's Meeting, 2013).

REFERENCES

ADMM Plus Meeting (2013). Statement by RRM (Minister of State for Defence), Brunei, 29 August.

Afghanistan Task Force Report (2014). G. Parthasarthy, and Radha Kumar, *What India Can Do.*

Ahmed, Khalid (2014). 'Afraid of Free Trade', *The Indian Express*, 25 April.

AIEPG (2012). 'ASEAN-India Eminent Persons Groups' Report to the Leaders'.

AINTT (2012). *ASEAN-India Strategic Partnership: Perspectives from the ASEAN-India Network of Think Tanks*, Proceedings of the First Round Table, 7-8 August, Published by RIS, New Delhi.

AJEPG (2008). *ASEAN-Japan Eminent Persons Groups' Report to the Leaders.*

ARF Meeting (2013). EAM's intervention at the 20th ARF Meeting, Brunei, 2 July.

ASEAN (2014). Speech by H.E. Le Luong Minh, Secretary-General of ASEAN at the Inaugural Session of the Realising ASEAN-India Vision for Partnership and Prosperity at Delhi Dialogue VI, New Delhi, 6-7 March.

ASEAN-India Summit (2012). Prime Minister's Response at the Summit, Phnom Penh, 19 November.

ASEAN-India Vision Statement (2012). Vision Statement – ASEAN-INDIA Commemorative Summit, New Delhi, 20 December.

ASEM (2013: 1). Chairman's Statement, 11th ASEM Foreign Ministers' Meeting, Delhi, 11 November.

——— (2013: 2). Inaugural Address by H.E. Mr. M. Hamid Ansari, Vice-President of India, 11th ASEM Foreign Ministers' Meeting, Chairman's Statement, Delhi, 11 November.

——— (2013: 3). Opening Remarks of Salman Khurshid, External Affairs Minister, 11th ASEM Foreign Ministers' Meeting, Chairman's Statement, Delhi, 11 November.

Bajpai, Shankar K. (2014). 'Japan, India and the Balance of Power', *The Hindu*, 27 January, 2014.

Banerjee, Ajay (2014). 'Indian, Chinese Troops to Hold Joint Exercises in Bhatinda This Year', *The Tribune*, 2 May.

Barua, Amit (2001), 'India-ASEAN Engagements will Come About: Mahathir', Interview of Prime Minister Dr. Mahathir Mohammad, *The Hindu*, 5 February.

BBC, 2014. 'US: China New Sea Rules Procedure', *BBC*, 10 January.

Bedi, Air Marshal R.S. (2014). 'China Flexes its Maritime Muscle', *The Tribune*, 5 April.

BIMSTEC Summit (2014). 'The Third BISTEC Summit Myanmar', *The Hindu*, 4 April.

BJP (2014). Election Manifesto of the Bharatiya Janata Party (BJP).

Brunei (2014). HE Dato Haji Erywan Bin Pehin Yossof, Permanent Secretary and SOM Leader for Brunei Darussalam for the ASEAN-India Strategic Partnership at Delhi Dialogue VI, New Delhi, 6-7 March.

Cambodia (2014). HE Dr. Sok Siphona, Advisor to the Royal Government, Cambodia at Delhi Dialogue VI, New Delhi, 6-7 March.

Chaturvedy, Rajeev Ranjan (2014). 'Reviewing the Maritime Silk Route', *The Hindu*, 11 April.

Chaudhuri, Pramit Pal (2014). 'Modi Card Help India Fend Off US Trade Sanctions', *The Hindustan Times*, 2 May.

Dasgupta, Sibal (2014). 'China Completes Tunnel to Link Pak, Plans Another', *The Times of India*, 2 March.

Declaration, 2000. Declaration on Strategic Partnership between the Republic of India and the Russian Federation, New Delhi, 4 October.

Dikshit, Sandeep (2014). 'India Not to Back Sanctions', *The Hindu*, 20 March.

EAM (2014: 1). Statement of External Affairs Minister, Salman Khurshid at the 14th BIMSTEC Ministerial Meeting, Nay Pyi Taw, Myanmar, 3 March.

——— (2014). HE Mr. Salman Khurshid, External Affairs Minister of India at Delhi Dialogue VI, New Delhi, 6-7 March.

Guha, Subhabrata (2014). 'Nalanda University to Start Classes in September', *The Times of India*, 2 May.

Gujral, I.K. (1996). Statement by External Affairs Minister I.K. Gujral at the Post-Ministerial Conference (PMC), Jakarta, 24 July.

Haidar, Salman (2012). 'Look East', in A.N. Ram (ed.), *Two Decades of India's Look East Policy*, ICWA and Manohar.

Haidar, Suhasini (2014). 'Abstention Louder than Any Vote', *The Hindu*, 31 March.

HOMs' Meeting (2013). 'Highlights of Prime Minister's Address at the Annual Conclave of Indian Ambassadors/High Commissioners Abroad, New Delhi, 4 November.

Indian Express (2000). 'India-US Summit, Clinton's Visit to India', 23 March.

——— (2014). 'Hope Prevails' (editorial), *The Indian Express*, 7 April.

Indonesia (2014). Statement by H.E. Mr. Rizali Wilmar Indrakesuma, Ambassador of the Republic of Indonesia to the Republic of India at Delhi Dialogue VI, New Delhi, 6-7 March.

Jayakumar. Remarks at EAM Jaswant Singh's Lecture at Singapore, 2000.

Joshua, Anita (2013: 1). 'China Takes Control of Gwadar Port', *The Hindu*, 18 February.

Joshi, Sandeep (2014). 'India to Suggest Renaming of Internet as "Equinet"', *The Hindu*, 16 April.

Krishnan, Ananth (2013: 1). 'Sino-Pakistan Friendship a Model for Bilateral Ties: Chinese Think-tank', *The Hindu*, 22 February.

——— (2013: 2). 'Chinese Anti-piracy Fleet to Join Pakistan Exercise', *The Hindu*, 17 February.

——— (2014: 1). 'Sri Lanka to Sign Landmark Trade Pact with China Soon', *The Hindu*, 12 February.

——— (2014: 2). 'China Moots Maritime Silk Road', *The Hindu*, 15 February.

——— (2014: 3). 'Japan Navy Chief's Message for New Indian Government', *The Hindu*, 24 April.

——— (2014: 4). 'An Unusual Request from Chinese Navy Chief', *The Hindu*, 25 April.

——— (2014: 5). 'India China to Deepen Naval Ties after Landmark Exercise', *The Hindu*, 26 April.

Landler, Mark (2014). 'Pact Obliges US to Protect Japan in Island Fight: Obama' (NYT), quoted in *The Indian Express*, 25 April.

Laos (2014). Statement by H.E. Mr. Thongloun Sisoulith, Deputy Prime Minister and Minister of Foreign Affaris, Lao PDR at Delhi Dialogue VI, New Delhi, 6-7 March.

Malik, General V.P. (2014). *India's Military Conflicts and Diplomacy: An Inside View of Decision Making*, HarperCollins Publishers.

Malik, Preet (2012). 'India's Look East Policy Genesis', in A.N. Ram (ed.) *Two Decades of India's Look East Policy*, ICWA and Manohar.

Malaysia (2014). Statement by HE Dato' Hamzah Zainudin, Deputy Minister of Foreign Affairs at Delhi Dialogue VI, New Delhi, 6-7 March.

Myanmar (2014). Statement by His Excellency U Wunna Maung Lwin, Union Minister Ministry of Foreign Affairs of the Republic of the Union of Myanmar at Delhi Dialogue VI, New Delhi, 6-7 March.

Nonalignment 2.0 Report, 2012.

NSA (2013:1), Address by India's National Security Advisor Shivshankar Menon, 'Strategic Culture and IR Studies in India'. 3rd International Studies Convention, New Delhi, 11 December.

Panneerselvan, A.S. (2014). 'When National News Dwarfs International News', *The Hindu*, 10 March

Patranobis, Sutirtho (2014: 1). 'Shakti or Shanti, China Analyses Modi's Plan', *The Hindustan Times,* 6 April.

——— (2014: 2). 'Ties with China Looming Over India-Japan Relations', *The Hindustan Times*, 24 April.

——— (2014: 3). 'Japan Wary of India-China Relations', *The Hindustan Times*, 24 April.

Philippines (2014). Statement by Laura Del Rosario, Under Secretary for International Economic Relations, the Philippines at Delhi Dialogue VI, New Delhi, 6-7 March.

PM, 2012, Remarks by Prime Minister, Dr. Manmohan Singh at Flag Down of the ASEAN-India Car Rally, 21 December 2012, New Delhi.

——— (2014: 1). Prime Minister's statement prior to his departure for 3rd BIMSTEC Summit at Nay Pyi Taw, Myanmar', 3 March.

——— (2014: 2). Statement by Prime Minister at 3rd BIMSTEC Summit at Nay Pyi Taw, Myanmar', 4 March.

Raja Mohan, C. (2014: 1). 'Chinese Takeaway 'Obama's Pivot', *The Indian Express*, 25 April.

——— (2014). 'The Great Game Folio', 'Sagar Mala', *The Indian Express*, 16 April.

Ram, A.N. (2012). 'The First Decade of India's Look East Policy: An Insider's Account', in A.N. Ram (ed.), *Two Decades of India's Look East Policy*, ICWA and Manohar.

Sahai, Paramjit (2008). 'Summitry in India-ASEAN Relations', in P.V. Rao (ed.), *India and ASEAN: Partners at* Summit, KW Publishers, New Delhi, pp. 77-101.

———(2013). 'India's Cultural Diplomacy in Southeast Asia: A New Thrust', Paper Presented at HCMC – International Conference on 'Indian Imprints on Vietnam-Southeast Asia Cultural Interactions', HCMC, 3 October.

Saran, Shyam (2014: 1). 'Opening Address, National Seminar on ASEAN-India Maritime Transport Cooperation, New Delhi, 31 January.

Secretary East (2014: 1). Remarks by Secretary (East), at the Inaugural of the MGC Museum of Asian Traditional Textiles in Siem Reap, Cambodia, 7 April.

——— (2014: 2). Keynote Address by Secretary (East), 6th IISS-MEA Dialogue, IDSA, Delhi, 4 March.

Sharma, Ateev (2014). 'Ahead of Polls, Chinese Copters Intrude into Ladakh', *The Tribune*, 6 May.

Sharma, Sanjeev (2014). 'India Defends IPR Laws', *The Tribune*, 2 May.

Sharma, Sheel Kant (2012). 'India's Look East Policy: Initial Years 1990-1994', in A.N. Ram (ed.), *Two Decades of India's Look East Policy*, ICWA and Manohar.

Sibal, K. (2014). 'Wrong to Tell Russia What it Can't Do', *The Tribune*, 24 March.

Singapore (2014). Statement by Mr. Vanu Gopala Menon, Deputy Secretary (Southeast Asia and ASEAN), Ministry of Foreign Affairs, Singapore at Delhi Dialogue VI, New Delhi, 6-7 March.

Srinivasan, Meera (2014). 'Diplomatic Gains from a Strategic Abstention', *The Hindu*, 7 April.

Suraiya, Jug (2014). 'Getting over Our Fear of China', *The Times of India*, 22 February.

Thailand (2014). Statement by Mr. Manasvi Srisodapol, Deputy Permanent Secretary, Ministry of Foreign Affairs, Thailand at Delhi Dialogue VI, New Delhi, 6-7 March.

The Hindu (2014: 1). 'We Welcome China's Peaceful Rise: Obama', 29 April.

——— (2014: 2). 'EU Ban on Indian Mangoes Unilateral, Commerce Secretary', 2 May.

——— (2014: 3). 'India's Abstention at UNHRC Vote on Sri Lanka, a Political Decision', 4 April.

The Tribune (2014: 1). 'China Seeks Greater Military Cooperation with Pakistan', 2 March.

——— (2014: 2). 'India Takes Part in China Navy Meet', 24 April.

——— (2014: 3). 'Modi and Sharif: Prisoners of the Past', 30 May.

US-Japan Joint Statement (2014). 'The United States and Japan: Shaping the Future of the Asia-Pacific and Beyond', Tokyo, 25 April.

Vietnam (2014). Statement by H.E. Pham Quang Vinh, Deputy Foreign Minister, Vietnam at Delhi Dialogue VI, New Delhi, 6-7 March.

CHAPTER 6

India's 'Look East' and 'Enhanced Look East' Policies

PARBATI SEN VYAS*

The 'Look East Policy' of the Government of India has been evolving since the early 1990s and has served to quickly and successfully deepen India's engagement with the countries of East and Southeast Asia. There has been satisfactory progress in the India-ASEAN relationship since 1991. India became a Sectoral Dialogue Partner of ASEAN in 1992 which was upgraded to full dialogue partnership in 1996 and a strategic partnership at the ASEAN-India Commemorative Summit in November 2012. India's trade and investment with that part of the world has been enhanced significantly with, among other agreements, Comprehensive Economic Partnership Agreements with Republic of Korea and Japan, as also Comprehensive Economic Cooperation Agreements with Singapore and Malaysia. India and ASEAN have also operationalized a 'Trade in Goods' agreement. As a member of the East Asia Summit process, India continues to participate actively in this evolving economic partnership and India-ASEAN bilateral trade crossed US $75 billion in 2012-13.

It may be recalled that even before independence in 1947, Pandit Jawaharlal Nehru travelled to the East and thereby connected India and its people with Southeast Asia. India's LEP is located firmly in the larger background of the country's long civilizational bonds – in spiritual and cultural values, in language, dance and art – with the countries of East and Southeast Asia. The Government of India firmly believes that India's future and especially its economic interests are best served by greater integration with Asia. This was of course a

* Amb. Parbati Sen Vyas, Former Secretary, Ministry of External Affairs and Ambassador of India.

complete break from an earlier period when the countries of East Asia, including India, were closely linked as colonies to various countries in the Western world. One of the many positive outcomes of the LEP is that young Asians do not have to look to the Western countries but can seek employment/travel in Asia and thereby rediscover their common Asian heritage. With this shift and the kind of interaction that is taking place among Asian countries at various fora, India's LEP can be a major force for future peace and stability on the Asian continent.

It may be recalled that in the early years after independence the Indian economy had a slow growth rate. Perhaps this was due to the then government's attention being focused on the security of the nation and therefore on India's immediate periphery. India has in the last two decades changed its image from that of poverty and underdevelopment and has taken its rightful place as one of the world's successful 'emerging economies'. The year 1991 saw the beginning of India's economic restructuring and reform programme which included reduction of licensing and greater emphasis on private initiative and entrepreneurship. This change made it easier for other countries to do business with India. As a result, the quantum of India's world trade and foreign investment in India grew rapidly and economic diplomacy became a much more important part of India's foreign policy formulation than it had been earlier. While there have been disturbances in recent years in India's growth story largely due to global factors, its economic development path is still filled with potential. India's policies regarding foreign trade, foreign direct investment, taxation, banking, finance and capital markets have grown and matured to make Indian industry more competitive globally. There is hope and confidence for the prospects of collaboration and positive cooperation. As part of its LEP, India seeks to make its neighbours partners in its development in order to work on the opportunities available due to globalization.

Some major opportunities which India has embraced under its LEP are seen in the working of the Bay of Bengal Initiative for Multi-Sectoral Technical and Economic Cooperation (BIMSTEC), Bangladesh-China-India-Myanmar grouping (BCIM), and the focus on the development of India's northeastern region.

BIMSTEC provides a unique link between South Asia and Southeast Asia and brings together 1.5 billion people and a combined GDP of over US $2.5 trillion. In today's interdependent world, the commonalities between the Asian countries provide enormous opportunities for cooperation in various important areas. At the Fourteenth BIMSTEC Ministerial Meeting in Myanmar in March 2014 India's then external affairs minister had mentioned some areas for regional cooperation amongst the BIMSTEC countries which would help in creating a prosperous future for the region:

- Connectivity, both physical and institutional. Since the ASEAN region has a deficiency of infrastructure, a priority is to provide this both in the physical and institutional areas. The India-Myanmar-Thailand trilateral highway project from Moreh in Manipur to Mae Sot in Thailand, which is expected to be completed by 2016, is a major and visible engagement undertaken by these three countries on land connectivity. Further, this connectivity will open up access not only to Myanmar and Thailand but will connect further to the ASEAN highway grid. The benefits of such connectivity for India's northeast with countries in Southeast Asia will ensure increase in trade and investment for the former. The challenge for India is to ensure that the northeast will have the requisite infrastructure by way of transport, telecommunication, IT networks, and power grids to take advantage of this highway project.
- Economic cooperation is one of the most important strategic requirement of our times in order to provide a better livelihood to the people of India. India is working with its partners on a BIMSTEC Free Trade Agreement. Such an agreement will benefit the people of the region significantly. Along with this agreement, the BIMSTEC countries will also need to promote customs cooperation, a dispute resolution mechanism and encourage business links to promote trade and investment in the region.
- It is imperative to promote economic development and technical innovation and thereby provide better livelihood to the people. The engine of economic development is energy. The BIMSTEC region has large natural resources and cooperation on use of such resources along with grid interconnections and viable coordinated energy policies will enable mutually beneficial development. The BIMSTEC Energy Centre being set up in Bengaluru can play an important role in this endeavour.
- The BIMSTEC and ASEAN regions still have major security concerns with incidents of terrorism and transnational crimes.

Significant advances in building legal architecture to combat these concerns has been made and work on this is continuing.

India's re-engagement with its eastern neighbourhood under the LEP more than twenty years ago ensured that India became a major player in the strategic dynamics of the region. Growth of trade between China and India has been very rapid and satisfactory. In 2012-13 India-China trade reached the figure of $65.8 billion. India has set a new target of US $100 billion for bilateral trade with China by 2015. At the same time, India's rising trade deficit with China remains a difficult problem to solve.

India and China have a strategic and cooperative partnership that ensures a broad-based engagement. While there is no denying that trade and investment are the major focus of the partnership, India is confident that the interaction will develop further. It is felt that there is enough space for both countries to grow and thereby bring more prosperity and benefits to both countries and to their other partner countries in Asia. Even during the recent general elections, India sustained the momentum in bilateral ties with China by participating in a naval exercise and holding a meeting of the joint border mechanism in Beijing. The two countries emphasized the importance of maintaining peace and tranquillity on the border as a prerequisite to foster and enhance their multifaceted bilateral relations. The meeting also emphasized what earlier meetings had discussed at length – that border peace and economic relations should be maintained while difficult issues like the boundary dispute would take a longer time to be settled to the mutual satisfaction of both countries. India's trade and investment with Japan, Australia, and the Republic of Korea are also increasing.

With Bangladesh the visit of Prime Minister Sheikh Hasina in 2010 and the landmark visit of Prime Minister Manmohan Singh to Bangladesh in 2011 had a major positive effect and forged a new path to a better and more meaningful bilateral partnership. While there is still a large trade imbalance in favour of India, India is doing its best to address the problem by providing better market access for Bangladeshi goods. Efforts to further help reduce the imbalance continue to be pursued by India. Two-way trade between India and Bangladesh reached US $5.8 billion in 2012-13.

Myanmar is also an important and essential country in India's LEP. The partnership with Myanmar includes areas such as security, capacity building, health, education, infrastructure development, greater connectivity and others. Energy security is also an area where India would like to cooperate and be a partner with Myanmar. The present level of India-Myanmar trade of US $1.9 billion for 2012-13 is well below the actual potential. A target of $3 billion by 2015 has been established. There is much work to be done and effort to be put in by India to improve its bilateral trade with Myanmar.

India's northeast is its land bridge and gateway to ASEAN and the countries of Southeast Asia. It is therefore natural that the northeast is seen as a natural partner in India's LEP. It is also important to note that, in strategic terms, the northeast is the region which has international borders with the largest number of countries of all the regions of India. These include Bhutan and China in the north, Myanmar to its east, and Bangladesh in the southwest. These borders pose challenges and opportunities. The benefits to the northeast from India's LEP will include connectivity and the India-Myanmar-Thailand trilateral highway project has already been mentioned earlier in this essay. Other regional initiatives include:

- The Kaladan Multimodal Transit and Transport Project connecting Mizoram to Sittwe port in Myanmar through multimodal transport which is likely to be completed by 2016.
- Inland Waterways Transit and Transport Protocol for movement of goods to and from the northeastern states through inland waterways route in Bangladesh.
- Development of rail link between Akhaura in Bangladesh and Agartala in Tripura.
- Development of Ashuganj port in Bangladesh to enable movement of goods to the northeast through Bangladesh.

While India's focus on transit and connectivity, as mentioned above, provides alternative access to and for the northeast, it also holds many benefits for the neighbouring countries who are partners in these projects.

For many persons in India, the northeast remains a remote region which it is geographically but should not be viewed as such. The northeast is an integral part of India. The government has been facing the challenge of promoting and bringing about development in the region to bring it on a level playing field with the rest of the country in every aspect – education, transport networks and connectivity, health, information technology, availability of electricity, telecommunications, trade, and all the other requirements to improve the lives of the people in the northeastern provinces.

It needs to be mentioned that India's LEP is an ongoing exercise with senior diplomats in the Ministry of External Affairs and other government ministries constantly meeting and working with their counterparts in other Asian countries. This is done so that the momentum and objectives of the LEP-India's developmental needs do not falter. During the recent general elections, India's Foreign Secretary made two separate official visits to China and Japan to highlight Government of India's long-term interest in and commitment to strengthening the economic and strategic engagement with Asia's leading economies. In all these interactions, India's objective remains clear and consistent – India is trying to use emerging opportunities to meet its urgent developmental requirements.

India has named its first full-time envoy to the 10-nation ASEAN and this step will naturally further strengthen India's interaction with ASEAN. India is now moving towards Phase II of its LEP which is called 'Enhanced Look East Policy'. Government of India is engaged in the formulation of such an enhanced LEP, which according to India's envoy to the 10-nation ASEAN, Anil Wadhwa 'fully recognizes the potential of our civilizational outreach, our economic aspirations, our desire for integration and our shared values and objectives' with the ASEAN.

A new government has recently taken over after the general elections. While there is speculation about changes in India's foreign policy, it is well known that the fundamental principles of the foreign policy will continue to endure despite any power shifts. This is the result of an unwritten national consensus on foreign policy which consists of the primacy of strategic autonomy, good relations with neighbouring countries, and consistent economic diplomacy to maximize gains for the country.

CHAPTER 7

The Strategic Importance of Myanmar: Its Implications for India's Look East Policy

PREET MALIK*

INTRODUCTION

India's Look East Policy (LEP) over the years since it was announced in 1994 by Prime Minister P.V. Narasimha Rao has to be seen as a process that India has deployed largely to position itself along lines of mutual advantage not only with the ASEAN countries with whom India today is a strategic partner but also to a significant extent with Japan, Taiwan and South Korea. China with whom there is a growing trade relationship is a case where there is both a sense of rivalry and a degree of understanding despite tensions created by the persisting political differences and security breaches conducted by China against Indian territory. The relationship is further complicated over the clashing of the two countries' interests in Southeast Asia where China is pursuing an aggressive policy to deny the rights and claims of countries like Vietnam and other ASEAN countries in the South China Sea, more particularly the Paracel and Spratly Islands. In specific terms China's aggressive intent to deny Vietnam its rights over its sea-bound territories and interests where India's relations with Vietnam are involved has resulted in face-offs for India's maritime presence in Vietnamese waters. In effect there is a direct problem being created in this context for India's comprehensive strategic partnership with countries of the ASEAN region.

The LEP has a geo-strategic dimension, a geo-economic dimension

* Amb. P.M.S. Malik, Former Secretary, Ministry of External Affairs and Ambassador of India to Myanmar.

and a geo-security dimension. In all these three areas Myanmar as a neighbouring country with whom India shares a land and a sea boundary assumes great importance for India and its future as a major Asian power. What is even more significant is the geographical proximity of Myanmar to India's northeastern states, for whom it forms a natural land bridge not only with Southeast Asia, but also following the development of appropriate infrastructure, with important areas of Indian involvement, with the outside world. Perhaps it would be appropriate at this point to reflect the geo-strategic significance of Myanmar arising out of its location as it lies on the tri-junction that connects China, India and Southeast Asia. This geographical reality provides a great opportunity for advancing the mining of cooperative interests of South Asia, Southeast Asia and of China and India in both regional and bilateral terms. Myanmar is thus central to the advancement of bilateral and regional interests leading to the promotion of a comprehensive strategic partnership covering the region, making it of key importance to India and its LEP.

It is perhaps necessary at this stage to point to certain aspects of the India-Myanmar bilateral relationship subsequent to both countries having attained their independence from a common colonial master, the British. The British developed the Irrawaddy Delta as an export-oriented rice bowl, which led to Burma becoming a major exporter of rice to India at a time when rice consumption in India outstripped by a substantial margin the domestic supply of this commodity. The dependence on the Indian market was of great strategic importance for Burma and remained a part of its trade focus during the U Nu period and even during the early part of the Ne Win period. However, as India's cereal needs were being covered under the American PL-480 programme, leading to substantial savings of its small foreign currency reserves and the consequence of the PL-480 programme resulting in the lowering of international prices, Ne Win adopted a policy of restricting exports unless Burma received what he felt was a realistic return. India did try and help out by agreeing to take up a certain limited import of rice, in keeping with its desire to maintain the bilateral relations on an even keel but Ne Win's policy of curtailing exports led eventually to a dramatic reduction in Burma's capacity to earn foreign exchange and had a negative impact on the economy. The result was that India's trade relationship with Burma till the 1990s remained limited. In fact, it was not till the middle of the first decade of the twenty-first century that the two-way trade reached and crossed the US $1 billion mark. The current target is to raise this figure to US $3 billion mark by 2015. It is an unfortunate fact of the Indian relationship with Myanmar that geo-economics did not occupy a major or decisive part of India's bilateral relations with Burma/Myanmar till the late 1990s.

The constant in the relations between the two countries has been the concentration on the geo-security dimension of the strategic relationship. This is so because of the conditions of insurgency that have preoccupied the two countries ever since they attained their independence.The security environment was created by insurgencies in the northeastern region of India and in the adjoining ethnic-dominated parts of Myanmar, creating a situation where cooperation between the two countries – particularly involving both administrative and security institutions – became an imperative. The fact was that the Chinese had exploited the insecure nature of the Myanmar ethnic-dominated frontier regions adjoining their borders, encouraging and materially supporting the CPB-led insurgencies threatening the integrity of Myanmar. This situation had lasted till 1988 when the successor military regime to the Ne Win-led government of Burma established a working relationship with Beijing that placed the country within China's sphere of influence and permitted Beijing to assume the role of dominance over Myanmar. The fact that Myanmar stood isolated with the Western powers and India placing relations on hold left an open space for China to assert its control and permitting it to promote its interests without hindrance.

The Chinese also used the general sense of insecurity that prevailed in Burma/Myanmar, over the years, to encourage passage of Indian insurgents through Myanmar territory while providing material support and training to the Indian insurgent groups. In the post-1988 period Beijing and Yangon/Nay Pi Daw arrived at arrangements that have enabled the Myanmar authorities to attain ceasefires with the ethnic groups and to obtain more sophisticated arms initially from the PRC and subsequently from other sources including some from India to help contain the insurgencies. However, the Chinese have continued to use the Kokang and the Wa ethnic groups to extend direct training and material support to Indian insurgent groups. This is despite a greater degree of collaboration between India and Myanmar to deny Myanmar space to Indian insurgents including the use of force to ensure that such activities come to be neutralized.

It is obvious that a major aspect of India's strategic interest where Myanmar is concerned lies in the security area. This is an area that has been operational except for a brief period during the years between 1988-92 and is an area that both sides are interested in keeping at the forefront of their relations as they are dealing with issues of mutual concern and in the interest of eventually advancing the cooperation to ensure the achievement of border development that would bring sustained peace and security underpinned by economic advantage for ethnic groups on both sides of the India-Myanmar border. It is also responsible for the agreement between Delhi and Nay Pi Daw to collaborate closely in the area of border areas development confirmed during the first visit by Prime Minister Manmohan Singh in 2012. Appendix I details the MOU signed by the two countries in this connection.

The other major area of the strategic dimension that should have been clear from the very beginning, once Burma attained its independence in 1948, was the geo-economic dimension of India's strategic interest in Myanmar. Unfortunately unlike China, India has not been able to concentrate or target this area of its foreign policy. Though it could be said that in the post-1991 reforms era India has been more involved in thinking out its geo-economic focus and projections in reality this still remains an area of weakness. The Nehruvian period appeared particularly lacking when it came to the trade aspects of India's strategic interests. The period from 1947 to 1991 was one where the emphasis on trade being a vital part of India's economic effort took a back seat. In fact, the tendency was to decry the need to look at export-led growth as an area of priority. Nor surprisingly India did not consider Myanmar as a market worth concentrating on. Because of the largely political nature of the relations between the two countries the main area of focus was on the rice trade that was in Myanmar's interest. Despite that commitments made to Yangon in the extension of concessional finance and trade being part of that arrangements this area never attained the importance that good neighbourly relations should have attracted. Of course, there was also the problem created by the domestic policies of nationalizing of the economy adopted by Ne Win and the negative impact that those policies had on the Indian business interests that till then had dominated the Myanmar economy. The fact remains that even today the emphasis on geo-economic targeting of Myanmar by India is rather weak as shall be spelt out in latter part of this paper.

MYANMAR: ITS GEOGRAPHICAL PROXIMITY TO INDIA

Myanmar is a neighbouring country with whom India has a deep historical relationship that has not only influenced Myanmar's monarchical traditions that get reflected to this day in the traditional administrative patterns that deal with the rural areas, but also in its religious and cultural practices. This civilizational presence of India is something that lends comfort and closeness without adding any negatives to the relationship. The colonial period, common to both countries, brought certain aberrations to the relations but the overarching elements that pertain to the civilizational norms have ensured that the colonial period could not prevent or disrupt the natural course of relations between the two countries.

There is no doubt that the period from 1988 to 1991 was one where the relations came under strain, largely out of India's concerns about the violations of the people's rights to determine their own political futures that made it clear that their preference was for democracy as the form governance for their country. The failure of the SLORC to honour its commitment to restore democracy to the country and to honour the results of the elections placed India in conflict with the then military-ruled Myanmar. However, the fact that Myanmar was a vital and important element in the progressing of India's LEP worked in favour of a restoration of relations to the logical level and today perhaps given the realities of a globalizing world the relations between India and Myanmar are in many ways closer than they have been ever since the two countries attained their independence from the British.

The realities of today now confront the two nations and have called upon them to move towards a comprehensive strategic partnership that is in keeping with the fact that geographically Myanmar is as much a part of the Indian subcontinent in regional terms and as such a major South Asian country as it is a major part of Southeast Asia and a partner in ASEAN.

Another factor of geography in the case of Myanmar is that both India and China are its neighbours having interests that have both a security and a strategic content to them. India's LEP is directional as well as guided by local interests that include the necessity to bring the whole of its northeastern region into the Southeast Asian mainstream covering the varied interests thrown up by the economic and developmental positives that such a relationship could bring about. The involvement of Myanmar is obviously very important for the fructification of this intent. This would be so not only in the sense that Myanmar provides the land bridge for this aspect of the policy being achieved but as both areas are resource-rich with economic and social developmental issues that can be addressed to the benefit of both countries. This raises the possibility of institution-building on a cross-border beneficial basis.

It could involve areas like education, public health, sanitation, potable water and local self-rule institutions, extension services and knowledge-based systems. Further taking account of the agricultural needs of the adjoining regions of India and Myanmar agro-industrial benefits with manufacturing supplementing agricultural practices and development based on cooperative involvement on a cross-border basis is clearly of great importance to the bilateral and regional relationship. The advantage lies in the fact that Indian involvement can be on a multi-pronged basis in areas that are jointly identified for development and investment covering the northeastern region of India and the Sagaing division of Myanmar along with the Chin state, the Arakan region and partly the Kachin state. This in itself constitutes a significant territorial space of Myanmar west of the Irrawaddy River.

The other aspect that gets reflected in the neighbourhood context is the physical communication links that can and are now being developed between India and Myanmar. These are represented by the development of infrastructure covering road, riverine and sea links that grant ease of access for the northeastern region to the outside world as well as an alternate route to mainland India via Myanmar. The alternative route to the 'chicken's neck' that links mainland India to its northeastern region would of course more logically be provided by Bangladesh; however the relations between India and that country have seen ups and downs that have stood in the way of these routes being used as during the pre-Partition days and being brought up to the sophisticated infrastructural levels that are required to meet today's and future needs. A case in point, in this regard has been the barriers the construction of a gas pipeline from Myanmar to India through the territory of Bangladesh that has forced India to consider the more expensive and longer route overland through Myanmar to the northeastern region of India. The result so far has been that India has been unable to gain the access to natural gas supplies from Myanmar that have the involvement of Indian companies in its exploration and development; instead these supplies have so far come to be contracted to China.

THE CHINA FACTOR IN MYANMAR

In contrast to India having so far a limited albeit gradually expanding role in Myanmar's economic development China has established itself as the key source of economic and commercial activity in Myanmar. In the post-1988 period up to 2011-12, China has dominated the economic and political bilateral scene in Myanmar. This is today, to some extent, within the logic of the restoration of greater normality to Myanmar's external relations. China remains Myanmar's largest investor and the single largest provider of defence supplies and assistance. Further, China has come to establish infrastructural linkages with Myanmar that grant it with an alternative source and route via the construction of oil and gas pipelines and the consequential port development activities that cover both the supply of Myanmar's domestic oil and gas resources as well as a route for the supply of oil and gas from the Gulf oil fields to China. This would serve as an alternative to the shipping of the Gulf energy supplies through the Malacca and Sunda Straits that could come under strain as relations between China and the Southeast Asian states deteriorate because of the disputed claims to the island areas in the South and East China seas. To this have to be added the growing gaps between China and the United States of America that are the main strategic aspects behind the US pivot or re-balancing towards the Asia Pacific region. The re-balancing also is the essential extension by the USA to the Southeast Asian region as the reassurance that it shall support them in case of any aggressive actions that China makes to deny them their rights in the South China Sea. The re-balancing in itself tends to embrace Myanmar as a key element in the strategy that lies behind it of containing China's ambitions to be the dominant and unchallenged power of influence in Asia. However, it remains to be seen to what extent Myanmar shall accept to be part of the overall strategy and intent that is projected by the re-balancing policy.

While the Thein Sein-led government has shown itself keen to have a greater involvement of countries like India, Japan and the ASEAN as preferred sources for economic development, financial aid, investment and bilateral trade, it has also kept alive its vital linkages to China and has shown itself sensitive to China's concerns.

The West is of course important to Myanmar both as a foreign policy factor and a source for support for the liberalization processes. It has so far been able to counter-pressures for further political reforms by pointing out that it has to be a gradual process that would involve the gradual building up towards a greater democratization based on compromises on the amendments to the 2010 constitution. The fact is the recognition by the Obama administration that Myanmar is a essential factor in the strategy behind the US Pivot and Myanmar's place within it has reduced the American pressure on Myanmar to accede to Aung san Suu Kyi's demands concerning the amendments to the constitution before the 2015 elections, enabling her to assume the presidency of Myanmar in case the NLD wins the elections.

China is also a serious factor in the security space of Myanmar with common ethnicities across the two countries' borders. It was only after the developments of 1988 in Myanmar that the Beijing-Yangon relations improved with China taking actions to strengthen the hands of the military government in Myanmar to effectively deal with the numerous insurgencies that had plagued it ever since its independence. Even though the ethnic groups and the GOM are in talks to achieve a comprehensive ceasefire and thereafter talks with the aim to find acceptable solutions that would help bring peace within the umbrella of securing the unity and integrity of the country while extending a degree of autonomy to the ethnic groups, the China factor has overall implications for the future of Myanmar. China continues to maintain the means to upset the arrangements because of its capacity to use its etnic groups and relations with entities like the Wa to create mischief whenever it feels that Myanmar is moving away with a potential to place its interests in jeopardy. The relations with India, or the West or Japan for that matter would always have to keep in mind the sword of Damocles that is held over the head of Myanmar.

THE STRATEGIC CONTENT OF THE INDIA-MYANMAR RELATIONS WITHIN THE LOOK EAST POLICY

India has in every sense of the term understood that Myanmar is vital to it bilaterally but also to a substantive sense to its LEP; particularly in the context of the linkages to the future development of the northeastern states. Both New Delhi and the ASEAN have adopted a policy of mutuality towards the economic and social development of these states and to develop the necessary infrastructure that would serve as the economic backbone of the region. Myanmar for obvious reasons is central to the establishment of cross-border infrastructure that would ensure land and sea communication links which in later would reinforce the India-ASEAN partnership to levels where areas like tourism, manufacturing based on readily available resources and institution building in support of developmental activities follow an interactive course. These activities could call on the experience, financial resources and technology that reflect the strength of the ASEAN countries and of emerging India as an economic powerhouse that could serve as an important driver of the Asian economies along with China and Japan.

In a globalizing world where trade is increasingly dependent on vendor-based flows reflecting the comparative advantages of the counties in question the future of trade in the Look East context shall become more in tandem with the hub phenomena leading to a more technology-savvy manufacturing pattern based on local advantages. This in itself warrants a deepening of the education system and the setting up of institutions that provide a more practical and work-oriented education. The northeastern region has a major opportunity to become an education hub that could cater to meeting the requirements of Myanmar that has a vast and growing need for high quality education which would also meet the new job patterns that socio-economic development on a cross-border basis is projected to bring about.

One of the areas of the LEP and its reflection on the relations with Myanmar is the expanding involvement of India in the infrastructural development of Myanmar. While the priority aspects of this factor are clear the progress on establishing the projects within a time bound and financially secure manner continues to raise questions. The primacy and validity of India's involvement is fully endorsed by the Government of India, however, there are gaps in the implementation that defy logic and financial acceptability because of delays and cost overruns. It would be important to point out that the imperative of India's geo-economic interests in Myanmar demand that the approach to projects is guided by the principles of time frames connected to delivery and financial backing that ensures that projects are implemented within the financial and time line commitments and handed over in keeping with the desire of both parties. Once agreements are in place implementation would be along predictable lines and India would be seen as one that keeps its promises. At present there are doubts that remain on India being serious on time lines and delivery. In fact the general impression among may decision makers in Myanmar is that there is a tremendous gap between promise and delivery. Despite this there is a degree of political goodwill that Myanmar has for India as there is the feeling that India is not exploitative as China has been seen to be. There is also the desire on the part of the Thein Sein government to see more of India in the socio-developmental aspects of Myanmar.

India has also to make it a part of its economic projections to encourage investment flows into Myanmar. There are many areas where it would be in the interest of the business community in India to establish themselves in an economy that has yet to reach its potential and thus offers opportunities to those who are willing to take advantage of being early birds. In the gas and oil area Indian companies are fairly well represented and are placed at an advantage to take on new exploration areas also. ONGC, GAIL ESSAR and Jubilant are already in Myanmar. The GoI has to reasonable financial terms to companies who are willing to take on investment possibilities particularly in key areas. The Tata Group has already got involved in the transportation sector but the Indian private sector has to get involved in other key areas. One obvious area is in the paper and pulp industry, utilizing the very large bamboo availability as well as tropical forest hardwoods of Myanmar. In Malaysia the Avanta Group is already utilizing the Sabah-based tropical hardwoods for its paper and pulp plant located there. This group has the capability of replicating a similar plant in Myanmar. The textile industry is another area where it would be advantageous for the private sector to establish itself in Myanmar. Then there is the wood-based manufacturing advantage that would best be done by establishing a SEZ that would be across from Myanmar covering the northeastern region of India. There is also a major opportunity for investment in the power sector where Indian private companies could be encouraged to step in, utilizing the advantage that India enjoys as a quality manufacturer of state-of-the-art equipment both in the thermal and the hydropower areas.

What is needed is for India to first establish in the economic and business areas that fit in with the overall strategic interests of the country. Obviously India has to define in categorical terms what it considers as its strategic interests Myanmar and its surrounds. The definition has to have a clearly thought out economic policy based on the recognized geo-economic aspects of the overall strategic interests. This would then make it easier to project the economic and investment absolutes that would be important to establish India as a serious player and one that provides substantive content to the LEP. This has to be backed up by the assurance that India can deliver and that it is now ensuring that the gap between estimates and the actual implementation of the project would not entail sharp cost overruns that have been an unacceptable part of India's implementation so far.

The abiding trend that has come to cover the direction and content of the relations between the two countries is part of a pragmatic approach that has within it the understanding that Myanmar is today set on the road to bring greater doses of democratic functioning to the state. The fact that no amendment of the Myanmar constitution is likely before the 2015 elections that will allow Aung San Suu Kyi gaining the president's post even if her party wins the election is not factor that India should consider a negative and that should come in the way of the expanding relations between the two countries. It is quite clear that the strategic interests that include the emerging parameters of the LEP as applied to Myanmar serve as the driving force that lie behind the new dynamic that has come to apply to the bilateral and regional relationship with the recognition that Myanmar has a significant part in the advances of the LEP. In May 2012 the then prime minister Manmohan Singh paid a role-defining visit to Myanmar. He was the first Indian prime minister to visit Myanmar after a gap of 27 years. The last visit was that made by Rajiv Gandhi in 1987. The 2012 visit succeeded in providing significant content to the relations covering vastly varied areas that included institution building, trade, border development, defence supplies, etc. It has granted a sense of direction to the relations. Appendix II covers the agreements adopted during the visit in a nutshell.

Trade has also ben targeted and to this has to be added the fact that for India having a stake in the agro-industrial area could become a major geo-economic factor in the LEP. Myanmar has the potential to develop an irrigation-based surplus in grain and farm produce, and the growing consumer base in India where the improvement in quality of life covering tens of millions of people shall continue to provide a huge market for the produce. Myanmar could thus become a major beneficiary of this demand that could be built on the back of agriculture-related infrastructure to be established on a large scale with the technical and material involvement of India. Further the agro-industry could be developed on a JV basis. As the demand on resources could become a stumbling block it would worth developing the schemes with the involvement of Japan that would ensure that the demand for financing the growth could be jointly taken care of with a concentration on produce that would also be of interest to Japan both as a direct consumer as well as an interested party in the evolution of a strong presence in the global market for such produce. For the current status of the trade flows between India and Myanmar compressed detailing can be seen at Appendix III.

CONCLUSION

There is little doubt that India has a very important stake in the future of Myanmar as its location places it right in the center of India's Asia policy and ambitions. It is also clear that despite the reservations that may have surfaced over the years commencing from the post-1988 developments placing China in a dominating position to the present ruling dispensation in Myanmar to curtail or place limits on China's influence, Myanmar shall continue to have a very intense relationship with Beijing via Kunming. For China Myanmar is of immense strategic importance particularly as it has become part of its projections in the Bay of Bengal and the Indian Ocean Region. Myanmar provides a significant alternative to the security problems that the Malacca Straits and the Sunda Straits could pose if the strain of maritime territorial issues result in the United States and the ASEAN countries restricting China's shipping movements including energy shipments that could cause great damage to its economy as well as its security as a nation. The laying of gas and crude oil pipelines traversing across Myanmar carrying not only the Myanmar product but also product from the Middle East and Africa forms today a very important part of China's strategic plans, placing its relations with Myanmar at a premium.

India too has a stake in the development of resources, not only energy based but also other natural resources, apart from Myanmar providing India with alternative routes of connectivity as an integral part of its bilateral involvement with Myanmar and as a vital part of India's LEP. In fact, India has also to take account China's strategy involving Myanmar as that influences the course of regional balances so essential to ensuring the security of its interests. This is especially important if the border issue with China is aggravated by China's penchant to keep issues alive by means of transgressions into Indian territory. There is also the element of India's interests in Southeast Asia being compromised by China's actions over its claims in the China seas.

In keeping with the fact that India is now a major stakeholder in the socio-economic development and in the progress that Myanmar is making in the areas of democratization of the political structures and systems as well as the efforts that it is making in securing its borders by arriving at workable solutions with its ethnic minority groups – it is an imperative that India has to ensure that its efforts – both political and economic – are tied to implementable action within acceptable time lines. The implications of failure to adhere to committed levels of costs and delivery are already staring India in the face with questions being raised on its capacity to deliver. The need is for a centrally monitored structure that ensures all clearances are in place within the time frames established after due diligence and there is also a competitive implementation system in place. Let it be assumed that now that India has a professionally worked aid and assistance system in place there would be faith reposed on it to carry out projects in a technically sound and professional manner. All barriers imposed on the achievement of original timelines that have till recently been the handiwork of restrictive policies adopted by the financial authorities in India centred around the Finance Ministry must be replaced with a single window sanctioning and project budgeting system that would ensure timely implementation. It has to be seen as a major element of India's geo-economic strategy that would make her a real player in the bilateral and the LEP context.

Politically India is well placed to put forward arrangements that would ease the situation within Myanmar on the issues of democracy and a federal structure that is essential to Myanmar's future as a united and secure nation. India is a living example of having a functioning federal system in place that recognizes that India's plurality is the nation's strength. This projects the fact that a federal structure for Myanmar would strengthen the nation's unity by recognizing diversity as a positive that could help resolve the existing differences plaguing the political situation in Myanmar and posing a substantial threat to its unity and security.

India thus has to have a strategic plan in place that has within it the elements that enable Myanmar to see its relations with India as an alternative to help reduce its dependence on China. India has to also see how it can fit within the US' Asia-Pacific pivot in Myanmar's place and its role within it. India has to also ensure that its economic and political relationship with Myanmar is not held hostage to bureaucratic functioning that has in the past resulted in failures of implementation and cost overruns. These have led to the questioning of India's intentions and created gaps in understanding. India has to have a very clear geo-economic strategy that covers the entire ASEAN region within the ambit of a progressing LEP that utilizes all opportunities to strengthen its Asia presence. In this regard it also has to promote the involvement of the Indian private sector to broaden and strengthen the country's economic presence. Within this imperative India could also involve a strategy that brings Japan and other ASEAN countries into the equation as joint venture partners. As part of this strategy India should also put a financial instrument in place that encourages the involvement of the private sector.

APPENDIX I

INDIA AND MYANMAR SIGN MEMORANDUM OF UNDERSTANDING ON BORDER COOPERATION, 10 MAY 2014

India and Myanmar have signed a Memorandum of Understanding (MoU) on Border Cooperation. The MoU was signed by Mr Gautam Mukhopadhaya, Ambassador of India to Myanmar, and Major General Kyaw Nyunt, Deputy Defence Minister of Myanmar, in Nay Pyi Taw on 8 May 2014. The MoU provides a framework for security cooperation and exchange of information between Indian and Myanmar security agencies. A key provision is that of conduct of coordinated patrols on their respective sides of the international border and the maritime boundary by the Armed Forces of the two countries Both sides have agreed to exchange information in the fight against insurgency, arms smuggling and drug, human and wildlife trafficking. Both sides have also agreed to take steps to prevent illegal cross-border activities. The level and frequency of meetings between the Armed Forces, Drug Control Agencies and Wildlife Crime Control agencies have been spelt out in the MoU. It is expected that this MoU will lead to enhanced and tangible cooperation between Indian and Myanmar security agencies in ensuring peace, stability and security along the long international land and maritime border between the two countries.

APENDIX II

Prime Minister of India Dr. Manmohan Singh paid a state visit to Myanmar from 27-29 May 2012. During the visit several new initiatives were announced and 12 MoUs and agreements signed including extension of a new line of credit (LOC) for US $500 million to Myanmar, support for setting up an Advance Centre for Agriculture Research and Education in Yezin, a Rice Bio-park in the integrated Demonstration Park in Nay Pyi Taw, and an Information Technology Institute in Mandalay. In addition important agreements such as Air Service Agreement, Establishment of Joint Trade and Investment Forum, MoU on Border Areas Development, and establishment of Border Haats and Cultural. . . .

Source: MEA

APPENDIX III

Bilateral trade has expanded significantly from US $12.4 million in 1980-1 to US $1070.88 million in 2010-11. India's imports from Myanmar are dominated by agricultural items (beans, pulses and forest-based products form 90 per cent of our imports). India's main exports to Myanmar are primary and semi-finished steel and pharmaceuticals. Following are the export-import figures as per the Central Statistical Organization (CSO), Yangon:

TABLE 1: INDIA-MYANMAR BILATERAL TRADE (*US $ MILLION*)

Year	India's Export	India's Import	Total	Trade Balance
2006-7	139.95	781.93	921.19	(-) 641.98
2007-8	185.43	809.94	995.37	(-) 624.51
2008-9	221.64	928.97	1,150.61	(-) 707.33
2009-10	207.97	1,289.8	1,497.77	(-) 1,081.83
2010-11	194.75	876.13	1,070.88	(-) 681.38
2011-12 (Apr-Dec)	217.65	763.32	814.6	(-) 545.67

Source: Central Statistical Organization of Myanmar.

APPENDIX IV

COOPERATION BETWEEN INDIA AND MYANMAR IN THE REGIONAL/SUB-REGIONAL CONTEXT

ASEAN: Myanmar became a member of ASEAN in July 1997. As the only ASEAN country which shares a land border with India, Myanmar is a bridge between India and ASEAN. A few proposals for cooperation have been implemented and some are under discussions with Myanmar within the framework of ASEAN's IAI programme.

BIMSTEC: Myanmar became a member of BIMSTEC in December 1997. Myanmar is a signatory to the BIMSTEC Free Trade Agreement. Myanmar is the lead country for the energy sector. Myanmar trades mostly with Thailand and India in the BIMSTEC region. Myanmar's major exports to India are agricultural products like beans, pulses and maize and forest products such as teak and hardwoods. Its imports from India include chemical products, pharmaceuticals, electrical appliances and transport equipment. The 13th BIMSTEC Ministerial Meeting was held in Myanmar in January 2011. The BIMSTEC Summit meeting was held in 2014 where the Indian delegation was led by the out going Prime Minister Dr. Manmohan Singh.

Mekong-Ganga Cooperation: Myanmar is a member of the Mekong-Ganga Cooperation (MGC) since its inception in November 2000. MGC is an initiative by six countries – India and five ASEAN countries namely, Cambodia, Laos, Myanmar, Thailand and Vietnam – for cooperation in the fields of tourism, education, culture, transport and communication. Member countries assume the chairmanship of MGC in alphabetical order.

SAARC: Myanmar was given the status of Observer in SAARC in August 2008, including Statistical Organization, Myanmar Exchange Programme, etc.

Source: MEA

PART III

Economic and Trade Linkages: Promise and Potential

CHAPTER 8

Economic Dimension of 'Look East' Policy

V.S. SESHADRI*

INTRODUCTION

India's Look East Policy (LEP), an expression of interest to develop closer relations with countries in Southeast Asia and beyond, has found resonance and retains continued relevance even after two decades of its enunciation. Four world leaders who were accorded the honour of being the chief guest at India's annual Republic Day splendour during the last five years have been drawn from this region – Indonesia, Thailand, Japan and Republic of Korea, countries that are regarded as part of the 'Arc of Advantage'. Strengthening of ties is also evident if we look at either the political, strategic or economic dimension of India's relations with the countries in this region. Initially, Look East was taken to address Southeast Asia but has subsequently been used to also develop closer economic and strategic ties with Japan and Republic of Korea in Northeast Asia. It remains to be seen if the LEP slogan will start to be used for other countries in the east as well, including China.

Three broad approaches have contributed towards developing the economic dimension of the LEP. One is through regional or sub-regional forums or organizations of which India is a member. These include Bay of Bengal Multi-Sectoral Technical and Economic Cooperation (BIMSTEC), Mekong-India Cooperation (MGC) initiative and East Asia Summit, apart from the dialogue partnership

* Dr V.S. Seshadri, Former Ambassador of India to Myanmar and Joint Secretary in-charge of WTO matters in the Ministry of Commerce. Currently Vice-Chairman, Research and Information System (RIS) for Developing Countries, New Delhi.

and close association with ASEAN. Second is through bilateral and regional initiatives towards promoting greater trade and investment including through free trade-type arrangements. Third is through promoting greater connectivity in a variety of ways, not only through land, air or maritime connectivity but also through people-to-people and institutional connectivity.

Scholars have pointed out that even historically India had developed many links with Asia and that footprints of Indian culture and scholarship, religious reach and maritime trade can be found in every corner of this region. The long colonial period saw a diminution of efforts on these fronts. However waves of migration of manual labour that took place during this period from India to Southeast Asia at the behest of the colonial power established another link but not without its attendant strains in terms of assimilation in their new homes and local resentment that occasionally gets played out even today.

In the first few decades after independence, much of India's foreign trade was taking place with the developed countries and they were also the sources of foreign investment and external development assistance. India was active in the non-aligned world and in G-77, seeking among various priorities, to redesign the international economic order that it felt was stacked against developing countries. India made no special attempts however to forge closer economic ties with Asia. ASEAN that came into being during this time received no special focus in our foreign economic policy.

REGIONAL AND SUB-REGIONAL FORUMS

There was one forum however, ECAFE which later became ESCAP, which brought together all Asian countries, minus the Gulf and Central Asian ones, which provided an opportunity for countries of the region to have an exchange of views about their development policies and priorities. The accelerated growth experienced by the Asian tigers and the flying geese patterns were much heralded and discussed. Experiences about growth triangles and Special Economic Zones were also exchanged. During and prior to the 1980s, ESCAP attracted high level participation at its meetings with no other competing forum available. Many Indian experts including on deputation from the central government, held high positions in the organization and were influenced by the economic policies and growth impulses that were transforming East Asian economies. There can be little doubt that some of them who later on returned to India in turn influenced Indian government's thinking when the economy was liberalized in 1991. By extension, it is surmised that they also had a role, along with the foreign policy establishment, in influencing the launch of the Look East policy. India also hosted the 50th annual session of ESCAP in New Delhi in 1994, with its focus on infrastructure development.

The growth impulses of the Asia-Pacific region also attracted others who sought to plug into it. Thus arose Asia Pacific Economic Cooperation (APEC) forum in 1989, mooted first by Australian prime minister Bob Hawke, enveloping 12 countries to begin with but eventually extending to 21 countries drawn from either side of the Asia-Pacific region. Non-inclusion of India was a disappointment although it was never so officially articulated. It is difficult to believe that geography was the sole criterion. Launched at a time when the Uruguay Round was still facing stiff challenges, APEC, that excluded EU, was also seen as rallying together of liberal minded East Asian and Pacific economies that could proceed to liberalize trade among themselves in case EU was shy about liberalizing trade in agriculture, a sector that was largely outside at that time of world trading rules, namely GATT, the predecessor to WTO.

India remaining outside of ASEAN and APEC, and South Asia itself remaining mired in internal contradictions, revealed a certain degree of isolation from Asian growth poles. India's LEP in this context was a unilateral pronouncement of its interest to plug into Southeast Asia. With Indian economic liberalization taking place in parallel, the ASEAN countries too saw merit in closer engagement with a potentially large market that could also become a counterweight to China whose rapid economic growth was not without concern for them. Thus came about India's sectoral dialogue partnership in 1992 that got elevated to full dialogue partnership in 1996 and eventually to holding summit level dialogues in 2002.

Two ASEAN countries that showed greater interest in India than others at this stage were Singapore and Thailand. Singapore played a lead role in influencing other ASEAN members in progressively elevating the partnership with ASEAN. Personal rapport between the leaders of the two countries and close interactions between trade and industry associations and think tanks played a part. Thailand, whose rapid economic growth was losing steam by the mid-1990s, and which was to be soon gripped by the Asian economic crisis, was looking for growth opportunities beyond ASEAN that it could plug into. It mooted the idea, in close cooperation with India, of a sub-regional grouping consisting of Bangladesh, India, Sri Lanka and Thailand in 1996 that eventually also included Myanmar, Nepal and Bhutan and came to be called the BIMSTEC. This sub-regional grouping sought to focus on issues like connectivity, energy security, food security, migration, drug trafficking and terrorism.

Thailand also took a lead role, along with India, in the launch of the MGC initiative in 2000 which basically sought to leverage the culture and people-to-people links between the five countries in the Mekong basin – Thailand, Cambodia, Laos, Myanmar and Vietnam – and their 'civilizational neighbour', India. The focus areas of MGC were agreed upon as education, transport and communications and tourism and culture.

These sub-regional forums helped towards forging closer ties by facilitating contacts between policy makers and leaders and featuring regular discussions among their think tanks about how further cooperation can be developed including in several economic areas like trade, investment, connectivity, transport and infrastructure. Initial enthusiasm for forging sub-regional forums, however, has somehow not been matched with subsequent follow-up actions. Leaders of BIMSTEC countries, for example, have not found it easy to hold regular summit level meetings which have had to be postponed several times on occasions. Cooperative initiatives have also not gone very much beyond holding meetings. Lack of required resources, absence of adequate political will to advance the agenda and lingering suspicion among neighbouring countries could be restraining factors. It may perhaps be important to focus on a few but doable areas.

ENTERING INTO FREE TRADE-TYPE ARRANGEMENTS

Closer ties with Singapore and Thailand were soon taken to the next stage of moving towards concluding free trade agreements with them. India's import regime was undergoing a change anyway with all quantitative restrictions maintained on balance of payments grounds being dismantled on 1 April 2001. India was also to embark on a declared policy of progressive reduction of tariffs down to ASEAN levels. It had further entered into its first reciprocal free trade agreement in goods with Sri Lanka that came into force from 1 March 2000. Having gained some experience in such negotiations, India agreed to examine entering into an FTA with Thailand when the then Thai prime minister visited India in December 2001. Soon after, in April 2002, when Prime Minister Vajpayee visited Singapore, it was announced that the two sides would study the feasibility of drawing up a Comprehensive Economic Cooperation Agreement (CECA) between them. Prime Minister Vajpayee also called for an India-ASEAN FTA in his address to the first India-ASEAN Summit in Phnom Penh in November 2002. It has been suggested in this context that India perhaps sought to match China that had already signed a framework agreement by then with ASEAN for an FTA. It could also have been a form of reciprocation for elevation to summit level partnership. Whatever the contributing factors, FTAs came to be used as an instrument towards advancing the LEP.

CECA WITH SINGAPORE

The first to be concluded was CECA with Singapore that entered into force in August 2005 involving liberalization in goods, services and investment. CECA was also accompanied by a bilateral investment promotion and protection agreement, a revised double taxation avoidance agreement, a more liberal air services agreement and open skies for charter flights. Tariff liberalization by Singapore as a result of CECA was not significant, however, since its MFN tariffs were already zero except for just six tariff lines. On the other hand, tariff liberalization by India covered 75 per cent of India's tariff lines which rose to 83 per cent after the first review in 2007.

On the services front, there was substantial liberalization in both horizontal and sector-specific commitments. Of particular importance were the concessions in the financial services sector, where three banks from each side were allowed to operate in the partner country with substantial privileges. Temasek Holding and GIC of Singapore were also allowed to invest in listed companies 10 per cent above Foreign Institutional Investor (FII) limits. CECA also made a breakthrough in terms of including commitments on movement of natural persons for the first time as also for opening discussions on mutual recognition between professional bodies and certifying associations in specific sectors like auditing, architecture, medicine, dentistry and nursing.

As for investments, India extended national treatment to not only investments but also to investors. India also agreed to bind its 2003 liberalization measures in the real estate sector. More importantly, under the revised double taxation agreement, India provided for tax exemption on capital gains on profits from sale of shares in India and a reduction in withholding tax from 15 to 10 per cent.

Negotiations with Thailand went on a somewhat different track with both countries signing a framework agreement along with an early harvest of 82 items, tariffs on which were quickly brought down to zero in 2003. But Indian industry did not react favourably to the early harvest since it brought about a situation of inverted tariff structure in certain sectors where the tariffs on raw materials turned out to be higher than the finished products that got included in the early harvest. The negotiations also got protracted on Rules of Origin. The situation therefore remained frozen for a while but an agreement has now been reached on trade in goods and investment even as some differences still remain on coverage of services sector.

INDIA-ASEAN FTA

The negotiations on India-ASEAN FTA also took considerable time for an agreement to be reached on rules of origin, negative list, modalities for tariff reduction and elimination and dispute settlement. In a way this was not surprising considering that in many products the ASEAN countries and India were competitors. Items like palm oil, pepper, tea, coffee, etc., needed extended discussion. The negative list of India as finally agreed consisted of 489 tariff lines (6 digit level) as against separate lists for each ASEAN country. As per the agreement signed in 2009, tariffs are to be fully liberalized for all items by 2018 except for 590 sensitive items for which reductions will only be partial. The agreement will eliminate tariffs on 80 per cent of the tariff lines accounting for 75 per cent of the trade in a gradual manner. Negotiations on services and investment have since been also concluded and signed in December 2012 and these now await ratification.

During the first decade of 2000, India entered into FTA negotiations with a host of other countries including Australia, EU, New Zealand, EFTA, GCC countries, Indonesia, ROK, Japan and Malaysia but the negotiations have been successfully concluded so far only with the last three countries. Frequency of engagement particularly at the level of leaders, extent of growing economic links, a certain degree of complementarity in terms of trading interests and, finally, the LEP slogan that makes it also easier to sell the agreement domestically have all contributed in some measure.

CEPA WITH ROK

The initiative for concluding a Comprehensive Economic Partnership Agreement (CEPA) with Republic of Korea began with the launch of a joint study group during the visit of Korean President Roh Moo Hyun in October 2004, by when bilateral trade was experiencing double-digit growth and Korean companies were already actively undertaking investments in the automobiles, white goods and electronics sectors in India and the Korean steel major POSCO also showed interest in a large steel investment in Orissa. With negotiations given a go ahead during the return visit of President Abdul Kalam in February 2006, the agreement was finally signed in August 2009 and came into effect from January 2010. It provided for tariff reductions up to 85 per cent of tariff lines for India and for Korea the coverage was 93 per cent. On services, it included sectoral commitments including in legal and financial services, travel trade, accounting and transport services. Particularly significant was the inclusion of 163 independent professions for allowing temporary entry in areas like database management, computer programming, advertising, construction, automobiles, electronic equipment engineering and management consultancy.

CEPA WITH JAPAN

The initiative to launch CEPA negotiations with Japan came soon after. Japan, like India, was a relative late entrant towards concluding FTAs and it was only on 21 December 2004 that in a basic policy decision the Japanese Council of Ministers deemed the Economic Partnership Agreements (EPAs) as a mechanism to complement the multilateral trading system. A joint study group set up in November 2004 to give its recommendations for strengthening bilateral economic relations proposed launching negotiations for CEPA in June 2006. In a state visit to Japan in December 2006 by Dr. Manmohan Singh, when bilateral relations were elevated to 'Global and Strategic Partnership' CEPA negotiations were formally launched. In his address to the Japanese apex chambers during the visit, Dr. Singh recalled gratefully on the one hand the financial assistance received from Japan during the time of India's balance of payments crisis in 1991 as also afterwards for projects like the Delhi Metro and further referred to the critical role played by Japanese companies in the development of automobile and other industries in India. On the other hand, he expressed surprise at Japan losing ground in India to China and ROK both in terms of trade and investment flows. He invited Japan to regain its historic status as India's most important business partner in Asia. This was, in a sense, encouraging competition within the Look East framework.

Under the India-Japan CEPA, which was finally signed in February 2011 and implemented from August 2011, 17.4 per cent of the tariff lines have been offered for immediate reduction of tariff to zero by India. Tariffs will be brought to zero in 10 years on 66.32 per cent of tariff lines. In all, India's commitment for tariff elimination over differing periods covers about 85 per cent of imports from Japan. India's exclusion list contains 1,538 (13.62 per cent) lines at the eight-digit level. Auto parts and agricultural and other sensitive items have been kept out of the liberalization schedule.

The Japanese side has put 87 per cent of its tariff lines that also cover about 95 per cent of India's exports under immediate tariff reduction to zero. A large number of these items are of India's export interest, e.g. seafood; agricultural products such as mangoes, citrus fruits, spices, instant tea; most spirits such as rum, whiskies, vodka, etc., textile products such as woven fabrics, yarns, synthetic yarn; readymade garments; petro chemical and chemical products, cement; jewellery, etc. The exclusion list of Japan mainly consists of items such as rice, wheat, oil, milk, sugar, leather and leather products and covers currently only 0.5 per cent of India's exports. Many of these, however, have potential for expansion. Japan, however, regards these products as extremely sensitive domestically.

In the services sector, Indian professionals will be able to provide their services and contribute towards further development of Japan's IT sector. Japan has also agreed to conclude Social Security Agreement within a specified period of three years. Contractual Service Suppliers (CSS), Independent Professionals (IPs) such as those in accounting, R&D services, tourist guide, market research and management consulting firms now can provide services in Japan.

CECA WITH MALAYSIA

A joint study to explore a CECA with Malaysia was agreed upon in December 2004 – immediately after the same was done with Korea and Japan – when the then Malaysian prime minister Abdullah Badawi visited India. Till 2003, during when Dr. Mahathir was the prime minister of Malaysia, political relations took a back seat even as economic ties grew in terms of greater trade (Malaysia was our largest trading partner then in ASEAN after Singapore), investment, participation in infrastructure projects and a large presence of each other's companies in the other's market. It took some time, however, for the actual negotiations to start and also for them to conclude. Malaysia's insistence on inclusion of palm oil and its products took some time to be sorted out. The ethnic riots resulting from protests by the Indian community in Malaysia against racial discrimination in 2008 also had a restraining impact. But Prime Minister Najib's visit to India in January 2010 and Prime Minister Manmohan Singh's visit soon after in October 2010, that elevated the relations to a strategic partnership, marked a turnaround and CECA was formally signed on 18 February 2011 and came into force on 1 July 2011.

The tariff reduction schedule in this agreement marks an improvement over India-ASEAN FTA in the form of fewer exclusions by both sides and a somewhat quicker pace of tariff reduction/elimination. Tariffs have also been agreed to be bound by India by 31 December 2018 on palm oil and three of its products. India has also obtained improved market access for basmati rice, mangoes, trucks, motor cycles and cotton garments. As for imports, India has shielded certain vulnerable sectors from deeper tariff reductions. Sensitive sectors figuring among exclusions are agriculture, fisheries, textiles, chemicals and automobiles and parts.

In the services sector, commitments have been made by both sides in sectors and modes of interest to them. The agreement will also facilitate temporary movement of business persons including contractual service suppliers and independent professionals in accounting and auditing, architecture, urban planning, engineering services, medical and dental, nursing and pharmacy, computer and related services and management consultancy services.

HOW FAR HAVE THE CECAS/CEPAS BENEFITTED INDIA?

An in-depth study will need to be undertaken to assess the full impact of each of these FTAs, which is beyond the scope of this essay. A broad brush analysis does however suggest that the coverage of these agreements have been quite broad, even if they may have significant exclusions, and the extent of concessions relatively deep wherever they have been taken. The CECA with Japan, the latest, is also perhaps the most comprehensive among them.

Bilateral trade trends with these countries can be seen from Table

8.1 that looks at how trade has grown in the ten years between 2004-5 and 2013-14 during when all these agreements were negotiated and signed. While India's exports worldwide multiplied by a factor of 3.75 between these years, its exports to Malaysia, ASEAN as a whole and ROK rose somewhat more rapidly. On the other hand, growth of India's exports to Japan and Singapore fell behind our overall export growth. In respect of India's imports, while our overall imports rose by a factor of 4.04, only in respect of ASEAN as a whole did our imports grow at a higher pace. On the other hand, India's imports from Singapore, ROK and Japan did not even keep pace with our overall imports.

While these figures generally indicate there has been no alarming growth in imports or a sharp surge in our exports compared to our overall trade growth, sector-level examination will be necessary that also looks at the extent of tariff concessions in the case of each agreement, year to year growth particularly in the immediate years following the implementation of CEPA/CECA, impact of rules of origin and non-tariff barriers that also factors in other aspects such

TABLE 8.1: FIGURES IN MILLION US DOLLARS

	A	B	A/B	C	D	C/D
	India's Exports in 2013-14	India's Exports in 2004-5		India's Imports in 2013-14	India's Imports in 2004-5	
India's trade worldwide	3,13,542	83,536	3.75	4,50,593	1,11,517	4.04
Singapore	12,601	4,000	3.15	6,774	2,651	2.55
Malaysia	4,197	1,084	3.87	9,212	2,299	4.00
ASEAN as a whole	33,279	8,425	3.95	41,618	9,115	4.56
ROK	4,204	1,042	4.03	12,471	3,509	3.55
Japan	6,816	2,128	3.2	9,495	3,235	2.93
Indonesia	4,906	1,333	3.68	15,024	2,618	5.74
Thailand	3,708	901	4.11	5,360	866	6.19
China	14,829	5,616	2.64	51,049	7,098	7.19
Hong Kong	12,734	3,692	3.45	7,333	1,730	4.24
Vietnam	5,440	556	9.78	2,594	87	29.8
Australia	2,299	720	3.19	10,161	3,825	2.65
New Zealand	282	93	3.03	619	128	4.83

Source: Department of Commerce, GOI.

as the global economic downturn and India's own economic situation. For example, it has been mentioned that certain non-tariff barriers in the form of restrictive SPS measures and procedures that favour local producers of generic pharmaceuticals and import quota restrictions on rice have hindered better utilization of CEPA with ROK. There have also been indications that due to lack of awareness or because of excessive paperwork and procedural requirements many trade and industry operators in India have not fully availed of the concessions in the CECA/CEPAs. On the other hand, complaints are also heard about how certain concessions granted to the partner countries have hurt the domestic industry. All these need to be carefully assessed before other FTA negotiations are taken forward.

In respect of services, several Indian IT, consulting and other companies have set up operations in CECA/CEPA partner countries. To determine whether anticipated gains have been realized, an in-depth examination would again be necessary. For example, the second bilateral review of CECA with Singapore which began in 2010 still remains incomplete. Reports indicate there are pending issues regarding grant of full status of qualifying branch for three Indian banks under the agreement and the issues relating to mutual recognition of professional qualifications have also not made much headway. It is hoped these will be addressed soon.

In respect of foreign investments Singapore which has certain favourable investment provisions and tax dispensations with India ranks second, accounting for a cumulative US $25.7 billion from April 2000 to April 2014 (see Table 8.2) that translates into 11.75 per cent of all FDI flows into India during this period.

TABLE 8.2: FDI INFLOWS INTO INDIA FROM CECA/CEPA COUNTRIES

Name of CEPA/ CECA country	FDI inflows into India in million US $ from April 2000 to April 2014	% of total FDI inflows into India
Singapore	25,762	11.75
Japan	16,482	7.52
Republic of Korea	1,424	0.65
Malaysia	642	0.29
ASEAN as a Whole	27,231	12.41

Source: Department of Industrial Policy and Promotion (DIPP).

While Japan accounts for 7.52 per cent, FDI from Republic of Korea and Malaysia appear far under stated presumably because many of the investments from companies from these two countries have probably come through the Mauritius or Singapore route that have favourable taxation agreements.

What is also significant from Table 8.1 is that our trade with some of the other ASEAN partners, namely Indonesia, Thailand and Vietnam has shown more rapid growth in the last 10-year period than those with whom FTAs have been signed. Likewise, in Northeast Asia India's bilateral trade with China and Hong Kong have far-exceeded her trade with Korea and Japan. FDI inflows from all these economies, however, have not been so significant yet.

There are many developments at play here that need to be carefully analysed and a suitable strategy devised. Many countries in Southeast Asia and East Asia are entering into bilateral FTAs with each other. Australia has, for example, concluded FTAs with Japan and China. China, Japan and ROK are negotiating a high standard FTA among themselves. Negotiations are also underway led by the United States for concluding a high standard Trans-Pacific Partnership (TPP) agreement that has Brunei, Malaysia, Singapore and Vietnam as members from ASEAN and Japan from Northeast Asia, that could also eventually be joined by ROK, and Australia and New Zealand. It may not be feasible for India to be a member of TPP, at least at the present stage, considering the high level of commitments required, particularly on many behind-the-border issues that have been generally regarded as within domestic policy domain.

On the other hand, India is participating in the 16-member Regional Comprehensive Economic Partnership (RCEP) agreement negotiations that would include the 10 ASEAN members and its 6 dialogue partners: Australia, China, India, Japan, ROK and New Zealand. The guiding principles agreed upon for these negotiations also aim for a comprehensive, high standard agreement but do not mention about inclusion of labour and environment standards, TRIPS plus intellectual property provisions, regulatory coherence disciplines and investor-state dispute settlement provisions, aspects that are figuring prominently in TPP negotiations. How do we craft a strategy for ourselves that leverages our large market size on the one hand but allows sufficient policy space for ourselves to enable our industry to grow and achieve accelerated development? This will be a great challenge indeed, particularly to ensure that we remain plugged to the vibrant growth impulses emanating from the region.

ACTION TOWARDS ENHANCED CONNECTIVITY

A third approach towards promotion of our LEP has been to enhance connectivity. While efforts have been made in respect of increasing air and maritime connectivity as well as institutional connectivity we shall in this essay essentially focus on land connectivity which is through Myanmar and which forms our gateway to Southeast Asia. While this need has been talked about for over two decades, it appears to be showing some decisive movement only now. Four links are sought to be established which should, if adequately followed up, make significant headway during this third decade of our development partnership with ASEAN. The four links are:

1. Imphal-Moreh-Tamu-Kalay-Kalewa-Yagyi-Monywa-Mandalay-Thaton-Myawaddy Highway, also Called as the India-Myanmar-Thailand Trilateral Highway

The Government of India-assisted Tamu-Kalay-Kalewa Road, also referred to as the India-Myanmar Friendship Road, which will form part of the trilateral highway, was inaugurated in 2001. On the Indian side, National Highway-39 already covers the portion from Imphal to Moreh. To enable a seamless trilateral highway to emerge, upgradation of several sections, realignment of certain routes and repair/renovation of bridges are necessary. Implementation of the following is currently underway which can make it possible for such a trilateral highway to be in place by about 2017.

(a) Upgradation and realignment of the Imphal-Moreh section of NH-39 being undertaken with loan assistance from Asian Development Bank;
(b) Repair/renovation of the 71 bridges on the Tamu-Kalewa-Kalaymyo section which Government of India has agreed to undertake;
(c) Reconstruction of the 120-km Kalewa-Yagyi section which has also been agreed to be undertaken by the Government of India;
(d) Reconstruction of the Yagyi-Monywa section for which Government of Myanmar has taken responsibility; and

(e) Realignment of the Kawkareik-Myawaddy section up to the Thai border which is being undertaken with Thai assistance by Myanmar.

2. Aizawl-Champai-Zokhawthar-Rhi-Tiddim-Kalay-Kalewa Highway

This link will enable road connectivity through Mizoram state. Once connectivity is established up to Kalay it will then link up with the trilateral highway to Mandalay and beyond. Not all sections have however been committed to as yet, as indicated below:

(a) Upgrading Aizawl-Champai section to two-lane highway standard which needs to be taken up by the Government of India, if necessary, with assistance from international financial institutions;
(b) Repair and reconstruction of the Champai-Zowkhawthar section upto the Indian border which is already being taken up by the Mizoram government with World Bank assistance;
(c) Construction of Rhi-Tiddim road on Myanmar side of the border for which Government of India has offered assistance to Myanmar and the two sides have signed an MOU;
(d) Upgradation of the Tiddim-Kalay section for which Myanmar needs to be requested to assume responsibility.

3. The Kaladan Multimodal Transit Transport Project (KMTTP)

This project funded by the Government of India will link eastern Indian ports with the Sittwe port in Myanmar which is being expanded to receive vessels up to 6,000 dwt tonnes. Transportation from Sittwe will take place through inland waterway over the Kaladan River till Paletwa in Myanmar from where a highway link will be constructed to Lawangtalei in Mizoram through Zorinpui on the India-Myanmar border. The waterway portion of the project is expected be completed by the end of 2014 and the road construction, both on Myanmar and on Indian sides, is expected to be completed by 2016. The KMTTP project, besides providing an alternative supply route from mainland India to the northeast, would also link western Myanmar with the northeast. In addition, Indian supply vessels coming to the northeast can also extend their services to Yangon and provide direct regular shipping connectivity between the two countries.

4. Railway connectivity linking Guwahati-Lumding-Jiribam-Imphal-Moreh-Tamu-Kalay

Establishing railway connectivity can help ease moving heavy goods over long distances. Here again while Guwahati already has a broad-gauge link with Lumding, and progress on certain other sections are underway but funding for the rest will need to be identified. Conversion from metre gauge to broad gauge of following segments are in progress and is expected to be completed by the end of 2016.

(a) Lumding-Badarpur;
(b) Badarpur-Jiribam (in Manipur); and
(c) Badarpur-Sairang (in Mizoram)

Laying of a new broad gauge railway line from Jiribam to Imphal is also in progress and is expected to be completed by around 2018. Finally, the two sections Imphal-Moreh in Manipur and Tamu-Kalay in Myanmar could be good candidates for funding by international financial institutions and will have to be taken up by the two governments. A Joint Working Group on Railways between India and Myanmar has already held some discussions in January 2013 and these needs to be taken forward. It will be a fitting celebration of 30 years of dialogue partnership if this railway connectivity, as also all road connectivity mentioned earlier, can be established by 2022 and Myanmar also takes action to strengthen its railway network, particularly the Kalay-Mandalay and Mandalay-Yangon segments.

While various India-ASEAN meetings and also of other sub-regional groupings have talked about establishing overland connectivity with other CLMV countries, it remains to be seen if Indian goods after transiting through the whole of Myanmar will still remain competitive when they reach such third countries. A more immediate priority may be to ensure that the connectivity corridors that are being established through Myanmar become active trade, investment and development corridors that, *inter alia*, reduce transaction costs and improve competitiveness. Establishing good inland connectivity within the northeast, setting up efficient border trade and clearance mechanisms and developing necessary infrastructure that will attract private investments both in India and in Myanmar are crucial here. Timely completion of the four roads, railway and multi-modal links already outlined will be absolutely essential.

CONCLUSION

The economic dimension of India's LEP has been sought to be developed through three broad approaches: regional and sub-regional economic cooperation, free trade and investment agreements and enhanced connectivity. Regional or sub-regional initiatives have had only limited success so far. As further efforts are made to rejuvenate them, it will be important not to push them in areas where common interests are minimal or sensitivities are high. It does not seem necessary or appropriate, for example, for a grouping like BIMSTEC to try to draw up a free trade agreement when there are several other ongoing initiatives. Instead, focusing on areas like transportation, transit, energy, fisheries and meteorology seems more important among these contiguous countries. As for free trade agreements with Southeast Asian and East Asian countries, it will be very important to ensure full implementation and utilization of the CECAs/CEPAs India has already entered into and also review those of the provisions where Indian industry is finding it difficult to cope. India needs to also craft a strategy for dealing with other free trade initiatives like TPP of which India is not a part. It will be important to ensure that multilateral disciplines do not get pushed through the back door through such plurilateral initiatives. Actively participating in the RCEP negotiations and ensuring that disciplines developed there are more in line with Indian interests would be one way of ensuring it. Third is the need to implement all the pending projects relating to overland connectivity by road, railways and inland waterways between northeast India and Myanmar. If India succeeds also in transforming these connectivity corridors into development corridors that can reduce transaction costs and enhance competitiveness, then India would be further strengthening its ties with Myanmar. It would also pave the way for extending the physical connectivity for trade and transit to Thailand and other CLMV countries.

CHAPTER 9

Trade and Economic Dimension of India's Look East Policy

RAJEET MITTER*

The ancient civilizational and economic links between India and the rest of Asia have been extensively documented and are quite visible even today. The thrust to renew and modernize these links in the 1990s arose from a number of interrelated factors. The break up of the Soviet Union and the end of the Cold War signaled momentous changes in the international geo-strategic environment. India, which had pursued a relatively insular developmental model since independence, experienced a major economic crisis in 1991, particularly in its external sector. This spurred the roll out of far reaching economic reforms, and over a short period of time India dismantled its industrial licencing regime, reduced import tariffs, liberalized the foreign exchange market and in short opened up its economy to foreign goods and foreign investment. The merits of economic openness had already been demonstrated by the impressive growth rates in China and some of the ASEAN 'Tiger' economies, who had embarked on economic reforms much earlier. Notwithstanding the temporary setback of the Asian financial crisis in 1997, commentators had begun to predict that the twenty-first century would be the Asian century. In India, the enormous success of the economic reforms which began to transalate into high rates of growth of 7-9 per cent, and the fact that per capita income grew by an annual average of 5 per cent between 1992 and 2013 gave India the confidence to engage enthusiastically with the fast-growing economies of Asia.

Apart from sustained bilateral engagement with the countries of Asia, India strove for participation in the new multilateral trade and

*Amb. Rajeet Mitter, Former Ambassador of India.

economic architecture that was evolving. India became a sectoral dialogue partner of ASEAN in 1992, a full dialogue partner in 1996 and since 2002 has been holding an annual summit with ASEAN leaders. A special commemorative summit marking the 10th such meeting was held in New Delhi in December 2012. India participated in the first meeting of the East Asia Summit or ASEAN+6 held in Malaysia in 2005. India also joined the Asia-Europe Meeting in 2007 and attended the 7th summit meeting held in Beijing in October 2008. BIMSTEC or the Bay of Bengal Initiative for Multi Sectoral Technical and Economic Cooperation was formed in Bangkok in 1997 and today comprises Bangladesh, Bhutan, India, Myanmar, Nepal, Sri Lanka, and Thailand. BIMSTEC uniquely builds a bridge between South Asia and Southeast Asia. Another grouping, the Mekong-Ganga Cooperation (MGC) was established in Vientienne in 2000 and comprises Cambodia, India, Laos, Myanmar, and Thailand. There is now the expectation that India will move towards joining the Asia-Pacific Economic Cooperation (APEC) following the Chinese President Xi Jinping's invitation to India to attend the APEC Summit meeting in Beijing in November 2014.

While all these groupings progressively expanded the areas of cooperation, the primary focus was on trade and investment liberalization and integration. China and India amongst others pioneered tariff liberalization in Asia by participating in the Bangkok Agreement concluded in 1975, and which is now called the Asia-Pacific Trade Agreement (APTA). The South Asia Free Trade Agreement (SAFTA) came into force in January 2006. Notably, India progressively extended non-reciprocal tariff concessions to the LDC members of SAARC and by December, 2011 India's negative list for these countries was reduced to just 25 tariff lines. This was a substantial liberalization facilitating for instance duty-free access to the large Indian market for Bangladeshi textile and garment exports. Further afield, the India-ASEAN FTA came into force in January 2010, and negotiations on services and investment were concluded in 2012. At the bilateral level, India concluded Comprehensive Economic Cooperation/Partnership Agreements with Singapore, Japan, Korea and Malaysia in the period 2005-11 covering trade in goods and services and investment. There are ongoing negotiations with other countries such as Thailand, Indonesia, Australia and New Zealand. The most ambitious of all is of course the launch of negotiations on the Regional Comprehensive Economic Partnership that will encompass the ASEAN+6 countries including China and India.

At first glance, the results of trade and investment liberalization have been quite spectacular. To cite a few numbers, India-ASEAN trade grew from $9.7 billion in 2002-3 to $75.6 billion in 2012-13. India-Northeast Asia trade grew from $15.6 billion to $129.3 billion in the same period. India-China trade grew from less than $3 billion in 2000 to $74 billion in 2011, and is expected to cross $100 billion by 2015. Although India has had a consistent trade deficit with ASEAN, more recent trade figures for the period 2008-9 to 2012-13 show that Indian exports to ASEAN grew by 72.49 per cent whereas ASEAN exports to India grew by 62.85 per cent. Similarly, in the same period Indian exports to Japan grew by 101.6 per cent whereas Japanese exports to India grew by 57.39 per cent. However, not all the figures were so encouraging. India's persistent and growing trade deficit with China has become a matter of considerable concern. India has a healthy share in China's global imports of pearls and precious stones, cotton, animal fodder, textiles, coffee and tea and spices. But there has been little change in the composition of India's export basket in the recent period of trade expansion and India accounted for just 1.3 per cent of China's total imports in 2011. Similarly, India's trade deficit with Korea has been growing and in the period 2008-9 to 2012-13, India's exports grew by a paltry 6.3 per cent, whereas imports grew by 51 per cent. Overall, India's trade deficit with ASEAN, China, Japan and Korea ballooned from $36.79 billion in 2008-9 to $63.58 billion in 2012-13.

To what extent India's services exports compensated for the trade deficit cannot be calculated, since such disaggregated country-wise data is not available. Although total services exports rose from $52.18 billion in 2005 to $137.32 billion in 2011, it is likely that most of this was directed to USA and Europe. Asian equity-based FDI into India between April 2000 and April 2014 totalled some $45.53 billion accounting for an impressive 20 per cent of the global total. India also remained the largest recipient of Japanese ODA with soft financing extended to large infrastructural projects like the Delhi Metro, the Delhi-Mumbai dedicated freight corridor and the Delhi-Mumbai industrial corridor. The overall impact of India's economic engagement with Asia under LEP is a complex subject which has to take into account a variety of factors such as the trade balance, investment flows, economic growth and trends in the country's external sector. As such it is still a subject of lively debate and discussion.

Indeed, the new BJP-led government that came to power in May

2014 indicated that there would be a review of India's participation in FTAs. The background perhaps was the perceived adverse impact that FTAs have had on the manufacturing sector in India. Anomalies arising out of an inverted duty structure where tariffs on finished goods have come down faster than intermediate products have also been voiced from time to time. Such a review is necessary as there is still no authoritative study on the impact of FTAs on the Indian economy. Part of the difficulty is that most of the FTAs are still being rolled out and have not been fully implemented. There is also no publicly available data on the extent of trade taking place under the new liberalized tariff regimes or at MFN rates. To assume that all trade takes place under concessional tariffs is not necessarily true. In fact a 2007 World Bank study showed that FTA preference utilization rates were low in Asia due to a variety of factors. Furthermore, Indian FTAs have aimed to liberalize a high percentage of existing trade to meet WTO benchmarks. But India still has relatively large negative lists which means that new trade is either not being encouraged or taking place at MFN rates. For instance, under the India-Singapore CECA, India has agreed to reduce tariffs in a phased manner on 5,115 tariff lines at the eight-digit level, but has maintained an even bigger negative list of 6,551 tariff lines.

Irrespective of the findings of the review, to conclude that India's headlong rush into signing FTAs in Asia was premature would be grossly mistaken. With the WTO Doha Round launched in 2001 interminably stuck, there was an explosion of regional trading arrangements in the Asia-Pacific region. ASEAN itself set the trend by launching as early as 1992 the goal of establishing an ASEAN Free Trade Area by 2015. In the first decade of the twenty-first century, ASEAN concluded FTA agreements with all the + 6 countries. Similarly, Japan concluded bilateral agreements with Singapore, Malaysia, Thailand, Indonesia, Philippines and Brunei, and China with Singapore, New Zealand, Thailand, Taiwan and Pakistan. For India to have stayed away from the economic integration process would have meant being effectively locked out from the Asia-Pacific which in turn would have undermined the vital security aspects of its LEP. After all the overall aim of the LEP was to promote mutual interdependence, cooperation and benefit as a factor for peace and security in the extended Asia-Pacific neighbourhood.

The new wave of economic integration in the region epitomized by the launch of negotiations on the Regional Cooperation for

Economic Cooperation (RCEP) and the Trans-Pacific Partnership (TPP) pose fresh challenges for India. TPP, now effectively led by the US, and presently excluding China and India, aims at a high standard WTO+ agreement. Twenty rounds of negotiations have been held since January 2009, but early conclusion of negotiations is clouded by the uncertainty regarding eventual US Congressional approval for the deal. In any case it would be very difficult for India to seek accession to TPP since many of its likely WTO+ provisions on intellectual property, environment, government procurement, labour standards, and competition would be extremely difficult to meet. Regarding RCEP involving the ASEAN+6 countries, five rounds of negotiations have been held since November 2012. The direction appears more modest than TPP, with the main aim being to consolidate and harmonize existing FTA agreements amongst the ASEAN+6 countries with the primary focus on trade in goods and services and investment. But here again there appears to be no leader driving the negotiations. Several commentators have opined that progress in RCEP is linked to the outcome of the politically difficult China-Korea-Japan FTA negotiations which were launched in 2012. The early emergence of an East Asian Economic Community may well be a Chinese priority. Japan may also prioritize its involvement with both RCEP and TPP. It would be in India's interest therefore to be more proactive in pushing RCEP. This would be the key opportunity for India to seek more effective market access for its goods in China and for its services exports in the entire region and focus on relatively neglected areas such as cross-border investment flows and establishment of cross-border joint ventures.

An important aspect of the trade and economic dimension of India's LEP has been the focus on improved connectivity. The two pioneering projects for regional connectivity within Asia were the Asian highway and the trans-Asian railway conceptualized by UNESCAP several decades ago. While there has been some progress on the road project, railway connectivity has been hampered by both gauge variations as well as large missing links in India's border regions and in Myanmar. India's recent emphasis on bilateral and sub-regional approaches to connectivity has highlighted the critical and geographically vital positions of Bangladesh and Myanmar in the overall context of the LEP. The breakthrough with Bangladesh came in 2010 when the two countries agreed on a number of measures to improve sub-regional connectivity. These included provisions for the use of Chittagong and Mongla ports by India, and the designation of Ashuganj in Bangladesh as a multi-modal trans-shipment point to connect eastern India with northeastern India by waterways and road. This route was in fact used to transport heavy power equipment to the gas-based Palatana power project in Tripura, and has since been used to send food grains to India's northeast. India and Bangladesh also agreed to link their rail and road networks at the Tripura border providing direct connectivity to Chittagong port. A separate agreement was concluded to facilitate rail connectivity from Chittagong to Nepal via India. While all these initiatives are not fully operational as yet, they do signify a breakthrough in the long vexed issue of transit through Bangladesh, and which will feed into other connectivity projects emanating from the northeast.

The Kaladan multi-modal transit project which will connect the port of Sitwe in Myanmar to Mizoram through inland waterway and road has made some progress, but there are concerns that the establishment of the final road link to Mizoram is lagging way behind schedule. Doubts have also been voiced on the ultimate commercial viability of the project. The more promising India-Myanmar-Thailand Trilateral Highway project is expected to be completed by 2016, with India agreeing to finance the repair of 71 old bridges in the Tamu-Kalewa section and the upgradation of the Kalewa-Yargyi section. The highway will link Moreh-Tamu on the India-Myanmar border to Mae Sot-Myawaddy on the Myanmar-Thai border. There are now plans to extend this highway to Laos and Cambodia. A separate Indian-financed project to upgrade the 80-km road between Rhi and Tiddim promises an ultimate branch connection with the trilateral highway at Kalemyo with a resulting outlet into Mizoram. Finally, brief mention may be made of the proposal called the Mekong-India Economic Corridor. This is still at a conceptual stage but envisages the reconstruction of Dawei on Myanmar's southeastern coast as a deep sea port servicing an industrial corridor going across to Ho Chi Minh city and linking up via sea to the southern Indian port of Chennai.

A bold new proposal is the idea of a Bangladesh-China-India-Myanmar (BCIM) Economic Corridor. The decision to set up a joint study group on this was taken during the visit of the Chinese prime minister to India in May 2013. The physical dimension of this corridor was demonstrated by the BCIM car rally held in 2013 starting in Kolkata in India and ending in Kunming in China with the route traversing Bangladesh, northeast India and Myanmar. Both the trilateral highway and the proposed BCIM Economic Corridor thus place eastern and northeastern India at the heart of India's LEP. While this is a longstanding demand of many in the northeast, it calls for urgent attention to backend infrastructural development as well as the clear identification of economic opportunities and challenges.

The importance of physical transnational connectivity is now recognized as an essential prerequisite for regional economic integration and cooperation. This has the added potential for the comprehensive economic development of peripheral and economically lagging border regions. While security issues remain relevant and need to be addressed, the sanctity of impermeable national borders has been substantially undermined by rapid technological changes and globalization witnessed over the last several decades. As tariff-based barriers have come down, enhanced connectivity stimulates trade and also encourages cross-border production and services networks, improved border trade facilitation measures, investment flows, the optimal use of natural resources, skill development and above all greater people-to-people contacts and the exchange of ideas and knowledge. Indeed, transportation is just one aspect of connectivity and other areas to be explored are transnational oil and gas pipelines, telecommunications and electricity generation and transmission links. Some beginnings have been made. The electricity grids between India and Bangladesh have been connected in West Bengal and India is now exporting 500 MW of power. There are plans to export an additional 100 MW from Tripura and evacuate up to 6,000 MW from Assam, through Bangladesh into Bihar. Given the huge power potential in the northeast, an integrated grid covering the entire sub-region including Bhutan and Nepal can be envisaged. Similarly, Assam has excess oil refining capacity, and a new proposal envisages the construction of a petroleum product pipeline from Siliguri to Parbatipur in Bangladesh. The climate for such cross-border initiatives is now much more promising compared to the aborted 2004 proposal of a Myanmar-Bangladesh-India gas pipeline.

For over two decades now India has steadfastly pursued its LEP aimed at integrating its economy with the dynamic economies of Asia. For an eventual equitable outcome, attention has to be concentrated on accelerated backend infrastructural development and quick implementation of Indian-financed overseas projects. Otherwise, primacy may get accorded to new Chinese-backed proposals of a southern silk route and a maritime silk route. Particular emphasis is needed on the needs and perceived opportunities of India's eastern and northeastern states whose vital role in the LEP has to be fully appreciated. The vision articulated by India's former prime minister, Manmohan Singh way back in October 2004 remains valid today. He said:

> India envisions an Asian Economic Community which encompasses ASEAN, China, Japan, Korea, and India. Such a community would release enormous creative energies of our people. One cannot but be captivated by the vision of an integrated market spanning the distance from the Himalayas to the Pacific Ocean, linked by efficient road, rail, air and shipping services. This community of nations would constitute an arc of advantage across which there would be large-scale movement of people, capital, ideas and creativity. Such a community would be roughly the size of the European Union in terms of income, and bigger than NAFTA in terms of trade.

PART IV

Security Convergences: A New Evolving Paradigm

CHAPTER 10

Indo-Pacific Security and Defence: India's Challenges and Policy Options

KAPIL KAK*

BACKDROP

For nearly a quarter century of the post-Cold War period, the economic resurgence of China and of late, India, has impelled enormous geo-political reconfigurations. This diffusion of economic power has tended to progressively shift the global strategic centre of gravity from Europe-North Atlantic to Asia. It is thus no surprise that the somewhat odd West-originated hyphenation of a continent and a water body, Asia-Pacific – in which Asia ended at Myanmar! – is decidedly morphing into the more appropriate Indo-Pacific.[1] This integrated Indian Ocean-Pacific Ocean geopolitical space is increasingly perceived as the world's future economic powerhouse, and likely fulcrum of great churning.

The prospect of future peace and security in the region raises a slew of questions. Would China's rise be a peaceful one? In the absence of an inclusive security architecture, is the US 'pivot' or 'rebalance' a means to cope with redistribution of power or a security assurance to its key allies or a more ominous 'containment' strategy? What would be the nature of China's strategic responses? Moreover, the unresolved boundary dispute between India and China along the Himalayas, and unsettled rival territorial claims by China and its

*AVM Kapil Kak, AVSM, VSM, Founder, Additional Director of the Centre for Air Power Studies (2002-12), analyst and independent commentator on security and defence issues.

neighbours in the oil- and gas-rich South China Sea and East China Sea have the potential to cause turbulence, and possibly even conflict. What are India's key national interests in the Indo-Pacific, more so after a newly-elected government, globally seen as decisive and business-trade friendly, has taken charge, and how best can India's interests be safeguarded and projected?

This paper seeks to explore the emerging security contours of the Indo-Pacific region – the likely theatre of geo-strategic competition between established and emerging powers – and how other regional players would pursue their security interests within this dynamic. An attempt would be made to explore the maritime and air power dimensions, as also traditional and non-traditional security facets. Trends and developments in India's defence relations with key countries of this region, and challenges and prospects in forging closer defence cooperation, as an indispensable dimension of security and foreign policy, would also be examined.

INDO-PACIFIC AS STRATEGIC SPACE

Indo-Pacific, the vast geostrategic and geo-economic realm spanning the western Pacific right up to the western Indian Ocean, along the eastern coast of Africa is rapidly eclipsing the once dominant Asia-Pacific as the centre of trade, investment, rivalry, competition and cooperation . . . more significance accrues from the fact that this narrowly defined entity places security and commerce at the centre of the Asian strategic matrix . . . the geographically distinct Indian Ocean holds two of the primary gateways in world maritime trade – the Strait of Hormuz and the Strait of Malacca – and has 85 per cent of world's seaborne trade, primarily oil, passing through it. Also 65 per cent of the world's oil reserves belong to just ten of the Indian Ocean littoral states.[2] Significantly, half the world's population, expected to grow increasingly prosperous in the decades ahead, lives in this region.

The view that much of Asia and Indian Ocean that form India's extended neighbourhood took root after the Cold War ended is only partially valid. This is because two centuries of colonialism and half a century of a bipolar order had substantially constrained India's strategic wiggle room. It is useful to recall here that soon after independence, Jawaharlal Nehru and his able Secretary-General, Ministry of External Affairs, Girja Shankar Bajpai were quick to endorse the early twentieth-century formulation by Lord Curzon that India's strategic neighbourhood extended from Hindukush to Irrawady, Aden to Singapore and Suez to Shanghai. Moreover, were not the efforts of Colombo powers (that organized the Bandung Conference of 1955) the first stirrings of efforts towards a construct identifying South Asia and Southeast Asia as not being separate strategic spaces?

Robert Kaplan, the American scholar, has aptly described the strategic scenario in the Indo-Pacific as one 'where the rivalry between the US and China interlocks with the regional rivalry between China and India'. A reading of the tea leaves suggests a future Asian strategic landscape in which the US, a rising China, an aspiring and emerging India would be the primary actors, with possibly a militarily strengthened Japan adding its heft. This quad would likely dictate the security narratives. Other regional players would find accommodation within this broad construct. But geopolitical anxieties on whether China's rise would be a peaceful one persist. In the concluding chapter of his book, *The Tragedy of Great Power Politics*, the well-known American strategic scholar, John J. Mearsheimer, espouses the theory of offensive realism in international affairs to analyse whether China would rise peacefully. His riveting argument is that if China sustains high economic growth rates, it will attempt to dominate Asia the way the US dominates the Western Hemisphere. Others also opine that China is aware that the best way to survive today's anarchic polycentric world order is to be the sole hegemonic power in Asia.

Where Mearsheimer appears somewhat unconvincing is his assessment that India, Japan, South Korea, Australia and Singapore and other countries will join the US to contain Chinese power. Such a policy would not only intensify security competition but also increase possibilities of conflict. Not unjustifiably, while addressing the Central Party in Beijing in October 2013, India's prime minister had averred 'India and China cannot be contained. . . nor should we seek to contain others.' Evidently, the US 'pivot' or 'rebalancing' does not imply containment, but perhaps a broader long-term initiative to rectify the emerging geo-political imbalance. That the Indo-Pacific nations would form defence and strategic partnerships to 'balance' China, and deter it against any military misadventure appears more plausible.

As to India-China strategic interplay, the latter's nautical forays into South Asia and the strategic islands of the Indian Ocean like Sri Lanka, Mauritius, Seychelles, Maldives, Madagascar among others, is seen by India as countering its traditional influence in these parts. This would only compel India to make counter forays in the Pacific. Some acknowledge that China's ability to put India under strain in the India Ocean is a growing factor shaping the broader dynamic of Asian security.[3] The 2014 US Pentagon report on China endorses this and foregrounds logistical support as a key obstacle for the PLA Navy to operate more extensively in the Indian Ocean and forecasts China establishing several access points in the region over the next ten years.[4] Should this mean the Chinese navy acquiring access to deep water port(s) in South Asia, India would be fully justified in doing likewise to begin with at the strategically located Cam Ranh Bay in Vietnam, an idea that has long enthused New Delhi's strategic community.

On the other side, we have the persuasive argument that

> India's future in the western Pacific is not about matching the military weight of China in the littoral. It is about generating strategic options for the littoral states. If India [under the Modi Government] continues to maintain high economic growth rates and builds on the framework of security cooperation that it has developed in the region, New Delhi's influence in the Pacific theatre can only expand.[5]

To be sure there is need to reiterate the criticality of substantially enhanced Indian military capabilities in the nuclear and conventional realms in order to sustain deterrence that has higher levels of credibility and effectiveness.

India's air power and maritime capabilities in five key areas that 'China should fear in a conflict' as articulated by Kyle Mizokami in *National Interest*, May 2014, comprise Mig 29K-equipped aircraft carrier *INS Vikramaditya*, Fifth Generation Fighter Aircraft (planned induction 2017), Brahmos Mach 3 cruise missile, *Arihant* nuclear submarine and Brahmos-equipped *Kolkata*-class destroyers. These, along with capabilities in information/cyber warfare and the space domain, require to be further built upon. India's air power and maritime power would play a key role in the execution of defence tasks in the Indo-Pacific. The key objective should be to strengthen the Indian Air Force, specifically in its ability to establish air dominance in sectors where China's Air Force could be vulnerable. That the Andaman and Nicobar Islands need to be the jump off points for

India's military outreach into the Indo-Pacific would be stating the obvious.

REGIONAL POWERS AND ASEAN

The first half of 2014 saw China again engage in *contre temps* and intimidation in both the northern and southern sectors of the South China Sea that showed total disregard of Vietnam and the Philippines, and spooked neighbours. While China does not condescend to explain the basis of its territorial claims, its tensions with Japan over the ownership of Senkaku/Diaoyu islands in the East China Sea have also heightened. We also see that the ASEAN Summit in May 2014 'agreed on a strong expression of concern about recent events', but would not have the gumption to state China was causing the disquiet. Such obsequiousness encourages China not to be swayed by legal arguments or US military pressure. For these do not square with China's deliberate expansionism, anchored in its conviction that the US is unlikely to go to war with it over 'reefs and shoals claimed by its neighbours' that helps it calibrate such show of force so as not to breach the American threshold of tolerance. Not surprisingly, neither the US nor India took sides on the merits of the disputed claims.

The not-so-adroit handling by the US of its ties with Russia in the Ukraine crisis has provided China with more wiggle room through cemented Russia-China strategic ties. The Skovorodino-Mohe gas pipeline project, worth $500 billion in overall value over three decades, and likely sale of advanced Russian Su35 fighter aircraft and S 400 surface-to-air missiles, long denied to it, are close to fruition. These developments could serve to raise apprehensions in the Indo-Pacific of a Russia-China twin-challenge, more so after China and Russia held their largest joint exercise in the Sea of Japan (July 2013) in which a total of 23 warships participated. But Russia's offer of extending the pipeline project to India could set the stage for a Russia-China-India energy partnership so endemic to resource security in the region.

The Chinese leadership appears convinced that the American pivot or rebalance is containment masquerading as security multilateralism, though the pivot seeks to reinforce US alliances in Asia. To be sure these alliances are coming under stress less from China's rise than its growing assertiveness. 'The real target of Chinese muscle flexing is the American forward presence in the western Pacific, as that prevents China from wielding untrammelled power in its neighbourhood and constrains its ambition.'[6] Perhaps partnerships between India, Japan, South Korea, Australia, among others, driven by shared concerns and interests, would best serve India's LEP.

This begs the question how Japan sees the fast changing geo-strategic contours in Indo-Pacific? Its foremost concern is the exercise of disruptive military power by a rapidly rising China. Enunciation of Japan's first ever National Security Strategy in December 2013 commits it to a stronger military posture. Prime Minister Shinzo Abe has also sought a reinterpretation of Japan's pacifist constitution making space for its greater military role in Asia. The strategy envisions higher defence budget for modernization of its maritime and air power for more effective control over the maritime and air spaces around the areas in dispute with China. Military cooperation with India is emerging as an important priority which should have a strong traction in the Narendra Modi-led Indian government.

In the case of ASEAN, it continues to show symptoms of low grade 'China fever' and, thus, seeks prophylactics. It was compelled to establish the ASEAN Regional Forum (ARF) in 1994 as a platform for confidence building and preventive diplomacy in the face of Chinese territorial claims in the South China Sea, which member-states contested. After the US and China joined the grouping, ASEAN welcomed India's entry as a factor for peace and security. As a credible nuclear and military power, India skilfully availed this opportunity to break out of the South Asian strategic straitjacket to assume the long-awaited new responsibility in Indo-Pacific, its strategic neighbourhood.

Helping shape ARF as the envisioned platform for confidence-building, transparency and cooperative security would remain India's objective. Moreover, cooperation in energy security, unhindered navigability of SLOCs and counter-terrorism – key issues of mutual concern – must remain the thrust areas. Non-traditional security dimensions that include transnational crime, narcotics and human trafficking, pandemics such as SARS or the bird flu would also pose challenges. The consultative non-governmental Track II mechanism, Council for Security Cooperation in the Asia Pacific (CSCAP) has shown promise in consolidating links with Track I. In an aspiring people-driven world, CSCAP's focused outcomes should greatly facilitate ARF, as it re-models itself for greater effectiveness in a fast-changing security matrix.

India's close interaction with individual ASEAN countries has helped dispel any divergences on cooperation with India.[7] This is because countries have varying concerns and interests, particularly with regard to the US and China. Recent improvements in Indo-US ties and security concerns with China also impact the India-ASEAN dynamic, as does continued economic assistance to Myanmar, Vietnam, Cambodia and Laos. But enduring and longstanding economic and cultural values and a generally similar approach to political Islam, given their common philosophy of ethno-religious accommodation and inclusivity resonates positively in the Indo-Pacific. This is important in the context of the terrorist-extremist religious firestorm that has enveloped both Iraq and Syria.

MARITIME DIMENSIONS

Extending at the northern end from the Gulf through the SLOCs of the northern Indian Ocean along the Malacca Straits, maritime geopolitics of the Indo-Pacific encompasses a wide canvas. Security challenges are relational and transnational; developments in one having resonance in another. These include traditional and non-traditional dimensions, maritime rivalries, and energy and resource security, as impacted by choke-points. The situation gets exacerbated by the unresolved maritime boundary disputes that could get out of hand. In an ironic development, it required China to indulge in intimidation and coercion in the South China Sea, during the first half of 2014, to get the Philippines and Indonesia to announce 'an agreement on their maritime boundary after nearly two decades of on-off negotiations'. This makes the case for having in place principles and mutually agreed frameworks for early resolution of maritime disputes even stronger.

It is thus no surprise that the US is committed to sustain credible combat power in the region, enhance its maritime and aerospace posture and strengthen cooperation with its partners. Inevitably, Japan, Vietnam, Indonesia and the Philippines are looking to build their offensive and defensive maritime capabilities. 'Many of these states. . . have also supported India in its aspiration for naval outreach in South China Sea.'[8] India has achieved a modest success in maritime security cooperation within South Asia with the India-Sri Lanka-Maldives maritime arrangement. This cooperative and comprehensive maritime security trilateralism could be replicated with other nations in the Indo-Pacific.[9]

There is need to reiterate that not just maritime capabilities but the entire verticality dimension comprising air, near space, space, outer space, cyber and information warfare must remain the highest priority for India's defence planners. Decisive impact of land-based, long-range, precision-force oceanic air power, in which China is investing heavily, can dramatically shape security outcomes in the Indo-Pacific. This important dimension needs to be seen in the light of China's successive Defence White Papers foregrounding the need for *Command of the Sea* and *Command of the Air* (emphasis added) to cause strategic paralysis of the enemy.

On the other hand, acute dependence of China and India on access to and transportation of hydrocarbon and mineral resources from the rest of Asia and Africa and vastly expanded sea-borne trade volumes along Indo-Pacific SLOCS could generate future rivalry. The so-termed security dilemmas, in which one nation's moves to protect its security interests are perceived by the other as undermining its position add to the disquiet. The key first step would be to evolve mechanisms to tone down such negative impulses and incentivize China to join a maritime security order that is inclusive, rule-based and flexible, even as China is presently disinclined to resonate to any such efforts. Early ratification by the US of the United Nations Convention on the Law of Sea (UNCLOS), a covenant on 'Order at Sea' that establishes a comprehensive framework for the regulation and management of maritime space, would constitute a move forward towards the desired outcome.[10]

DEFENCE COOPERATION

For India, opportunities offered by anchoring defence cooperation in national strategy and Indo-Pacific policies are manifold: pursuit of understanding, transparency on intentions and capability, perception of mutual interests, and energizing defence industry, as also the spin-offs these offer for cooperation in areas other than defence. Some of the common defence focus areas that could be pursued in the region include enhancing defence trade, defeating violent extremism, combating proliferation of weapons of mass destruction, combating piracy and providing humanitarian assistance and disaster relief (HADR). Given India's recent track record and rapidly developing capabilities, HADR would serve as key component of India's defence diplomacy in the Indo-Pacific.

It is significant that ASEAN countries see defence relationship with India less as a factor in enhancing their defence capacities than as contributing to their freedom and well being. For under the Treaty of Amity and Cooperation signed at Bali in October 2003, India is formally committed to the stability and freedom of ASEAN. It was, thus, no surprise when following India's acceptance of the membership of the first East Asia Summit in 2005, it also joined the first conclave of the ASEAN Defence Ministers Meeting Plus (ADMM+) in 2010. Even with China, military engagement should be encouraged for it accords with India's 'overall policy of sustaining equilibrium among major powers'. While army and navy exercises have been held regularly, it is time the envisaged, but long delayed, joint exercises between the two air forces take place soon.

Shedding its erstwhile long-lasting defence isolation, India has tended to jettison what has tongue-in-cheek been termed its predilection 'to Look East, then Look Away' or 'be half-in and half-out', of the Indo-Pacific. It has gingerly stepped up security engagement in the region with institutionalized strategic and defence dialogue, increased port calls by its naval ships and enhanced participation in international military exercises by all three armed forces. But many challenges remain on the horizon. To be sure, despite defence agreements with Indonesia and Singapore, close cooperation with Vietnam, and Memorandums of Understanding with South Korea and Malaysia, among others, construction of overall military engagement in the region has been slow, possibly on account of what could be termed 'self deterrence'.

India-Japan defence cooperation is a case in point. For despite the two navies conducting joint military missions, and governments holding the so-called two plus two dialogue involving the Defence and Foreign Secretaries from both sides, 'there is residual scepticism about the political will and bureaucratic capacity to build consequential defence cooperation, especially in the context of the inevitable suspicion or hostility'.[11] India's challenges and options for ensuring effective security and defence of the strategically vital Indo-Pacific region, with a rising and unprecedentedly aggressive China staring in its face, are indeed daunting. India would have to put in place robust policies for safeguarding and projecting its key national interests, and in the process be the net security provider for the Indo-Pacific.

NOTES

1. For a more detailed rationale for Indo-Pacific, see Rory Medcalf, 'A Term Whose Time Has Come', *The Diplomat*, 12 December 2012 and Hemant Krishan Singh, 'Reimagining the Region: "Asia-Pacific" or "Indo-Pacific"?',*ICRIER Issue Brief*, vol. 3, issue 3, 31 October 2013.
2. Sureesh Mehta, 'An Evolving Geostrategic Realm', in Pradeep Kaushiva and Abhijit Singh (eds.), *Geopolitics of the Indo-Pacific* New Delhi: Knowledge World, 2014, p. 17.
3. Ibid., p. 18.
4. Department of Defence, Annual Report to Congress: *Military and Security Developments Involving the People's Republic of China*, 2014, p. 38.
5. C. Raja Mohan, *Samudra Manthan: Sino-Indian Rivalry in the Indo-Pacific*, New Delhi: Oxford University Press, 2013, pp. 107-8.
6. Kanwal Sibal, 'Let the Cherry Blossoms Bloom', *Hindustan Times*, 23 January 2014, p. 18.
7. For an analytical exposition on areas of divergences within ASEAN, see Sudhir Devare, *India and Southeast Asia: Towards Security Convergence*, New Delhi: Capital Publishing Company, 2006, pp. 81-3.
8. Note 2, p. 19.
9. For an exposition on the maritime trilateral arrangement in South Asia, see P.K. Ghosh, *Strategic Analysis*, May-June 2014, pp. 283-8.
10. For details on UNCLOS, see Vijay Sakhuja, 'Security in the Maritime Commons', in Ashley Tellis and Sean Mirski (eds.),*Crux of Asia: China, India and the Emerging Global Order*, Washington: Carnegie Endowment for International Peace, 2013, pp. 155-61.
11. Note 5, p. 106.

CHAPTER 11

India's Look East Policy: The Maritime Dimension

C. RAJA MOHAN AND DARSHANA M. BARUAH*

INTRODUCTION

The Look East Policy has been one of India's more successful foreign policy initiatives since the end of the Cold War. The success of the policy was rooted in the transformation of India's economy that began in the early 1990s and the consistent support from the Association of Southeast Asian Nations (ASEAN) that welcomed India into its fold despite years of mutual neglect. Despite the widespread skepticism at that time on prospects for long-overdue reforms in India, the ASEAN leaders kept faith with the proposition that Delhi will increasingly matter to the economic growth, political stability and regional security in the East Asian region. This bet has paid off with India emerging as an important economic, political and security partner for the ASEAN. While many would like to see a faster pace of progress, there is no denying what has been achieved in the last two decades. India is now a full partner in all of ASEAN's institutions. It has a free trade agreement with the ASEAN and is committed to negotiating a more comprehensive regional economic partnership agreement with the ASEAN and six of its leading trade partners.

India and ASEAN elevated their relations to the level of a 'strategic partnership' at the commemorative summit in Delhi in December

* Dr C. Raja Mohan, Distinguished Fellow, Observer Research Foundation, Contributing Editor, *The Indian Express*, Visiting Research Professor, Institute of South Asian Studies, Singapore and Non-resident Senior Associate, Carnegie Endowment for International Peace, Washington D.C; and Dr Darshana M. Baruah, Junior Fellow, Observer Research Foundation.

2012 that marked twenty years of India's engagement with Southeast Asia.[1] It marked India's increasing weight in Southeast Asia as well as the growing expectations in the ASEAN for a proactive political role in stabilizing the region at a moment of profound political turbulence in East Asia marked by intensification of regional conflict and renewed great power tensions. The new emphasis on the strategic partnership underscored ASEAN's interest in security cooperation with India, especially in the maritime domain. The security dimension, which was always latent in India's Look East Policy (LEP), has now become explicit. This essay begins with a brief review of India's LEP and its growing security dimension. In the second section we assess the impact of India's emergence on the geopolitics of the region and the consequent changes on our mental maps about Asia and its waters. The final part of the paper makes the case for stronger security cooperation, particularly naval engagement between India and Southeast Asia.

THE THIRD PHASE

The evolution of the LEP can be can be defined as having gone through three distinct phases. The first phase of the policy lasted until the early 2000s and saw India's incremental integration with the ASEAN institutions, first as a sectoral dialogue partner and then as a full dialogue partner and a member of the ASEAN Regional Forum. The second phase saw the expansion of geographic scope of India's LEP. In 2003, India's then External Affairs Minister Yashwant Sinha outlining the second phase of the policy remarked that,

> The first phase of India's 'Look East' policy was ASEAN-centred and focused primarily on trade and investment linkages. The new phase of this policy is characterised by an expanded definition of 'East', extending from Australia to East Asia, with ASEAN at its core. The new phase also marked a shift from trade to wider economic and political issues, including joint efforts to protect the sea-lanes and coordinate counter-terrorism activities.[2]

The second phase saw India join the East Asia Summit as a founding member. ASEAN chose to invite Delhi into the EAS despite objections by some that India did not belong to 'East Asia'. The move underlined the recognition that India would be an important partner in shaping Asia's political future.

In what might be the beginning of the third phase, East Asia is looking for a more explicit security role in the region. Amidst the rise of China and its growing assertiveness on maritime territorial disputes with its neighbours and the concern that the United States might not be able to sustain its primacy in Asia, there is a new sense in the region that India could help contribute to a stable balance of power in the region. There is growing eagerness in the region for stronger bilateral defence cooperation with India. Japan, Australia, Indonesia, Vietnam and Singapore are among countries that are looking for a more intensive military engagement with India. The United States wants India to take on a larger security role in East Asia. The ASEAN as a whole is eager that Delhi plays a more active role in the multilateral forums on regional security in Asia. While a security role for India seems some kind of novelty, even a cursory look at recent history reveals the significant Indian military contribution to the evolution of modern Asia.

In the colonial era, the European colonial powers came into the Indian Ocean from the west, established their presence in the subcontinent before conquering the regions to the east of India. The military resources of the undivided subcontinent were central to the imperial defence system of Great Britain that prevailed over other powers in East and Southeast Asia. India played a significant part in the Second World War, when nearly 750,000 Indian troops under Lord Mountbatten's Southeast Asia Command delivered a hard fought victory in what is often called the 'forgotten war'.[3] As India's massive contribution began to alter the course of the Second World War in Asia, it was not difficult to visualize a critical role for Delhi in shaping the post-war order in Asia. K.M. Panikkar, one of the early Indian strategists, for example, argued that 'a free and stable government in India conscious of its responsibilities and capable of playing its part in Southeast Asia, is the essential prerequisite' for the success of such a collective security system. 'In the absence of such a government in India', Panikkar argued Southeast Asia 'will remain the cockpit of colonial ambitions, incapable of defending itself, and a prey to the predatory urge of any power which is strong enough to attack it'.[4] However, with the Partition of India and turn of events in the world order, New Delhi began to focus more on the global Cold War issues and India found itself increasingly isolated from the ASEAN.

When India did return to Southeast Asia with its LEP in the early 1990s, the country faced a very different dynamic with the region. If Asia had looked up to India during the middle of the twentieth century, it was India's turn now to be inspired by East Asia's rapid economic growth in the 1970s and 1980s. That India and the ASEAN had traded places was also reflected in the fact that not all members of the regional organization were enthusiastic about bringing New Delhi into the regional institutions. India's friends in the region advised Delhi to discard its traditional high-decible diplomacy. They wanted India to avoid the habit of posturing on big global issues and focus on practical questions of regional cooperation. Determined to become a part of the region's institutions, New Delhi was quite happy to heed Deng Xiaoping's advice to the Chinese leaders, 'keep a low profile, and never take the lead'.

A modest approach did indeed seem to serve the objectives of India's LEP in the early years of engagement with the ASEAN. But as geopolitical turbulence envelops East Asia, the case for a modest Indian approach to the region has begun to unravel. The stronger the Indian economy and higher its international profile, the greater have been ASEAN's security expectations of Delhi. But India's continuing caution has left a big question mark on whether India is willing to bridge the gap between its potential security role and its current performance.[5] New Delhi's slow pace and seeming lack of purposefulness have generated considerable disappointment in the region. Many in the ASEAN see India unwilling or unable to deploy its growing power resources in promoting regional security and public goods in Southeast Asia. Some have argued that the problem appears to be India's lack of self-consciousness of its own strength and the absence of a strategic culture.[6] Whatever the merits of that argument, there is growing pressure on Delhi to respond to the mounting expectations in Southeast Asia for a vigorous Indian role. Much of this is a consequence of India's own successful integration with the ASEAN, the rise of China and the reconfiguration of the Asian geopolitical space.

IMAGINING THE INDO-PACIFIC

India's inward orientation from the 1960s resulted in the steady dissipation of its commercial, political and security links with Southeast Asia. Foreign offices around the world and the international relations community began to treat South and Southeast Asia as very different regions that had little to do with each other. The process of reconnecting Asia with itself began with the formation of ASEAN in the late 1960s and the eventual expansion to cover the entire region of Southeast Asia, and its deeper engagement with Japan and later with China. Bringing India in was pulling in the last big economy into the framework of regional cooperation. Although the pace of India's integration has been slow, it has slowly but certainly begun to change the geopolitical conceptions of Asia and erase the differences between East Asia and South Asia. Intensifying this process was the rapid economic growth of China. The opening of Myanmar, that last major economy in Southeast Asia to globalize more recently, will make sure that the geographic distinctions between different parts of Asia will increasingly break down. Meanwhile, India's trade and economic relations with East Asia are acquiring greater weight, with more than 50 per cent of its trade flows now heading east. India's stake in the political stability and security of the Western Pacific has also steadily risen. New Delhi's LEP has acquired a distinct naval dimension over the last decade. Since the beginning of the 2000s, the Indian Navy has made continuous forays into the Western Pacific.

The traditional clear distinctions, then, between the Indian Ocean and the Pacific are beginning to erode. The economic growth in East Asia in the 1980s generated the concept of the 'Pacific Rim'. The expansion of this growth to Southeast Asia led to the construction of the term Asia-Pacific. China's increasing reliance on the Indian Ocean and the acceleration of India's economic growth and strategic interests in the Pacific has now led to the increasing use of the term 'Indo-Pacific'. The intersection of the maritime interests of a rising China and an emerging India with those of the United States that has long provided security in the two oceans has begun to give the 'Indo-Pacific' a distinctive geopolitical character.[7]

The idea of Indo-Pacific, that has gained some traction in recent years, is not entirely new. The German geopolitical thinker Karl Haushofer had expanded upon the idea of 'Indopazifischen Raum' or the 'Indo-Pacific space' in the 1920s. Before him, Mahan saw Asia and its waters as a single space. What is new and more current has been the tendency to see Asia as consisting of separate zones and dividing its littoral into the Indian and Pacific. The integration of Asia with itself and the expanding global interests of China and India are what make the Indo-Pacific. The concept of the Indo-Pacific has gained policy attention in recent years, especially since the US

Secretary of State Hillary Clinton talked about the interconnections between the two oceans and outlined the framework of Washington's pivot to Asia at the end of 2011. In India, the term has gained salience as Delhi begins to appreciate the importance of its economic and strategic interests in the Western Pacific.

While the theoretical debate on the Indo-Pacific and its meaning has just begun, it is not an abstract notion for Southeast Asia. For the region is at the very intersection of the Indian and Pacific Oceans and links the subcontinent and East Asia. As we re-conceptualize the mental maps of Asia and its waters amidst the region's integration with itself, 'Southeast Asia becomes not an appendage to either East or South Asia but a hinge linking both together'.[8] Many of the new geopolitical trends we discussed above find their fullest expression in the littorals of the Bay of Bengal, the Andaman Sea and the South China Sea that connect the two oceans and demand greater attention to the waters that connect the two oceans.[9] China's vital Sea Lanes of Communications (SLOCs) pass through the Malacca Straits and other passages in archipelagic Southeast Asia. India's own east-bound trade travels in the other direction through the Malacca Straits.

India is also strengthening its joint military command at the Andaman and Nicobar Islands whose southern tip is at the mouth of the Malacca Straits. If Delhi worries about the security implications of China's strategic investments in Myanmar and the Bay of Bengal, Beijing is concerned about the Indian ability to interdict its SLOCs in the Andaman Sea and the growing naval collaboration between Delhi and Washington. If the Bay of Bengal and the Andaman Sea have acquired a new geopolitical salience in the eastern Indian Ocean, the deepening conflict in the South China Sea between China and its neighbours has pushed the littoral to the centre of regional power play. For instance, in 2012 Beijing and Manila were locked in a maritime standoff over the Scarborough Shoal, increasing tensions of a possible armed conflict. The two-month stand-off came to an end with an American-mediated agreement wherein both sides settled to withdraw their forces.[10] While Manila withdrew its vessels, China continued to maintain its forces eventually gaining control over the island. Later that year, China put up nine oil and gas blocks in the South China Sea for international bidding – including Block 128 in Vietnam's EEZ and under operation by India. Vigorous assertions by China such as the recent move in placing the oil rig HD 981 within Vietnam's EEZ and Continental Shelf[11] in the South China

Sea carry the threat of destabilizing the security of vital SLOCs in very important waters.

Although India is not a direct party to the territorial conflicts in the South China Sea, trouble in those waters has a direct effect on New Delhi's economic and security interests in the region. Whereas New Delhi refrains from taking positions on the nature of the territorial disputes between China and its neighbours in the South China Sea, the Government of India has emphasized the importance of their peaceful resolution and the need to assure freedom of navigation and stability in the region. Officials within the government have noted that 'Our position on the South China Sea is quite clear. We believe that we should have freedom of the right of navigation in these areas. And we believe that disputes, whatever they may be, should be resolved between the concerned parties.'[12] Moreover, the Indian Navy identifies the South China Sea and other areas of Western Pacific Ocean as 'secondary areas of maritime interest'.[13] Indicating New Delhi's growing interest in the region, the Indian Naval Chief of Staff in 2012 remarked that if the political leadership so decides, the navy is prepared to protect its interests in the South China Sea. 'Not that we expect to be in those (South China Sea) waters very frequently, but when the requirement is there, for example in situations where our country's interests are involved, for example ONGC Videsh etc., we will be required to go there and we are prepared for that. Are we preparing for it? Are we holding exercises of that nature? The short answer is yes.'[14] Senior officials in India's Ministry of External Affairs have also underlined the growing demands on New Delhi to maintain stability in the region.

> Over the past few years, one can discern that ASEAN also wishes India to play a more active role in maritime security and related issues. Ensuring maritime security and freedom of navigation in the sea lanes of communication (SLOC) is an imperative for the growing economies in the region given its interface with energy and economic security. Considering that India is strategically located overlooking vital trade arteries, it is a natural corollary that India should play a greater role in maritime security in the region.[15]

Much like India, which is concerned about the rising Chinese naval profile in the Indian Ocean, Beijing is warily watching India's growing diplomatic and strategic interest in the South China Sea. A deepening security dilemma, between China and India, the Bay of Bengal, Andaman Sea and the South China Sea has begun to intersect with the increasingly uncertain dynamic between China and the

United States in the Western Pacific. The intensifying territorial disputes between China and Japan in the East China Sea naturally spill over into the South China Sea. The current churn in the waters to the east and west of the Malacca Straits has set an entirely different context for political and security cooperation between India and the Southeast Asian countries.

A central theme of India's LEP has been a conscious deference to the leadership of the ASEAN in the building of an East Asian order. Through the last two decades, India has repeatedly underlined the ASEAN centrality in shaping the future of East Asia.[16] There was more than prudence dictating this policy posture. It is rooted in the recognition that ASEAN's coherence is in India's vital national interest. India is aware that a weaker ASEAN might allow a great power to pry away its member-states into special relationships and introduce rivalry with other powers, including India. India recognizes the significance of the ASEAN in transforming a region that was once known as 'Asia's Balkans' into the principal agency promoting regional integration. Yet, India will increasingly have to confront the fact that the new political dynamic in the region is testing ASEAN's coherence and its ability to act as a moderating force in the region. Until recently it seemed that the ASEAN was quite capable of managing structural changes in the East Asian system through multidirectional engagement and finding a way to draw in most of the major powers into the regional process.[17] Although the ASEAN has offered the broadest possible platform for Asian regionalism in recent decades, its ability to do so in the future is being threatened by the rapid changes in the distribution of power and intensifying territorial conflicts between some of its members and China. During 2010-12, as China's maritime territorial conflicts with Vietnam and Philippines intensified, it has not been clear that the ASEAN as a whole is willing to lend strong support to their member states against Beijing. China's refusal to collectively engage the ASEAN on the South China Sea issue and its growing ability to wean away individual members of the organization underlines the dangers of the new dynamic in the ASEAN.[18] As internal political fissures within ASEAN come to the fore amidst the changing regional balance of power, India can't assume that repeating the slogan of 'ASEAN centrality' is enough of a strategy.[19] It will need to do a lot more to deepen its own security and political cooperation with the ASEAN as a whole and key member states, especially in the maritime domain that has emerged as the principal arena of contestation in the region.

SECURITY COOPERATION: THE NAVAL DIMENSION

In the early 1990s when India opened up to the world, the Indian Navy reached out to the maritime neighbours of Southeast Asia. Over the last two decades and more there has been a steady expansion of India's naval interaction with its East Asian neighbours. The multilateral 'Milan' exercises launched in 1995 sought to dispel the fears of the region, generate transparency about India's naval plans and lay the foundation for long-term maritime engagement with the Southeast Asian nations.[20] At the end of 2004, Indian Navy was quick to respond, on its own, to the tsunami disaster and later joined the navies of the US, Japan and Australia to provide relief in Southeast Asia. In 2005, India sent its aircraft carrier, *INS Viraat*, for the first time to the waters of Southeast Asia. It visited the ports of Klang (Malaysia), Singapore and Jakarta. In the Spring/Summer of 2007, Indian Navy sailed all the way up to Vladivostok and conducted a series of bilateral and multilateral exercises with a number of nations that included major powers like the US, Japan, Russia and China as well as regional actors like Singapore, Vietnam and the Philippines. India also began to conduct coordinated maritime patrols of the Malacca Straits with the littoral states since piracy in the region seemed to threaten the security of the SLOCs. The Indian Navy also took the initiative to convene an Indian Ocean Naval Symposium in February 2008.[21] Since then, the biennial IONS has a become forum for discussion of regional naval cooperation and confidence building among the chiefs of littoral navies in the Indian Ocean. In 2010 when the ASEAN expanded the forum for its defence ministers (ADMM), India was invited to join in.[22] As the disputes in South China Sea escalated, India lent its diplomatic voice in favour of peaceful resolution of disputes in accordance with the United Nations Convention on the Law of the Sea. Delhi also joined the United States and other powers in emphasizing the importance of protecting the right to freedom of navigation in the South China Sea. Since 2011, India has also sought to revive the Indian Ocean Rim Association for Regional Cooperation and inject some security content into its deliberations.[23] Beyond the expanded reach and scope of its multilateral military engagement, India has stepped up its bilateral security cooperation across the region. During the last few years, India has signed security cooperation agreements with a number of Southeast Asian countries, including Singapore, Indonesia, Malaysia, Vietnam and Thailand.[24] These involve Indian assistance in port calls, joint exercises, military training, servicing of military equipment and dialogues between the defence establishments.[25] Additionally, the Indian Navy frequently visits major ports in Singapore, Thailand, Vietnam, the Philippines, Cambodia and Indonesia. The 2012 India-ASEAN Summit also saw the Indian naval ship *Sudarshini* embarking on a commemorative expedition to ASEAN countries from September 2012 to March 2013, retracing the historical ASEAN-India maritime link.

This vigorous Indian military diplomacy in Southeast Asia is a significant departure from India's recent tradition of military isolationism. After a century and a half of dominating the regional security environment, India's armed forces withdrew into a shell in the post-Nehru years. India's first prime minister had actively pursued defence cooperation with key partners in Asia, for example with Indonesia and Burma in Southeast Asia. After him, military disengagement became synonymous with non-alignment. From being a lone ranger, India has now begun to emphasize the virtues of security partnerships – of working with other great powers, cooperating with regional actors, and contributing to multilateral security forums. While this shift is real, many of India's military partnerships remain subcritical. The ASEAN leaders want more not less security cooperation with India both at the bilateral and multilateral level. While they are impressed with the professionalism of the Indian armed forces and value cooperation with them, they are frustrated at the slow and tentative responses of the civilian bureaucratic leadership in the Indian Ministry of Defence. India now must expand its naval cooperation into defence and naval technological collaboration with the navies of the east. The ASEAN also wants more active participation of the Indian defence establishment in the deliberations of the ADMM Plus, propose pragmatic steps for promoting regional security and exercise leadership.

The vision statement issued at the end of the 2012 commemorative summit in Delhi declared that the two sides 'are committed to strengthening cooperation to ensure maritime security and freedom of navigation, and safety of sea lanes of communication for unfettered movement of trade in accordance with international law, including UNCLOS'. India and the ASEAN also agreed to 'promote maritime cooperation, including through engagement in the ASEAN Maritime Forum (AMF) and its expanded format, to address common challenges on maritime issues, including sea piracy, search and rescue at sea, maritime environment, maritime security, maritime connectivity, freedom of navigation, fisheries, and other areas of cooperation'.[26] The pace and intensity of this cooperation now largely rests on Delhi which must bring into synergy its real and existing naval capabilities with the growing maritime security needs of the region. To effectively contribute to ASEAN's maritime security, India needs to change the core political assumption on which it launched its LEP at the turn of the 1990s. As India returned to the region, Delhi chose to defer to the regional leadership, underline the centrality of the ASEAN, maintain a low profile and avoid interjecting itself into the regional disputes. The last few years have seen a dramatic transformation of that political context. The region seeking effective contributions from India in helping stabilize the region and demonstrate leadership on maritime security issues at a time when the Southeast Asian seas are becoming the locus of regional conflict and great power confrontation. With the contours of the LEP having changed, New Delhi must now find the political will to take an active role in the maritime security of Asia-Pacific. It needs to balance the competing imperatives of securing its growing interests in the East Asian waters on the one hand and the danger of being drawn into the conflicts of the littoral on the other.

NOTES

1. See, 'Vision Statement: ASEAN-India Commemorative Summit', issued in New Delhi, 20 December 2012, available at <http://www.mea.gov.in/bilateral-documents.htm?dtl/20982/Vision+StatementASEANIndia+Commemorative+Summit>
2. Yashwant Sinha, 'Resurgent India in Asia', Harvard University, 29 September 2003; available at: http://mea.gov.in/Speeches-Statements.htm?dtl/4744/Speech+by+External+Affairs+Minister+Shri+Yashwant+Sinha+at+Harvard+University
3. Christopher Bayly and Tim Harper, *Forgotten Wars: The End of Britain's Asian Empire*, London: Allen Lane, 2007.
4. K.M. Panikkar, *The Future of South-East Asia: An Indian View*, New York: Macmillan, 1943, pp. 11-12.
5. C. Raja Mohan, 'An Uncertain Trumpet? India's Role in Southeast Asian Security', *India Review*, vol. 12, no. 3, 2013, pp. 134-50.
6. 'India as a Great Power: Know Your Own Strength', *The Economist*, 30 March 2013.
7. For a discussion of the emergence of the concept see, David Scott, 'The Indo-Pacific: New Regional Formulations and New Maritime Frameworks

for U.S.-India Strategic Convergence', *Asia-Pacific Review*, vol. 19, no. 2, November 2012, pp. 85-109.

8. Bronson Percival, 'U.S.-India: Parallel Links along China's Southern Periphery', *Asia Pacific Bulletin*, no. 114, Honolulu: East-West Center, 1 June 2011, p. 2.
9. Shaun Lin and Carl Grundy-Warr, 'ASEAN and Interconnecting Regional Spheres: Lessons for the Indian Ocean Region', *Journal of the Indian Ocean Region*, vol. 8, no. 1, pp. 54-70.
10. Keith Bradsher, 'Philippine Leader Sounds Alarm on China', *The New York Times*, 5 February 2014; available at: http://www.nytimes.com/2014/02/06/world/asia/philippines.html
11. Vietnam Ministry of Foreign Affairs, Petro Vietnam Press Release, 5 May 2014; available at: http://www.mofa.gov.vn/en/nr040807104143/nr040807105001/ns140505225816
12. Sanjay Bhattacharyya, 'Transcript of Media Briefing by Official Spokesperson and Joint Secretary (South) of January 11, 2013', Ministry of External Affairs, 11 January 2013; available at: http://www.mea.gov.in/media-briefings.htm?dtl/21050/Transcript+of+media+briefing+by+Official+Spokesperson+and+Joint+Secretary+South+of+January+11+2013.
13. Indian Navy, 'Indian Maritime Doctrine', Integrated Headquarters, Ministry of Defence (Navy), 2009.
14. Manu Pubby, 'Ready to Protect Indian Interests in the South China Sea: Navy Chief, *The Indian Express*, 4 December 2012; available at: http://archive.indianexpress.com/news/ready-to-protect-indian-interests-in-south-china-sea-navy-chief/1040119/
15. Anil Wadhwa, Secretary (East), 'Keynote Address at the 6th IISS-MEA Dialogue on "India's Extended Neighbourhood: Prospects and Challenges" at IDSA, New Delhi', 4 March 2014; available at: http://www.mea.gov.in/Speeches-Statements.htm?dtl/23030/Keynote+address+by+Secretary+East+at+6th+IISSMEA+Dialogue+on+Indias+extended+neighbourhood+Prospects+and+Challenges+at+IDSA+New+Delhi
16. See for example Prime Minister Manmohan Singh's statement that Tenth India-ASEAN Summit, Phnom Penh, November 2012: 'We believe that ASEAN centrality is essential in the evolving regional architecture for peace, stability, development and prosperity'; available at <http://www.mea.gov.in/Speeches-Statements.htm?dtl/20825/Opening+Remarks+by+Prime+Minister+at+10th+IndiaASEAN+Summit>
17. Evelyn Goh, 'Great Powers and Hierarchical Order in Southeast Asia: Analyzing Regional Security Strategies', *International Security*, vol. 32, no. 3, Winter 2007/8, pp. 113-57.
18. 'ASEAN in Crisis: Divided We Stagger', *The Economist*, 18 August 2012, available at http://www.economist.com/node/21560585>
19. For the unfolding debate within the ASEAN on its central role, see

Benjamin Ho, 'ASEAN's Centrality in a Rising Asia', *RSIS Working Paper*, no. 249, September 2012.

20. See Udai Bhanu Singh, 'India and Southeast Asia: Enhanced Defence and Strategic Ties', in N.S. Sisodia and Sreeradha Datta (eds.), *Changing Security Dynamics in Southeast Asia*, New Delhi: Magnum, 2008, pp. 329-45; see also David Brewster, *India as an Asia Pacific Power*, London: Routledge, 2012.
21. See Gurpreet Khurana, 'Indian Ocean Naval Symposium: Where From . . . Whither Bound?', *IDSA Strategic Comments*, 22 February 2008; available at <http://www.idsa.in/publications/stratcomments/gurpreet khurana220208.htm>
22. Established in 2006, the ASEAN Defence Ministers Meeting (ADMM) is an annual forum for the ASEAN ministers to consult each other on key regional security issues. The second meeting of the ADMM agreed to conceptualize the 'ADMM Plus', a meeting between ASEAN and its eight dialogue partners to facilitate better understanding amongst each other. For further information please see, 'About the ASEAN Defence Ministers Meeting', ASEAN official website; available at: https://admm.asean.org/index.php/about-admm/2013-01-22-10-51-17.html and 'About the ASEAN Defence Ministers' Meeting Plus', ASEAN Official Website; available at: https://admm.asean.org/index.php/about-admm/about-admm-plus.html.
23. See for example, Vijay Sakhuja (ed.), *Reinvigourating IOR-ARC*, New Delhi: Pentagon Press, 2012.
24. For a broad discussion on India's security politics in East and Southeast Asia, see, David Scott, 'Strategic Imperatives of India as an Emerging Player in Pacific Asia', *International Studies*, vol. 44, no. 2, April/June 2007, pp. 121-40; see also, Harsh Pant, 'India in the Asia-Pacific: Rising Ambitions with an Eye on Rising China', *Asia Pacific Review*, vol. 14, no. 1, 2007, pp. 54-71.
25. For details, see Pankaj Kumar Jha, 'India's Defence Diplomacy in Southeast Asia', *Journal of Defence Studies*, vol. 15, no. 1, January 2011, pp. 47-63.
26. Sinha, op. cit., n. 2.

CHAPTER 12

Strategic Security Dimensions of the India-Southeast-East Asia Partnership: Scope and Prospects

SATISH NAMBIAR*

For almost four decades after gaining Independence, India's national security strategy was conditioned by a mindset induced by the experiences of the war in Jammu & Kashmir in 1947/8, and the Chinese aggression of 1962 in Ladakh and NEFA. As a consequence, the contours of our defence policy, organization, equipping and planning remained centred for a long while around an obsession about Pakistan and a concern about China repeating an aggression. As such, the total focus had a continental land border connotation that precluded the broader geo-strategic and geo-political dimension imposed on us by virtue of being a peninsular country occupying such a vital strategic position in the Indian Ocean region. A radical change in this rather narrow visualization of our national security strategy came about with the far-sighted and visionary 'Look East' policy articulated and put in place by late prime minister Narasimha Rao in the early 1990s. As prime minister, he is reported to have remarked in an address at the time, 'the closer relationship which India seeks today with Southeast Asian countries, has to be fashioned on twin foundations – the benign interaction of the past and mutuality of interests that exist at present'. The policy therefore drew its inspiration from the idea of capitalizing on historical cultural ties and the concept of an extended neighbourhood to harness the economic

* Gen. Satish Nambiar, First Force Commander and Head of Mission of the UN Forces in the former Yugoslavia and former Deputy Chief of the Indian Army.

benefits that would accrue by the pursuit of such a policy. Even so, the connotations of dependence on the sea for trade and commerce, and the consequent need to ensure the security of sea lanes of communication, soon highlighted the imperative of a radical review of the country's defence policy to include the vital element of maritime security. The eloquent articulation of this policy by Prime Minister Narasimha Rao and the impetus he gave it, in terms of implementation, heralded such a radical review of Indian strategic and military planning and thought, from that of a 'continental' mindset fixed on our western and northern land borders, to the broader plane of India's strategic interest extending from 'the Persian Gulf and the east coast of Africa in the West, to the Straits of Malacca and the South China Sea in the East, and Afghanistan and the Central Asian states in the north and northwest, to the Southern Indian Ocean in the South'. There is also a growing awareness that northeast India is to be factored in as a bridgehead to Southeast Asia.

As it happened, the Look East Policy (LEP) was put in place by the Government of India more or less concurrently with the end of the Cold War and the removal of many of the limitations imposed by that era. It is therefore a matter of some disappointment that our foreign policy apparatus and security establishment did not fully capitalize on the opening provided by the events of the time to exploit the tremendous goodwill towards India in countries like Vietnam, Singapore and many other countries in Southeast Asia, to put in place strategic security partnerships or institutional defence cooperation arrangements, much to the dismay of our diplomatic representatives in those countries one may add.

Be that as it may, over the last two decades plus, a number of initiatives for increased defence cooperation with many of the countries in the region have been taken. The Singapore that emerged from the shadow of Malaya into an economic powerhouse in Southeast Asia was initially dismissive of India, largely because it perceived our country as a non-performer; not without some justification one has to admit. However, since the LEP was put in place, Singapore has engaged with India in meaningful defence cooperation for conduct of training and exercise facilities; even paying for the use of many of the facilities. Whereas Singapore is a city-state with a relatively small defence force compared to India and many other countries of the region, its strength lies in the quality of the equipment it possesses and its well-trained forces. Equally significant is Singapore's maritime importance given its location in relation to the Malacca Straits. It is a matter of great satisfaction that Singapore was very supportive in facilitating India's entry into the ASEAN grouping and its security extension, the ASEAN Regional Forum (ARF). This obviously provided India with the opportunity to pursue the goal of greater integration into the Southeast and East Asia groupings. The crowning achievement in this context was the ASEAN-India Commemorative Summit held in New Delhi in December 2012 to mark the 20th anniversary of ASEAN-India relations and the 10th anniversary of India becoming a dialogue partner of ASEAN. The most notable achievement of this summit was the issue of a vision statement which significantly declared that 'the ASEAN-India Partnership stands elevated to a strategic partnership'. The vision statement lays down in great detail the blueprint for ASEAN and India to surge ahead in all fields in a comprehensive manner.

Given the immense goodwill towards India in Vietnam, one would have hoped for greater political, economic and defence cooperation between the two countries after the withdrawal of US forces and its allies from Vietnam. Whereas much has been achieved and even more is quite apparently on the agenda, following the joint declaration of 2007 and the exchange of visits at senior levels of the government, there is scope for a great deal more, particularly in the areas of international and regional peacekeeping, counter-insurgency operations and maritime cooperation.

India has also forged strong political linkages with Indonesia, Thailand, Myanmar, and Malaysia. High-level exchanges of political dignitaries take place regularly. Dialogue mechanisms exist for regular exchange of strategic views and advancing economic and defence relations to higher levels.

Whereas India is not, and should not attempt to be, party to the regional disputes in East Asia and Southeast Asia, we cannot remain a detached observer of regional events that have scope for conflict, as there would be an impact on India's security and national interests. India and ASEAN share overlapping security environments and share virtually the same strategic concerns. In fact, given the proximity of the maritime boundaries, Indonesia, Thailand and Myanmar are part of India's immediate neighbourhood. As such, the continuing military interaction with Myanmar (a long-standing arrangement) and the increasing strategic and military dialogue, not only with Singapore and Vietnam, but with Indonesia and Thailand as also with Malaysia and the Phillipines are to be welcomed.

Political, economic and military relations with Japan and South

Korea were inevitably handicapped by the Cold War dynamics with the two East Asian countries bound by treaty considerations, following Second World War and the Korean War, to the Western bloc led by the USA, and India perceived by the Western bloc and regional allies as a camp follower of the Soviet Union. Following the end of the Cold War and the dynamics associated with it, and the articulation of India's LEP, some tentative economic initiatives were taken by Japan and somewhat more aggressively by South Korea. Strategic and military initiatives took a long time coming. It is only in recent years that Japan, and even more recently South Korea, have initiated moves to establish strategic partnerships with India and the conduct of joint military exercises. This has gained further momentum and needs to be built upon with greater vigour to take it to more meaningful levels of cooperation and coordination, both bilaterally and multilaterally. This is especially so in the knowledge that both Japan and South Korea, together with many others countries in the region, are increasingly concerned with China's growing military capacities and propensity for belligerence; as also with increasing doubts (not obviously openly expressed) about the dependability of the USA in terms of active military support to deal with possible Chinese aggression in the years to come.

In putting in place and further building on strategic partnerships and defence cooperation, including joint development of military equipment, conduct of joint exercises and coordination of military doctrines, both bilaterally with individual countries of East and Southeast Asia, and with multilateral groupings like ASEAN and ARF, the Indian political leadership and the foreign and defence policy planners must capitalize on the credibility of the Indian military establishment in the regional and international arena. The outstanding success of the 1971 operations, particularly in the eastern theatre, is a military achievement without parallel in recent history. This was complemented with the determination and resolve displayed by the Indian military in the Kargil conflict in 1999 in the most inhospitable terrain at great heights and under severe climatic conditions, to inflict defeat on the aggressor. The nuclear tests of May 1998 displayed India's resolve to take necessary action to safeguard its national security interests, even in the face of disapproval by sections of the international community – a position that proved to be well-taken given the subsequent endorsement of the Indian position and the strategic partnership that emerged with the USA and the acceptance of India's position at the IAEA. Another demonstration of India's military capacity was provided, if indeed it was necessary, by the Indian response to the tsunami disaster; a maritime response capability that the international community sat up and took note of at that time.

Given such established expertise and military capability, there can be little doubt that in the years to come India may well be called upon by the international community, represented by the UN or by regional organizations or by our neighbours on a bilateral or multilateral basis, to deploy our military, together with others in a multinational force, and possibly take a lead role for dealing with what are perceived as threats to regional or international peace and security, as also to provide disaster relief when required. This is an aspect which we need to start deliberating and focusing on; to study in detail and evolve concepts for: joint training, command and control, coordination; operational compatibility, etc., together with other like-minded countries in the region and beyond. A few years back, a working group was set up under the aegis of the Council for Security Cooperation in the Asia Pacific (CSCAP) to examine and make recommendations on the scope for cooperation and coordination in the arena of international peacekeeping, in which activity a number of countries in the region were involved. It is a matter of some considerable satisfaction that the recommendations of that working group seem to have been acted upon and an Association of Asia-Pacific Peacekeeping Centres (AAPC) has been set up to coordinate and share experiences on peacekeeping. One is given to understand that meetings of this association are held on a regular basis by rotation in each member-country to good effect.

Another working group was set up under the aegis of the CSCAP Steering Committee to examine and make recommendations on the aspect of the 'Responsibility to Protect' (RtoP) as endorsed by the 2005 World Summit. The Working Group held three meetings, one in February 2010 in Jakarta, the second in Manila in September 2010 and the final one in Phnom Penh in April 2011. It engaged in some very meaningful discussion, including on the validity or otherwise of the intervention in Libya by some Western countries, and made some comprehensive recommendations on how to mainstream RtoP into official establishments, namely national governments, ARF, etc.; the need to sharpen early warning and assessment apparatus; and the imperative for a sustained relationship with the United Nations on the subject.

To meet contingencies in the future that call for an agreed and spontaneous response from member countries, with provision of material and trained manpower resources, there is a compelling case for India to put in place and maintain a credible rapid reaction force primarily dedicated to deploying at short notice for 'expeditionary' stabilization or peacekeeping operations, RtoP intervention on request, or disaster relief within the extended region; a force organized, trained, equipped and located appropriately; and under strategic direction. Such a force should ideally be part of a regional arrangement agreed to by ASEAN or ARF, together with similar forces earmarked by other countries in the region. Needless to say, in so far as the Indian security establishment is concerned, such a force would also be available for use as national reserves in an operational situation if and when India is at war. This paper is not the platform for going into the finer details of such a force. Nor is it a new idea or concept. It has been studied and discussed in the past. But the context in which it needs serious review and attention is that of a greater role for India at the regional level, which possibly merits a more focused study of the concept.

Given the sort of regional or global commitments the force may be required to respond to, such a force needs to be a multidimensional tri-service one under a joint operational command, and include components from the army, navy and air force; elements from the coast guard, civil affairs officers, civilian police components, personnel trained in human rights aspects, legal affairs personnel and representatives from the diplomatic corps.

To that end, such a rapid reaction task force should broadly comprise the following elements:

- A tri-service *corps-sized headquarters.*
- A land forces component to include *an airborne brigade*, together with *a light armoured or mechanized division* that includes an air transportable armoured brigade equipped with light tanks and infantry combat vehicles, an amphibious brigade and an air transportable infantry brigade.
- Essential for such a force would be army aviation elements, assault engineers, communication, and logistics elements.
- A naval component that desirably includes an aircraft carrier, appropriate surface and sub-surface craft and aerial maritime capability.

- An air force component that includes strike aircraft, helicopters and strategic airlift capability.
- A special forces component.
- Civilian component to include diplomatic representatives, civil affairs personnel, civilian police, human rights personnel, etc.

It is time the Government of India recognized that in context of the demands being placed on us for provision of troops for international peacekeeping, and requests that have been made from time to time for us to consider the scope for participation in other multinational operations, there is a compelling need to set up such a capability. While formalization of the concept and authorization of the organization, personnel and equipment, may take its course, though hopefully at some speed, it may be useful to set up the nucleus of such a rapid reaction force by drawing on existing assets to the extent available. This can be more than justified from the operational capability of view given the situation in the neighbourhood, and the possibility that the armed forces may be called upon to act unilaterally in pursuance of our national interests, or to assist in a bilateral context on the request of one of our neighbours. That we should be prepared to do so needs no further emphasis. But that can only be facilitated if we create the capacity, analyse concepts of employment, evolve an appropriate doctrine, carry out joint training with countries in the region, put in place compatible communication and logistics infrastructure, and so on. The sooner we commence work on this the better.

Together with such initial moves, it is important that we work on a number of other measures in cooperation with regional players in ASEAN and ARF and may be other regional and global players. It would be useful for joint working groups comprising diplomats and selected military personnel to interact at the international level at multilateral forums to share perceptions about coordination and training, exchange data on trouble spots on a regular basis, establish mechanisms for consultation, etc. It would be most useful to organize events like the symposium conducted by the Indian Navy some years back for chiefs of the Indian Ocean littoral states. Similar meetings, seminars, symposiums and conferences could be held to discuss the scope and extent of cooperation with like-minded countries including the USA, Japan, Australia, Singapore, Vietnam, Indonesia, Malaysia, Myanmar, and others.

While the training of our own personnel from the three services and other components of such a rapid reaction force should receive focused attention to achieve jointness, it is also essential that commanders and staff officers are gradually exposed to operating with their counterparts from other countries either bilaterally or at multilateral forums in order to foster better understanding, cooperation and coordination. Equally if not more importantly, training of senior military leadership must focus on the nuances of multinational operations, particularly in context of the possibility of India being asked to assume a leadership role. The need to adjust to a 'consultative' style of leadership, and paying increased attention to aspects of coordination and liaison at headquarters will need to be understood, as also the methodology to be adopted for assimilating staff officers and subordinate commanders within such a system.

Finally, it is without doubt important that in working towards the arrangements discussed in the preceding pages and leading up to implementation, the possible reactions of the People's Republic of China need to be taken into consideration. The main point that merits emphasis in this context is that of transparency, in as much as, all the arrangements that are to be put in place would be the outcome of decisions taken at meetings of ASEAN or ARF. Stressing the fact that such initiatives and moves are not directed against China, but in context of the imperative need to ensure the maintenance of peace and security in the region. In fact, the PRC would not only be very much a part of the consultative process leading up to putting in place the mechanisms and wherewithal for implementation, but be called upon to provide, together with the other regional powers, many of the resources required. Should the Chinese leadership have reservations about the process and participation in it, they should be made aware that the process will be pursued and put in place even without their active endorsement and participation.

In actively participating in the process, unreservedly endorsing it, and providing resources to fulfil the perceived mandate, not only would India be preparing itself for assuming a role that is likely to be imposed on us in regional and global affairs, but also convey a seriousness of purpose in the pursuit of our LEP.

CHAPTER 13

Emerging Defence/Security Scenario in East Asia: Challenges and Opportunities for India

SKAND TAYAL*

BACKGROUND

East Asia has been relatively peaceful since the end of the Vietnam War in the mid-1970s. The last major war in which India was involved was also forty-three years ago in 1971 for the liberation of Bangladesh. This prolonged period of relative peace has resulted in unprecedented economic growth in most of the countries of the region and rise of hundreds of millions of East Asians from abject poverty to a life of some dignity and hope. It is hugely important that this era of regional peace and stability continues in the coming decades.

A significant positive feature of East Asia is that the ongoing political differences between nation states are not ideological. The doctrinal confrontation between communism and capitalism/ democracy of the post-Second World War era had destroyed Indo-China and spawned the 1950-3 Korean War. But today, no country wishes to impose its ideology or way of life over any other country. The differences are mostly territorial, confined to land borders (Thailand-Cambodia or India-China) or maritime boundaries in South China Sea. It is unlikely that such conflict-prone areas would degenerate to any kind of regional conflict or become an international quagmire.

The major potential flash points on the horizon are the escalating differences between Japan and China over Senkaku Islands presently

*Amb. Skand Tayal, Former Ambassador of India to the Republic of Korea and currently Visiting Professor, University of Delhi.

in Japan's possession and control and the continuing quest of Democratic People's Republic of Korea to acquire nuclear weapons with a delivery system which could eventually threaten the territory of the United States. Japan's security alliance with the US and China's aversion for any bloody conflict on the Korean Peninsula are likely to prevent any future sustained hostilities in Northeast Asia. However, sporadic violent incidents between North and South Korea and aggressive surveillance and air/sea patrolling around Senkaku Islands by both China and Japan may continue to occur.

REGIONAL DEFENCE ARCHITECTURE

The ultimate objective of multilateral security cooperation is to construct a security cooperation regime which allows participant countries to exchange their views and coordinate their differences on common security issues. The institutionalization of security cooperation contributes to so-called confidence building measures, preventive diplomacy and conflict-resolving mechanism.[1]

The present 'hub and spokes system' constructed on a set of bilateral alliances with US at the centre is over time expected to be replaced by a new security architecture in Asia which would most likely be multilateral in shape, a concentric order where different layers of multilateral architecture overlap and intersect. Researchers in Japan[2] have conceptualized the following three-tiered approach to security architecture in the Asia-Pacific region:

First Tier: Security cooperation based on military agreements and alliances.

Second Tier: (i) Networking and capacity building (e.g. PSI, Coast Guard, HADR, military and other law enforcement organizations' cooperation).
(ii) Security dialogues (e.g. Six Party Talks, Japan-Korea-China trilateral, Shangri-la Dialogue)

Third Tier: Regional institutions (e.g. EAS, APT, ARF, ADMM+).

The multilateral forums concerned with security issues are likely to continue to be ASEAN-led, like ARF, EAS or ADMM+. But these may remain forums for discussion and debate and not evolve into a credible mechanism for preventive diplomacy and conflict resolution. The overarching structure of ASEAN-centric security fora would, however, form the core of institutionalized multilateral discussions on security and strategic issues. This process has been bolstered by the inclusion of US and Russia in the East Asia Summit process.

As we peep into the future, the robust and credible defence for several countries of East Asia would continue to be provided by the United States through its existing bilateral arrangements with countries like Japan, ROK, Philippines and Australia. To prepare for the rise of China, United States has already embarked on its policy of 'rebalancing' towards Asia-Pacific. US would, therefore, continue to be a net provider of security and stability in the region.

CONFLICTING CLAIMS IN THE SOUTH CHINA SEA

South China Sea includes about 250 atolls, shoals, reefs and small islands. Most of these are un-inhabited as they are partially or fully submerged. However, different countries are staking their claims over individual features and sometimes erecting weather stations and other such structures. This has led to enhanced defence expenditure and preparations in countries like the Philippines and Vietnam.

Philippines expects United States to play a more active and robust part in supporting its territorial claims under the terms of the Philippines-US mutual Defence Treaty of 1951. However, the US is understandably reluctant to get drawn in any Philippines-China conflict which does not pose an existential threat to the Philippines.

The ASEAN Declaration on the conduct of Parties in the South China adopted in 2002 lays down the guidelines to deal with the competing territorial claims of littoral states in the South China Sea. But it is non-binding and, therefore, ineffective. Consequently, Philippines was forced to take its dispute regarding sovereignty over the Scarborough Shoal to the International Tribunal for the Law of the Sea (ITLOS) in preference to dealing with the issue under the auspices of ASEAN. The consensus-based decision making of ASEAN makes it unsuitable to deal with contentious bilateral or multilateral issue.

China has the naval and air capacity to defend all its claims in the South China Sea unless the US openly comes to the military assistance of the countries who contest the extravagant Chinese claims. China has recently declared a vast area as its Air Defence Identification Zone in the East Sea which has been challenged by the US, Japan and South Korea. If China declares a similar ADIZ in the South China

Sea, it may lead to some serious response from affected littoral countries.

US IN THE INDO-PACIFIC

In the future defence and security scenario of the Indo-Pacific, the United States would continue to play a major role. Several countries of East Asia including Japan, ROK, Vietnam, Indonesia, Philippines, Brunei, Australia, New Zealand and India would favour an enhanced and more muscular presence of US in the region. President Barak Obama's well-known 'pivot' or 'rebalancing' towards Asia is gradually taking place. On a visit to Australia in 2011, President Obama declared that the US would not only place 2,500 Marines in Darwin but may also position military planes in northern Australia to enhance US forces' visibility and reach in the region.

The Obama administration treats China as a strategic competitor. Chinese experts have concluded that competition between the US and China is inevitable for resources, markets and influence. Historically, China has been a continental power with significant land-based armies. As it gradually acquires a blue water navy, its footprint and reach would incrementally challenge the dominance of the United States, first in East China and South China seas and later in the Western Pacific and the Indian Ocean.

Many countries of East Asia are anxious about the declining financial clout of the US. Strains on US economy and manufacturing would have an inevitable deleterious impact on its military might over the years. The present yawning gap between the defence and offense capabilities of the US and other military powers, particularly China, would inevitably narrow. China's policy of A2AD 'anti-access and area-denial' strategy and its possession of anti-satellite and anti-air craft carrier weaponry would, in not too distant future, make the US wary of any direct confrontation with China.

CHINA-ROK-JAPAN

The Trilateral Summit in December 2008 in Japan among Japan, ROK and China commenced with considerable promise. It was an attempt to have a Northeast Asian regional body independent of ASEAN and bringing together three economic and military giants of Northeast Asia. Annual summits were held for five years and a secretariat was also established in Seoul. However, this new forum for dialogue has entered a rough patch with increasing differences between Japan and China on the one hand and between Japan and ROK on the other. No annual trilateral summit was held in 2013.

In five years, the three countries had moved rapidly to devise inter-governmental cooperation including 18 minister-level cooperation processes also covering the field of foreign affairs. At the fourth summit in 2011, the three countries had emphasized the importance of the de-nuclearization of the Korean peninsula for the continued peace and stability in Northeast Asia. However, this issue was not specifically mentioned in the joint press release after the fifth summit held in China in May 2012. The recent exacerbation in the differences between China and Japan over Senkaku/Diaoyu Islands and the articulation of a more robust security policy by Prime Minister Shinzo Abe's regime has introduced a new element of heightened friction in that region. Japan's new National Security Strategy Document of December 2013 indicates a shift from a passive role to 'proactive, contribution to peace' and 'strengthening deterrent capacity'. It notes China's attempts to change status quo by coercion in East and South China seas. It observes that China's 'external stance and military activities' are a source of concern.

US-JAPAN-ROK

The US-Japan defence alliance is primarily for security in Northeast Asia but is also important for the security of Southeast Asia particularly to manage any threat emanating from DPRK or deterioration of the situation in the Taiwan Straits. The US-ROK defence alliance would also endure in view of the continuing threat from North Korea. The role of ROK top brass is likely to increase with the proposed transfer of operational control over the ROK-US alliance forces to ROK scheduled for 2015.

US is keen to promote closer ties and inter-operability among its two allies – Japan and ROK but deep-seated hostility among the Koreans against Japanese colonial rule stands in the way of closer trilateral cooperation among the US, Japan and ROK. South Korea, US and Japan did conduct trilateral naval exercises in June 2012 with the participation of the US air craft carrier *USS George Washington*. But subsequently the relations between ROK and Japan have cooled further with the change of guard both in Seoul and Tokyo. President

Park Geun-hye and Prime Minister Shinzo Abe had not met bilaterally till the writing of this essay even after about 18 months of coming to power. They first came face to face in March 2014 in The Hague on the sidelines of the Nuclear Safety Summit in a trilateral meeting convened by President Barak Obama. Reports indicate that President Park agreed for this meeting only after much persuasion by the US.

This lingering distrust between India's two strategic partners in East Asia – Japan and ROK – is a cause of concern for India. Indian leaders and diplomats would be well advised to play a discreet role in narrowing the differences between the two countries.

EXISTING REGIONAL ARRANGEMENTS

ASEAN Regional Forum (ARF) is the well established inter-governmental body to discuss security related issues. It strives to formulate norms for dealing with trans-national and non-traditional security threats. At present ARF is focusing on counter-terrorism, disaster relief, humanitarian assistance, anti-piracy cooperation, freedom of navigation, etc. But ARF needs to go a step further to become action oriented and also must undertake preventive diplomacy. The member nations need to have the confidence and the will to develop in ARF a crisis management mechanism also.

ADMM-PLUS

A potentially important forum which brings together the defence ministers of the region together is ASEAN Defence Ministers' Meeting-Plus which had its second meeting in Brunei in August 2013. ASEAN defence ministers had their first meeting in 2006 to deliberate over the defence and security related challenges faced by the region. In 2010, the first expanded meeting of regional defence ministers was held in Vietnam with the participation of ASEAN's eight dialogue partners including India and this biennial meeting was designated as ADMM-Plus.

ADMM Vision is to contribute to progress towards establishment of an 'ASEAN Political Security Community'. Initially it has commenced collaboration in the areas of Humanitarian Assistance and Disaster Relief (HADR), maritime security covering piracy and armed robbery, peace-keeping operations, military medicine and counter-terrorism. The focus is on developing capabilities to collaborate with regional partners through joint exercises. In 2013, the first ADMM-Plus Humanitarian Assistance and Military Medicine Exercise was held in Brunei and a counter-terrorism exercise in Indonesia. In the coming years ADMM-Plus plans to look into the issues related to clearing of mines, cyber-security and bio-terrorism.

The then defence minister A.K. Anthony had participated in the first meeting of ADMM-Plus in Hanoi and the then minister of state for defence Jitendra Singh had represented India in the second meeting in Brunei in August 2013. The significance of this forum is evident from the fact that minister of national defence of China General Liang Guanglie as well as US Defence Secretary Robert Gates had attended the first ADMM-Plus in 2010 and state councillor & minister of national defence of China General Chang Wanquan and US Defence Secretary Chuck Hagel had participated in the second meeting in Brunei in 2013.

SHANGRI-LA DIALOGUE

The IISS Asia Security Summit – The Shangri-la Dialogue (SLD) is a Track 1 inter-governmental security forum organized by Singapore-based International Institute for Strategic Studies (IISS) where defence ministers, military chiefs and experts from 28 Asia-Pacific states including India are invited. The forum is named after the Shangri-la Hotel in Singapore where it has been held since 2002. The dialogue is modelled after the well-known Munich Conference on Security Policy and concentrates on security and defence related issues of Asia, particularly East Asia. The dialogue is financially supported by the Government of Singapore.

In 2005, Pakistan was represented for the first time. Since 2009, participation has been elevated to minister level by several countries. In 2011, the Chinese defence minister participated when some countries raised the South China Sea issues. General Liang Guanglie indicated China's willingness to work with neighbouring countries to resolve competing claims in the South China Sea. In 2012, US Secretary of Defence Leon Panetta announced at the dialogue that 60 per cent of US naval forces would be located in the Pacific region by 2020.

In 2012, then defence minister A.K. Anthony presented India's vision for a 'Comprehensive Maritime Security Architecture' at SLD. Minister Anthony said that given India's geographical location, extensive maritime interests, dependence on the seas for trade and the evolving asymmetric threats in the form of maritime terrorism, piracy and drug trafficking, maritime security issues have become a strategic priority for us. He pointed out two distinct imperatives for India: safeguarding India's territories and adjacent waters against seaborne threats and a desire to ensure traditional freedoms at sea for access to all. In this context he emphasized that 'large parts of the common seas cannot be declared exclusive to any one country or group' and reaffirmed 'the importance of maritime security and freedom of navigation for all, in accordance with the relevant universally agreed principles of international law including UNCLOS'.

At the 12th SLD in June 2013, the participants discussed the themes (i) US Approach to Regional Security, (ii) Military Modernization and Strategic Transparency, (iii) Defending National Interests and Preventing Conflicts, and (iv) Advancing Defence Cooperation in Asia-Pacific.

INDIA'S ROLE

India's economic growth is closely tied with the security and prosperity of the Indo-Pacific region. India's foreign trade is dependent on open maritime routes to the extent of 90 per cent by volume and 77 per cent by value. India's exclusive economic zone is more than 2.5 million sq km. India has also been allotted areas for deep sea mining under UNCLOS which are located at a distance of almost 2,000 km from India's shores.

India sees for itself an increasingly effective role in contributing to the safety and security in East Asia. Its strategic location as a peninsula gives India the capacity to protect the maritime sea lanes in the Indian Ocean. It may be noted that India has land boundary with Myanmar and shares maritime boundaries with three Southeast Asian countries – Indonesia, Thailand and Myanmar.

India's Andaman and Nicobar Islands are closer to Indonesia as compared to the Indian peninsula. A three-services strategic command has been created to develop Andaman as an un-sinkable aircraft carrier. Aircraft located at Andaman would be able to patrol a vast area covering the Malacca Straits also.

India's Ministry of Defence took an important initiative to send a sail training ship *INS Sudarshini* on an expedition to ASEAN member countries for six months in 2013 along the monsoon trade wind route to trace India's trade and maritime linkages with its neighbours in the east. The expedition was to commemorate two decades of India's Look East Policy. A car rally was also organized in the year covering nine ASEAN states and a distance of 8,000 km to focus on land connectivity of India with the East.

INDIA-JAPAN

During his visit to Tokyo in May 2013, Prime Minister Manmohan Singh spoke about the idea of Indo-Pacific strategic confluence at an address before the Japan-India Association. He outlined three key areas of cooperation to (i) forge greater regional interaction to 'develop habits of consultation' and 'evolve commonly accepted principles for managing differences'; (ii) promote regional economic integration and connectivity; and (iii) ensuring maritime security in the Indo-Pacific by upholding principles of 'freedom of navigation and un-impeded lawful commerce in accordance with international law and resolve maritime issues peacefully'. During this visit, Prime Minister Manmohan Singh made India's strategic inclination clear by describing Japan as 'a natural and indispensable partner'.

India and Japan have been steadily deepening defence cooperation. The two countries had their first bilateral naval exercise in June 2012 which is now expected to be held on a regular basis. Contacts among the top brass of the Indian armed forces and the Japanese Self Defence Forces have also increased. In 2013, India's army chief General Bikram Singh visited Japan and the chief of the Japanese Self Defence Forces also came to India. Another sign of the trajectory of India-Japan defence relations is the reported Japanese offer to sell US-2 amphibious aircraft to India. For this sale to materialize, the planes will be configured in a civilian mode since there is a self-imposed weapons export ban from Japan since 1967. In the past, Japan has exported military technology but not complete equipment or weapons systems.

To deepen defence cooperation, India-Japan and India-ROK need to conduct joint naval exercises regularly to enhance inter-operability. The exercises should cover search and rescue operations, anti-piracy and anti-terrorist operations, humanitarian relief and disaster management. Indian Navy held PASSEX exercises with the Korean Navy in 2009 and JIMEX with Japan Maritime Self-Defence Force (JMSDF) in June 2012. Another proposal to be considered in due course would be the organization of a symposium for South and

Southeast Asian navies similar to Indian Ocean Naval Symposium (IONS) and West Pacific Naval Symposium (WPNS).

Japan and India signed a joint Declaration on Security Cooperation in 2008 and followed up with a Plan of Action in 2009. The first Japan-India Maritime Security Dialogue was also held in 2009. Australia, Singapore and JMSDF joined the US-India maritime exercise 'Malabar' in 2007 in the Bay of Bengal devoted to operations to counter terrorism and piracy. JMSDF also participated in Malabar -09 exercises in 2009 in the Western Pacific near Okinawa. After Prime Minister Shinzo Abe's state visit to India in January 2014, it was announced that the Japanese Navy would participate in the Malabar exercises in 2014.

CONCLUSION

India needs to promote a dialogue-oriented approach to deal with festering defence-related issues. Building of networks and direct contacts among the defence ministers and chiefs of staff of neighbouring countries is likely to contribute to reduction of tensions and prevention of actual hostilities.

India's approach till now has been to build defence cooperation strictly on a bilateral basis. However, some security issues are discussed in trilateral format, e.g. US-Japan-India, Russia-China-India, US-Afghanistan-India, etc., as well as multilateral format, e.g. ASEAN Regional Forum and East Asia Summit. It may be argued that to discuss defence-related matters in a trilateral framework may be counter-productive as it may raise the suspicions of particular countries which feel excluded and apprehend the emergence of a hostile alliance against them. It may, therefore, be prudent to discuss defence related subjects in a multilateral framework where all concerned parties are present and contribute to a cooperative regional regime taking on board the concerns of all the regional states.

India has a significant defence cooperation component in its bilateral ties with the East Asian countries. These includes periodic flag visits by Indian Navy, study visits by the senior officials of India's National Defence College, training of senior military officers in the staff colleges in India and vice versa and periodic visits by the chiefs of army, navy, air force and coast guards. India needs to progressively strengthen these relations and vigorously explore the possibilities of export of defence equipment to some of these countries.

The biggest asset for India is that there is a high level of trust between India and all the individual countries of ASEAN as well as with ROK and Japan. There is also strong bipartisan support among the political leadership in India as well as in these countries to forge a strong friendly relationship which would include a defence component in varying degrees. It is for India to take advantage of this favourable environment to deepen the defence cooperation in harmony with the capacity and inclination of the countries of East Asia.

NOTES

1. 'The Korea-China-Japan Trilateral Summit and Northeast Asian Security Cooperation', Jo Yang Hyeon (IFANS, KNDA) Paper presented at IDSA, New Delhi; 29 June 2012.
2. 'Asia-Pacific Security Architecture: Three-tiered Structure of Regional Security'; Jimbo Ken and Tokyo Foundation Asia Security Project (ed.), Tokyo; Nihon Hyouronsha, 2011, p. 33.
3. 'Towards a New Asian Security Architecture? India and Japan', Issue Paper no. 223; June 2013; Institute of Peace and Conflict Studies, New Delhi.

PART V

Culture, Diaspora and 'Soft Power' Dimension: An Underemployed Asset?

CHAPTER 14

India and Southeast Asia: Contacts and Contiguous Cultures in Outreach and Overlap

SURYAKANTHI TRIPATHI*

> Tibet, Mongolia, Malayas, wherever India had preached her wisdom, had been through genuine human relations. To-day my pilgrimage is to witness those historical evidences of man's holy access everywhere. Also to note that India of yore did not preach some cut and dried sermons, but inaugurated the inner treasure of man through architecture, sculpture, painting, music and literature, stamps of which remain in the deserts, woods, rocks, isles, rugged terrain and difficult resolves . . . . [*Tagore's Java Diary*, 1927]

MOSAIC OF SOUTHEAST ASIAN CULTURE

From the early twentieth century, there have been many scholars and strategists who have variously defined Southeast Asia. Till then, this area was referred to by the Europeans as Further India or simply as the Far Eastern Tropics. The Indians called it Suvarnabhumi, the Golden Land, and the Chinese referred to it as Nan Yang, implying the warmer and fertile geographical region to their south.

The term for the region as Southeast Asia, however, is first attributed to K.M. Panikkar, the Indian historian, in his book *The Future of South East Asia*, published in 1943. The term was justified for the fairly well-defined geographical region lying to the southeast

* Amb. Suryakanthi Tripathi, Former Ambassador of India and Director-General, Indian Council of Cultural Relations, author, playwright and social activist.

of the Asian landmass, to the east of India and the south of China. Once the term Southeast Asia was adopted by the Allied Supreme Command during the Second World War, its usage became commonly accepted.

The Oxford historian, Professor Brian Harrison described Southeast Asia as always being a part of something bigger than itself, and drawing its own significance only against the background of the history of Asia as a whole.

Even as late as the 1970s, some political analysts called Southeast Asia a 'cultural shatterbelt', implying that it is essentially stuck between two opposing forces, being in the sphere of competition of these larger states. The colliding external cultural-political forces being referred to were, obviously, India and China. Its location between these two great cultures has indeed resulted in considerable exchange of people and ideas over the centuries. However, calling Southeast Asia a shatterbelt is somewhat off the mark for several reasons. First, the people in all the ten countries of Southeast Asia are a tough, independent-minded people, not susceptible to collapsing before alien or foreign pressures. Second, historically India has never had a relationship based on aggression or rancour with any of the countries of this region.

Southeast Asia is an intricate and elaborate cultural mosaic, with each state having a variety of peoples and cultures. It's fishing cultures contrast and interact with their jungle and upland agricultural interiors, a pattern established since prehistoric times. Its coastal and riverine world and its easy accessibility by water have resulted in a constant convergence of various peoples in this southeastern swathe of Asia. In historic times a succession of influences from China, India, the Middle East and Europe increased the cultural themes. From about the first century AD it were the Hindu-Buddhist influences that became important. Thereafter, Islam became dominant on the Malayan and Sumatran coasts and later on in Java. The many languages of the area have been enhanced by other Asian and European languages.

From the sixteenth century, European and Christian influence began to be felt in the Philippines, Indonesia and the Malacca Straits. Subsequently, with only Thailand escaping colonial rule, the rest of the area came under the British, Dutch, French, Spanish, Americans and Portuguese. The Vietnamese were once under Chinese suzerainty, and their culture, to this day, shows the impact. Elsewhere, Chinese influence was trade-connected until Chinese immigration began in the nineteenth century.

It is the unique Southeast Asian genius that could almost effortlessly mould what it had received from so many distinct civilizations with its own cultural expressions, and thus become a plural society. Since gaining independence in the years following the Second World War, they have once again reaffirmed their independent identities. Today, we refer to the region with the ten modern Southeast Asian nations collectively as the ASEAN.

INDIA AND SOUTHEAST ASIA

One study says that the peoples of Southeast Asian culture are also found in the eastern hills of India (notably the Nagas, Garo, Khasi, Mizo) and Bangladesh (Kuki in the Chittagong Hill Tracts) and in southern China (notably Tai and Miao). This in itself constitutes the first great connector for Southeast Asia, since culture generally travels light and easy – as free accompanied baggage and subject to little security checks.

In the report, 'Our Creative Diversity: The UN World Commission on Culture and Development', it says: 'Culture is the whole complex of distinctive spiritual, material, intellectual and emotional, features that characterizes a society or a group.'

In 1950, the Publications Division of the Ministry of Information and Broadcasting, Government of India, published a small report on India and Southeast Asia, which begins thus: 'From Persia to the Chinese sea', wrote Sylvain Levi, the French Orientalist, 'from the icy regions of Siberia to the islands of Java and Borneo, from Oceania to Socotra, India has propagated her influence on one fourth of the human race in the course of a long succession of centuries.'

This report adds that this was possible mainly because of India's strategic geographic position. Indeed, from about 200 BC to AD 1200, India maintained unbroken cultural and economic relations with its western, northern, eastern and southeastern neighbours. It is, however, our southeastern neighbours that provide the best testimony to this extraordinary energy in the India of antiquity.

Perhaps the first and most comprehensive affirmation of the cultural links between India and Southeast Asia was at the Asian Relations Conference held in Delhi in March-April 1947.

At that conference, Justice Kyaw Myint, the leader of the Burmese delegation said, 'Friends, I feel here I am a man in my own home. Here I stand as the leader of the delegation from the nearest of your neighbours. We are contiguous to the centre of culture. We are near in thought; we are literally near, geographically, socially and culturally.'

At the conference there was also an exhibition of artefacts that showed the cultural kinship of our countries. A copper-plate inscription of AD 840 found in the ruins of the Nalanda University stated that King Balaputra of Sumatra requested the King of Magadha in India to donate five villages to the Nalanda University to help maintain a monastery for students from Indonesia. Inscriptions from Champa temples in Vietnam were rare specimens of classical Sanskrit poetry from the second and third century AD in an early south Indian script. There were also sets of bronze and stone images of the pre-Khmer (fifth-seventh century) and Khmer (ninth-twelfth century) periods in Indo-China.

It is this manifest and manifold resource that Southeast Asia and India have shared with each other over the centuries, and thus becoming contiguous cultures across land and sea borders. But even so, there has to be a considerable degree of differentiation to be exercised in our interaction with the ASEAN countries. We tend to look at ASEAN as a grouping, and sometimes overlook the fact that each of the countries in Southeast Asia is also very distinct from the other, and that our approaches need to be specifically tailored individually to the social, economic and cultural perspectives of each of them. The Cambodians have a saying – negotiate a river by following its bends, enter a country by following its customs. It is good advice, since every bend in the river reveals yet another vista.

That creativity freely crosses man-made boundaries comes alive in a small newspaper article dated 5 November 2012 in the *Jakarta Post*, about Chinese products imbued with Indian culture. Giant joss sticks belong to Chinese culture but an Indian-origin shopkeeper, S. Yogeswari, in Ipoh, Malaysia, has specially-designed joss sticks and sells them in her shop in Little India Bazaar in Jalan Lahat. Much like Chinese joss sticks, they are colourful and over 2-ft long, but come in the several fragrances of Indian incense sticks, and carry a Happy Deepavali inscription. Yogeswari said that she had done a little modification by using Indian aromas after first learning about joss sticks from a Chinese friend. This, briefly, hints at the continuing vivacity of the cultural mosaic that is Southeast Asia.

THE RETURN OF THE *RAMAYANA*

It is fascinating to note that different adaptations of the *Valmiki Ramayana* are included as national epics in Cambodia, Indonesia, Laos, Malaysia, Myanmar, the Philippines and Thailand.

It is no wonder, therefore, that the *Ramayana* was brought back to India in revitalized splendour in November 2002 by the artists of Southeast Asia. It was a salute to the ancient epic through a collaborative and creative reinterpretation by artists from all ten Southeast Asian countries. Called *Realising Rama*, the purpose of the ballet was said to 'explore the theme of selfless leadership'.

The presentation distilled the essence of the Rama story with a rich harvest of sights and sounds, conflicts and delicately-nuanced revelations. It was ensemble acting and dancing of many different talents and styles. Through a brilliant feat of synthesis of ideas with roots in the different regions of Southeast Asia, the production brilliantly choreographed elements of traditional Thai, Malay, Indonesian and Cambodian dance sequences overlaid by more contemporary dance movements. If the first half emphasized the richness of their dance traditions through costumes, headdresses and jewellery, the second half used the animal and masked motifs of some of their theatrical performances.

Every presentation of this epic is recognition of its contemporaneity, its many levels of reality and symbolism. Among the many stories that have been told and retold, the *Ramayana* has seen phenomenal transference, transmitted and received across borders for two millennia. The elemental power of its themes of heroism, justice and honour were universal enough to accept, accommodate, even invite, alteration and adaptation of narrative, according to regional practices, beliefs and mores. The *Ramayana* thus became a phenomenon expanding beyond its literary and religious identity, and embedded itself in the consciousness and confluence of many societies.

In *Realising Rama*, Rama must himself overcome the temptations of power, for his followers are too full of admiration to offer sage advice. However, Lakshmana and Sita often function as his conscience keepers, through his intellect and his emotion. As the introductory text of the ballet puts it, Rama slays Ravana, who is, in fact, Rama's own dark side. The closing reminds one of the life of Gautama Buddha, with the three central characters all freed from earthly vanity and temptation, surrounded by silver figures who pay them homage by forming a lotus around them. Together, all have found the unity of salvation in the diversity of their action.

The text of the brochure also underlined the diverse forms of assimilation, indigenization and interpretation that the epic has undergone in Southeast Asia because of the traditions, folk tales, experiences and general culture of each country.

The Ramakien (the Thai version) introduced Thai-Buddhist rituals for the newly-born babies into the epic. Malaysian natives, seers and Islamic prophets figure in the Hikayat Seri Rama. Food and dress and behaviour and tradition have made the Phra Lak, Phra Lam (Laotian version) a true encyclopaedia of life in Laos. More importantly, each country infused its own value system into the story, thereby modifying or transforming the epic's characters and plot. The Burmese version emphasises fraternal love, while the Laotian version underscores smooth interpersonal relations. Depending on a country's social priorities, Rama may be depicted as a god, a romantic hero, an ideal husband, beset by doubt, a temperamental brother; Sita a goddess of love, a faithful wife, or vengeful demi-goddess; and Ravana a cruel tyrant, sincere ascetic, and a gentle young man.

The idea and the ideal of Rama grown into a myriad formats. Transmuted from gold to gold, across centuries, countries, cultures, languages, philosophies and art forms. Transmuted in the magical alchemy of human experience, emotion and interpretation. From China to Cambodia to the Caribbean, from the silent recesses of the human soul to the staccato wisdom of the wooden puppet. *Realising Rama* was one of its most breathtaking formats.

ISLAM IN SOUTHEAST ASIA

Islam in Southeast Asia is said to have travelled from the coastal areas of India, and first established itself in Pasai. In 1300, the kingdom of Pasai at the northeastern tip of Sumatra is said to have first become Muslim. The first Muslim graveyards in East Java date to the same period. Indigenous sources state that the 'apostle' of Islam came from Ma'bar, a place on the Coromandel Coast. As there existed a long tradition of trading between south India and Southeast Asia, this historical representation was deemed to make sense.

In addition, there was also active seaborne trade between China and the Mediterranean countries in which Arab traders and sailors were quite prominent. The Indian Ocean, then as now, provided vital sea routes for this Eurasian commerce, with Southeast Asia and India both providing vessels as well as goods. Southeast Asia also grew to be a very important source for the more expensive spices as well as for aromatic plants from its rainforests. The trading links that had earlier resulted in the spread of Hinduism and Buddhism, with an increasing number of Muslim traders from the west coast of India, resulted in elements of Islamic religion and culture making their home in Southeast Asia from around the eighth century.

It was thus a peaceful and voluntary acceptance of the new faith that took place in the region rather than through conversions by force or conquest. In this process, the Sufis who went there from India also played a role with their emphasis on the mystical aspects of Islam. They syncretized Islamic ideas with existing local rituals and religious notions, and there was hence a considerable degree of tolerance for pre-Islamic Hindu and Buddhist beliefs and practices, something that orthodox preachers may have been more rigid about. Evidence of this was to be found in the many forms of cultural representations that continued with the largely Hindu themes as they had been already regionally adapted and refined.

What made Southeast Asian Islam distinct? Numerous authors have reiterated that in Southeast Asia, Islam was a layer over indigenous traditional cultures. For example, with the exception of a few pockets in Sumatra, Kalimantan, and Sulawesi, it entered an area of 'high culture' centred around the Hindu-Buddhist Javanese state and therefore did not construct a civilization but 'appropriated' one. In this manner, Islam fit in with a general Southeast Asian pattern of selective borrowing of cultural elements that came from the outside. The modes of its transfer to Southeast Asia, distinct in both its cultural and religious emphasis, resulted in a kind of original Southeast Asian dimension of Islam.

EXHIBITION OF ARCHIVAL DOCUMENTS (1820-1970), DECEMBER 2012

In December 2012, there was an exhibition organized in New Delhi by the National Archives with a sampling of their documents on India's interaction and exchanges with the countries of Southeast Asia covering fifteen decades from the 1820s to the 1970s.

Merchants, sailors, artists and monks, since antiquity, set out from India to the countries of Southeast Asia. They carried with them what was grown on her soil, the exquisite creations of her craftsmen, the knowledge of her scholars, and the illuminating messages of her great seers. They sowed the seeds of perennial goodwill amongst our peoples, giving us the message that we are interdependent in our freedom and security, interdependent economically and culturally. This archival exhibition reinforced this powerful message. A few of these documents are highlighted here:

Indonesia: The documents pertaining to Indonesia had an interesting spread of themes. They also revealed the close interest with which both India and Indonesia followed political developments in the other, aware that these would determine not only their own futures but also that of Asia.

Even before India had gained independence, in July 1946, India had made a proposal that Indonesian students be given scholarships to study in India. As a result, ten Indonesian students reached India in July 1948, nine to study engineering and one for agricultural science. They were among the earliest foreign students to acquire professional degrees in India!

Malaysia: On display was a copy of the Treaty of 1862 concluded by the Governor-General of India with the King of Johore. Signed in continuation of the treaty signed in 1824, this document highlighted the fascinating interplay of power and territory in the Asian continent, and marked another phase in the history of British presence in Singapore.

Then there were the documents directly relating to India and Malaysia. Malaysia implemented special schemes in 1953 to settle Indian labourers on land of their own, as it would be 'to the advantage of the labourers themselves, the rubber industry and the country as a whole'. The documents reminded one of how Indians found a welcome home in Malaya from the time they went there in the first century AD. As a result, Malaysia has one of the largest communities of persons of Indian origin in the world, numbering close to two million and constituting about 7 per cent of Malaysia's population. The images included portrayed the warmth of Malaya culture at its inclusive and hospitable best.

Myanmar: India and Myanmar are inseparably connected by land and water, and this geography has defined their historical, ethnic, cultural, linguistic and religious ties. This became evident in the archival material. Topics ranged from the vacation plans of Burmese students studying in India, the restoration of Bodh Gaya by the King of Burma in 1880, trade and emigration relations in the 1930s, and clarifications sought in 1949 about the nationality provisions in the Indian Constitution.

The certificate of the death of Bahadur Shah Zafar in Rangoon on 7 November 1862, that silently marked the end of the Mughal Empire, was also included in this collection. It is an interesting fact that Thibaw Min, the last king of Burma, was exiled in India, and Bahadur Shah Zafar, the last ruler of Delhi, was exiled in Burma by the same foreign power.

Philippines: Philippines prides itself on being the first democratic country of Asia and India as the world's largest democracy. Relations between the people of India and the Philippines are said to date back to the early centuries of the Christian era, and that these connections were further sustained through the spread of Malay culture to the Philippines. Also included was a report about the visit of Dr. Wade in 1931 from the Philippines on a medical mission to serve in India.

Singapore: Then there were the fascinating images of Singapore, its multi-cultural ethos, and its passion for success.

One of the oldest documents in this collection, and testimony to the march of colonialism, was the 1824 draft of a treaty between the Sultan of Johore and the East India Company in which the former ceded all his rights of property and sovereignty in Singapore and adjacent islets to the latter.

There was also the British capitulation of 1942 in Singapore to the Japanese, and the Indian Independence League in East Asia announcing that a new era of life and glory had dawned all over Asia. The passion for freedom of the League in Borneo, evident from the papers of the Indian National Army, is even today an inspiring document of a group of people whose motto was Unity, Faith and Sacrifice, and who were determined to struggle for the complete independence of India, free from any foreign control, domination or interference. History, of course, had many more upheavals in store for Asia.

Also included was a report of a press conference of September 1965, announcing that India would be one of the countries where Singapore would be first establishing its embassies – countries that had been very close to Singapore and had always supported it.

Cambodia: India-Cambodia relations are a product of religious and cultural exchanges that began in the first century AD. It is from the

Khmer inscriptions that we can today study the story of India's contacts with Indo-China. The Khmer genius for synthesis resulted in magnificent cities, palaces, bridges and temples. Angkor Thom was said to have over a million people, a royal city larger than the Rome of the Caesars. And then, there was the Angkor Vat, the masterpiece of Khmer architecture, said to be the largest monument in the world.

Laos: Interaction between India and the Lao PDR dates back to the reign of King Asoka. According to a legend, emissaries of King Asoka brought a relic of the Buddha to Laos, which is believed to have been placed beneath the That Luang temple in Vientiane. Laos has developed, almost as a fine art, its own version of the *Ramayana* epic in ballet form. The speech of India's first ambassador to the Kingdom of Laos, when he presented his credentials on 10 September 1957, is revealing of the intrinsic goodwill and friendship that continued across centuries between the two peoples.

Thailand: Located in each other's extended neighbourhood, India and Thailand share ancient links. Indian themes are reflected in Thai arts and architecture, the Thai language assimilated some Pali and Sanskrit influences, and Thai monks and pilgrims visiting Indian Buddhist sites kept contacts alive. And, Indians in large numbers continue travelling to Thailand, drawn by its stunning landscapes, diversity and rich cultural heritage.

Several of the Thailand papers in this archival display related to India's pre-Independence period. Exchanges took place in topics as diverse as the restoration of telegraphic lines between the two countries, on the drafting of a new electoral law, and the need to study issues such as the cooperative movement or cattle breeding in India. Thailand, proud to have been a land of the free from time immemorial, also supported a conference in Bangkok for the liberation and independence of India, so that 'India may rightly be a country for Indians'.

Vietnam: According to Vietnam, the cause of peace and of freedom are indivisible. Ho Chi Minh once said that he owned the greatest weapon – nationalism. In India, the name and the memory of Ho Chi Minh has always commanded the deepest respect. The foundations of India-Vietnam relations were laid in finding our kinship in the common struggle for liberation from foreign rule. Pandit Nehru was one of the first visitors to Vietnam after its victory against the French at Dien Bien Phu in 1954.

Given the period that they covered, the documents told of political changes, of colonial ambitions, of commerce and culture, of the struggles for independence and recognition, of natural and man-made marvels, of courage and sacrifice, and of the enduring exchanges among the peoples of our countries. These documents spoke of history being shaped, of some eras ending and others beginning, and of the bonds that kept these nations in close contact with each other in all these times. Together, all the texts and images speak of this indivisible relationship between India and Southeast Asia dating back over two thousand years to a period even before the inspired architectural synthesis of the Cham temples.

To sum up our long friendship, as evidenced in these documents, it seems appropriate to quote a few lines of Nguyen Thang, a famous Vietnamese poet of the nineteenth century, that could nudge India to focus more on Southeast Asia.

Where did you come from and what's your name?
To questions you just smile, smile. . .
Your arms are folded and you glance at the sky,
Perhaps you are brewing up something for the world?
Stop thinking of far-off matters,
Let posterity settle the problems of the universe,
This meeting is good fortune for us,
Let's bring out the wine cups.
Here's to you, to you, to me, then to you again. . .

RABINDRANATH TAGORE'S VISIT TO INDONESIA

Professor Gde Dwitya Arief Metera of the Gadjah Mada University in Yogyakarta, Indonesia, has written an interesting paper, 'Rabindranath Tagore and Balinese Contemporary Religious Identity', with inputs taken from the detailed account of Tagore's visit to Indonesia, entitled 'Rabindranath Tagore in Indonesia: An Experiment in Bridge-Building', by the Indian historian, Arun Das Gupta.

Tagore visited Indonesia from August to September 1927, at the invitation of several people familiar with his writings, many of which had been translated into Javanese by his friend, Soeriosoeparto, a Javanese nobleman. Tagore is also said to have provided some inspiration to the Indonesian nationalist movement through his school in Santiniketan which tried to find an alternative to Western education by integrating modern educational needs with elements of local culture.

According to Das Gupta, Tagore viewed his visit to Indonesia as a cultural mission with two goals. There was something about the remains of ancient Indian culture in Southeast Asia that caught his interest, and as Tagore put it, he was 'going on a pilgrimage to India beyond its modern political boundaries', and thus discover an Asian cultural identity. Secondly, it was the poet's desire to forge afresh cultural cooperation between India and Southeast Asia.

It is during this tour that Tagore wrote a tribute to forgotten and lost ties and his hope for future harmony in the poem 'Bali' that was later called 'Sagarika':

I come as your guest, I said . . .
In your woods by the sea where the south wind blows.
My veena is all I have with me.
Look at me, see if you recognize me.

Tagore was intensely interested about the Hindu culture in Bali. Das Gupta mentions in his paper how Tagore recorded his impression of Bali:

Along every village road processions of men and women were arriving with multifarious offerings. Some Puranic age seemed to have come back to life before our very eyes, some picture from the Ajanta caves come out from the realm of art to the realm of life to revel in the sunshine.

Tagore's meeting with the King of Karangasem also left him with a great impression on the strong link between Balinese culture and India. Tagore realized that the king knew some Sanskrit, and this was an indication of the cultural link between them. Das Gupta wrote about this moment when Tagore was both pleased and surprised:

The Raja, seeing that this was surprising and pleasing to his eminent guest, went on to recite the other Sanskrit names for the sea: *sagar, abdhi, jaladhya*. Then he said: '*Saptasamudra, saptaparvat, saptaban, sapta-akash,* (seven seas, seven hills, seven forests, seven skies). A little later, he recited the names of the Indian rivers Ganga, Jamuna, Narmada, Godavari, Kaveri and Sarasvati. India's geography seemed to be imprinted on the Balinese mind.

At another moment the king surprised Tagore by asking a question about man's ultimate quest and on some prompting answered the question himself. Dasgupta recounted the king's answer as follows:

'*Dewa-Dewa tida apa, Nirvana satu*'. It meant that *nirvana* is the supreme goal, not merely the worship of gods. This moment left such an impression on Tagore that he referred to it in his poem.

Tagore, nevertheless, did have had some reservations about the island being trapped in an 'archaic manifestation', through old Indian links in the dances, rituals and life of the Balinese people. He expressed discomfort with it saying, 'The Past was a great one [. . .] but it is after all the Past and its duty was to fall behind the Present, not to come in front of it and hamper the self-manifestation of the Present.'

Incidentally, Tagore did influence the process of Balinese religious modernization, according to Arief Metera. Thirty years after Tagore's visit, Balinese religion did undergo a transformation, changing from an unquestioning, traditional and practice-based one to a modern, rationalized form. Among the Balinese intellectuals who inspired this transformation were Ida Bagoes Mantra and Nyoman Pendit. They both were among the first Balinese intellectuals who studied in India, specifically in Santiniketan in the 1950s, and then returned to become prominent leaders who significantly influenced this development. Pendit was a journalist, while Mantra was a towering intellectual. They also paved the way for later generations of students to come to India and strengthen the ties between the two countries. Tagore's mission of bridge-building was indeed successful.

Tagore himself was influenced by what he saw in Java and Bali, and introduced some of their forms and ideas in Santiniketan. This included Batik in textile design, innovative dance costumes, the new versatility of dance-dramas, as well as several motifs in the visual arts.

This 1920s view of Tagore that Bali should not linger in India's past is particularly significant for us in India now. Tagore's discovery of the remains of the ancient Indian civilization in Bali yielded a vision of India's past, trapped in the Balinese present.

Do we in India continue to be over-enamoured, similarly? Proud but somewhat trapped in India's past presence and cultural influence in Southeast Asia?

HIGH-LEVEL COMMITTEE ON THE INDIAN DIASPORA

Reports of the migration of Indians to foreign lands are innumerable. One such interesting account is by Dr. Pattabhi Sitaramayya in his book, *Feathers and Stones*, written in Ahmednagar Fort Jail where, along with eleven other Congress leaders, he was imprisoned by the

British for three years after the Quit India resolution of August 1942. Like his other compatriots in jail, many of whom were prolific writers, he too did not have access to any reference material for what he wrote:

> India has a coastal length of 4,800 miles and an area of 18 lakhs of square miles and now (1943) a population of 389 millions. And India was once a great shipping country. Conditions therefore are quite favourable to emigration. Gujarat is a great field of recruitment. This was known in the days of the contemplated mass Civil Disobedience of 1921 when it was said that the Gujaratis who had been in South Africa knew what the movement was and therefore Gandhi wanted to try it in the Ananda and Bardoli Tahsils and wanted India to infuse her spirit and strength into him. From Gujarat, people were going to South Africa. After World War 1, they began migrating to East Africa. The Bengalees, Uriyas and Andhras migrated in large numbers to Burma, besides Africa, while the Tamils and Malayalis migrated in addition to Malaya, Singapore and Ceylon.

Nearly sixty years later, the Report of the High Level Committee on the India Diaspora, presented in 2002, had the following to say about Indian emigration to Southeast Asia during the colonial period:

> Indian emigration during the 19th and early 20th centuries to the British, French and Dutch colonies in that region was unprecedented. There were of two types:
>
> (a) emigration of contract labourers under the 'indenture system' or 'Kangani' system, and
>
> (b) 'free' or 'passage' emigration of traders, clerks, bureaucrats and professionals.

With the abolition of slavery, particularly in the British Empire and the French and Dutch colonies in 1834, 1846 and 1873 respectively, there was a severe shortage of labourers working in sugar, tea, coffee, cocoa, rice and rubber plantations in the colonies. India and China became the obvious alternative sources of labour. During the period 1852 to 1937, approximately two million Indians went to Malaya and approximately 2.5 million to Myanmar. Since these colonies were situated not far from India, a majority of the migrants returned home after serving as plantation labourers. After 1920, the 'Kangani' emigration gradually gave way to individual or un-recruited migration due to a fall in the demand for Indian labour.

The second type of migration, namely, 'free' or 'passage' migration of traders and artisans took place to Myanmar and Malaysia during the late nineteenth and the first half of the twentieth centuries, from the United Provinces (modern UP), from Rajputana, from Madras, as well as Gujaratis, Maharashtrians and Punjabis.

Prior to Second World War, specially in Malaysia and Singapore, Indians had little political interest in their countries of residence, their activities being largely oriented towards the mother country with which they retained strong economic, sentimental and political links. This orientation of the Indians in Malaya was strengthened by periodic visits by Indian leaders like Rabindranath Tagore, Pandit Nehru and Srinivasa Sastri. It was finally brought into the open with the establishment of the Indian National Army (INA) in Malaya. Between 1942 and 1945, thousands of Indians volunteered to join the INA for the purpose of fighting for the independence of India. In addition, Indian Independence League (IIL) organizations were established in all leading centres in Southeast Asia to recruit men, collect funds and generally to coordinate the independence movement. Men and money poured into the independence movement on an unprecedented scale from all over Southeast Asia. After Independence small numbers of Indians have continued to migrate to Thailand, Malaysia, Singapore and Indonesia. These have been mainly professionals working for Indian joint ventures and other institutions. In recent times many local companies have also engaged Indian professionals. In Thailand there are also blue collar workers from the Gorakhpur region.

The 2002 Report on the Indian Diaspora also has a table showing that, when it was written, the Indian diaspora constituted 9.7 per cent of the population in Singapore, 7.3 per cent in Malaysia, 5 per cent in Myanmar, 2.3 per cent in Brunei, 0.07 per cent in Thailand and negligible in the other countries of Southeast Asia.

THE CONNECTIVITY ISSUE

With ASEAN we have achieved a considerable measure of economic and commercial coherence. At the same time, however, even among contiguous regions there remain interrupted or missing transportation links that keeps the markets fragmented and hence, in very tangible terms, functioning below optimum efficiency. This is particularly true of India's road and rail connectivity with Southeast Asia, particularly from our northeast.

A former Thai deputy prime minister saw linking India with

Southeast Asia as strategically, commercially and culturally significant, expanding as it would India's access even up to the South China Sea. Every countryside and town that the road or rail will pass through is humming with economic activity, and that every border to be crossed is an active one with people on both sides looking for better facilities to access larger markets both for their products and purchases.

It was in other times, many centuries ago, along hundreds of other paths, that the gospel of the Buddha reached several lands, bringing together peoples as rivers uniting in the sea. It is a message that still endures.

To reinforce our Asian identity across Asia, to help rediscover the confluence of the Ganga and the Mekong, we need to link with each other at many levels. When we travel by road and rail, it is not a soulless shift from airport to sterile airport. It is, on the other hand, a journey where one feels the lives of the people across countries, experiences the wonder of contiguous cultures, and realizes it is not difficult to transcend both physical and psychological frontiers. Then, we do not merely reach a destination, we truly arrive.

Travelling by land and river is like seeing a film in which one is also present, a riveting travelogue across South and Southeast Asia. Images of young children, the itinerant *bhikshu*, the busy amiability of the street vendor, the farmer ploughing the land with his bullocks, the faces peering out of train windows, the golden pagodas, the temples, churches and mosques before whom a million heads bow in prayer, all make for the colourful kaleidoscope that defines and unites this ancient continent.

While a federation of Asian nations that India spoke of in March 1947 is now not mentioned with the same parameters, no one denies that Asia should engage more with itself, and that this is best done through transportation networks that unite people, markets and countries.

It is facile to say that the road to success is always under construction. That means that success must keep waiting. It is now accepted that with the bridging of all the major Asian rivers, land connectivity is no longer difficult. Yet, India has not energetically worked to remove impediments to the connectivity of culturally and physically contiguous countries. The limited impact so far of India's LEP on improving the economy of our resource-rich northeastern states is seen as attributable to this inadequate connectivity.

Unhindered and integrated markets that span the distance from the Himalayas to the Pacific Ocean would constitute an arc of advantage, across which there would be a large-scale movement of people, goods, capital, ideas and creativity. It has been said that the distance from New Delhi to Hanoi is no greater than that to Kerala, and hence regional connectivity cannot remain just a dream. There is a great surge in support of an East-West land corridor, one which would also control the illegal trade in drugs and arms, and give a fillip to legitimate trade in both agricultural and manufactured goods.

There is a yellow-painted signpost, installed by the Indian Border Roads on the road they constructed in Myanmar that reads, 'Where there is a will, there is a highway'. Where there is a will, there can be a long railway as well.

THE PUBLIC DIPLOMACY ANGLE

India, wanting to show that its naval diplomacy also had a soft-power aspect to it, sent its newly-inducted sail training ship, *INS Sudarshini*, to retrace the ancient sea route taken by Indian traders to Southeast Asia. It commenced its odyssey from the Indian port of Kochi on 15 September 2012, sailed to 13 ports and 9 countries of the ASEAN, and returned to its home port on 25 March 2013, after a voyage of over six months. Undertaken to mark 10 years of India's summit-level ties with ASEAN and the 20th anniversary of its Dialogue Partnership with the grouping, it was hailed as a unique expedition that kindled the imagination of a large number of young people of Southeast Asia about the Indian Navy and about India itself.

Such journeys, including the India-ASEAN car rallies, have their place since they reinforce images. Public diplomacy needs, however, to be followed up by serious public activity. The journeys we make to each other are good, but the journeys we make together take us to a higher level of friendship.

And, as a point of comparison, the Indian Council for Cultural Relations, which was founded in 1957, runs some 30 Indian Cultural Centres abroad, of which a few reportedly have been shut down in the past one year. In comparison, China, which began a similar programme only in 2004, had some 330 Confucius Centres in 93 countries as of 2013, and the number is growing. Being culturally and linguistically visible and accessible across the globe is fundamental to a country's soft power status.

At least as far as Southeast Asia is concerned, India has to strengthen its diaspora infrastructure. The 'Know India' programme of the Ministry of Overseas Indian Affairs has to be specially tailored for the youth in these countries, and must highlight the variety and richness of our own northeast. This would reaffirm another dimension of our cultural overlap and contiguity.

THE ECONOMIC PERSPECTIVE

Compared to most other countries in Southeast Asia, India in 1947 was relatively better off. The Working Group for Asia and the Far East set up by the UNESCO in 1947 observed that

> India emerged from World War II a creditor nation as a result of large British wartime purchases in the country. This gave an impetus to the gradual process of industrialisation which had been going on for some time. Many entirely new industries were started in India as a consequence of the war, and a few existing industries were expanded. These may well be vital factors in a chain of industrial programmes that will have a far-reaching effect not only for India but for the whole of Asia.

The analysis of this report at that time was that the industrial development of India was the best guarantee for the economic recovery of Southeast Asia, mainly because the economies of India and Southeast Asia were complementary and not competitive, and 'the greatest cooperation between the two is necessary for the good of all'.

This led to increased exchanges in the 1950s, and Indian businesses became more active and present in the countries of this eastern neighbourhood. However, other geopolitical developments soon grabbed hold of our global agenda. It was not till the early 1990s that India once again acknowledged the significance of Southeast Asia to its economy and people and announced its LEP.

This recognition is validated by the May 2014 report of McKinsey, the global consulting firm. It says that Southeast Asia is one of the world's fastest-growing markets, and that despite their distinct cultures, histories, and languages, the member-states of ASEAN share a focus on jobs and prosperity. With more than 600 million people, ASEAN has been called an economic powerhouse, a growing hub of consumer demand and at the crossroads of important global flows.

Foreign direct investment has also boomed, with ASEAN-5 (Indonesia, Malaysia, the Philippines, Singapore and Thailand) receiving more FDI than China in 2013. In addition to attracting multinationals, ASEAN has become a launching pad for new companies, accounting for 38 per cent of Asia's market for initial public offerings. Singapore alone has ranked fifth globally for corporate-headquarters density and first in terms of foreign subsidiaries. Then there is also ASEAN's relentless passion about being globally connected, whether it be in terms of inflow and outflow of goods, services, finance, and people, or in the underlying flows of data that speeds up all types of cross-border exchanges.

According to Mckinsey, there remains the need for the region to develop its human capital. In Indonesia and Myanmar alone, a shortage of 9 million skilled and 13 million semiskilled workers is projected by 2030.

The report also highlights the diversities within ASEAN, with Indonesia representing almost 40 per cent of the region's economic output while Myanmar, emerging from decades of isolation, is still building its institutions. Per capita income in Singapore is said to be over fifty times higher than in Cambodia, and in fact, surpasses those of Canada and the United States. That diversity extends to culture, language, and religion too. Indonesia, for example, is almost 90 per cent Muslim, the Philippines is 80 per cent Roman Catholic, and Thailand about 95 per cent Buddhist. Hence, local preferences and cultural sensitivities continue to remain important. A one-size-fits-all strategy would not work across such widely varying societies.

Many aspects touched upon in this report are extremely pertinent to India which is in ASEAN's immediate geographic, economic and strategic neighbourhood. They also have a direct bearing on the presence, spread, influence and economic opportunities of Indians who are already there or are likely to move to Southeast Asia in the coming decades. Such assessments need to be factored in by the government when it makes or modifies policies in the context of overseas Indians.

A FINAL THOUGHT

I would like to end with some lines of A.K. Ramanujan's poem, 'Extended Family', that has been subject to various interpretations, but which conveys a longing that persists for eternal India:

Yet, like grandfather,
I bathe before the village crow,
The dry chlorine water my only Ganges,
The naked Chicago bulb a cousin of the Vedic sun.
Slap soap on my back like father
And think in proverbs.

Ramanujan, the eminent poet, translator, linguist and folklorist, who was a Professor of South Asian Studies and taught at several American universities, would remark to his friends that he was *the hyphen in Indo-American*. Millions of Indians living outside the country perhaps feel, at some point or another, that they also are such hyphens. For those in Southeast Asia, this hyphen, fortunately, would be a soft overlay across contiguous and exuberant cultures.

We have to salute all hyphens because they are essential to India and to India's life with the world.

CHAPTER 15

India's Southeast Neighbourhood: A Cultural History and Basis for Future Prospects

SURESH K. GOEL*

The India-ASEAN Vision Statement issued at the end of the India-ASEAN Summit in New Delhi in November 2012 began by 'Acknowledging that the civilizations of ASEAN and India have been enriched by cross-cultural exchanges over several millennia, where knowledge and ideas, goods and spiritual traditions have moved seamlessly across borders, providing a strong foundation for co-operation in a globalized world.'

There is a multiplicity of ideas embedded in this one paragraph. Most importantly, it acknowledges that the history of India and ASEAN, and in fact, Southeast Asia have been intertwined not through a political discourse, but primarily through ideas, knowledge, traditions, civilizational elements and commerce traversing among these countries on the high seas of the Indian Ocean, Malacca Straits and maritime exchanges. Even more importantly, it underlines that the history of such relations between India and Southeast Asia is based in history of civilizational and cultural exchanges as the strong foundation for relationship in the contemporary context.

Political divisions between nations on the basis of geographical boundaries is a relatively new context, originating in Europe in the nineteenth century, with these geographical boundaries increasingly providing the basis for political intercourse in the twentieth century. The problem is that the creation of geogaraphical boundaries in many cases has led to partitioning of societies, fracturing cultural and social

* Amb. Suresh K. Goel, Former Ambassador of India to Laos and Director-General, Indian Council of Cultural Relations.

consensus, if not homogeneity in most of these cases. The internal and inter-state conflicts in Africa, West Asia and other regions is a testimony to problems created by such cultural and social breakdown amongst the traditional and tribal societies in that continent.

The idea of nations in other parts of the world, and most importantly in South and Southeast Asia was in contrast, not based on any rigid geographical lines but derived more from the administrative authority of the ruler exercised through collection of revenue, adjudication of disputes and institution of social laws to govern the society. What it meant was that an expansion of a village through any means would provide a mobility to the territorial boundaries of the ruler. The nation's geographical limits were therefore fluid through both the social and the cultural behaviour. It provided an organic growth to the state without creating a conflict or friction among states as the basic unit of the nation retained its integrity.

Nowhere was this cohesion of civilizational integrity and interaction more visible at an international level than in India and Southeast Asia. The Chola ships travelling across to Southeast Asia – which during the first millennium was not a group of sovereign national identities but a heterogeneous region with a rich and diverse folk and tribal culture – founded links with the rulers in this region on the basis of a trade and cultural regime. The relationship was governed more through an expansion of influence rather than through acquisition of territory or other exploitative instruments. Historians recall that there has been no evidence of expansion of Indian influence into Southeast Asia through war or conflict. The Chola ships travelled as part of exploration and trading activity and the powerful navies then provided protection to these maritime activities from pirates and marauders. It's, however, a certainty that these navies never indulged in conflicts with other sovereign entities.

The traditions, culture and archaeology of Southeast Asian nations today is evidence of the strong Indian influence in this region for more than a millennium. The Myson Valley temple complex near Danang in Vietnam is a magnificent archeological testimony to the benign Indian influence which existed in the Champa empire of Cham people from second century AD onwards. While there is no clear historical indication of how the Indian architectural influence travelled to Vietnamese areas so early, one could only speculate that the traders who reached Indochina through the South China seas may have travelled further north and having come to the pleasant green area of Myson Valley, decided to make home there.

There have been several suggestions that the Indian influence travelled from Myson Valley to present-day Cambodia and further east to Laos.

The archeological history of India and Southeast Asia cannot be discussed without mentioning Angkor Wat and Siem Reap. The beautiful and sharply sculpted figures of *apsaras*, from *Mahabharata, the Sagar Manthan* (Churning of the Ocean episode) and the majestic architecture of the temples clearly establish the existence of a rich and powerful kingdom with Indian linkages in those areas from sixth century onwards.

The temples in Java are further evidence of the rich intercourse between the Indian influence in Southeast Asian traditions of that era.

The strong linkage between India and Southeast Asia is even more visible in the cultural traditions of Southeast Asia. *Ramayana* is a cultural factor which links India and the Southeast Asian nations intimately and intricately. A study has found that the *Ramayana* is probably the only one epic which exists in all South East Asian nations in one form or the other. It has to be noted, however, that there are variations both in nuances of the story and the characters in the various versions of the *Ramayana* prevalent in these countries. *Vayangkulit* in Indonesia and Malaysia takes its stories extensively from the *Mahabharata*. The Lao Pimai or Sonkarn festival in Thailand, which also celebrates the New Year resembles the Holi festival in India to a remarkable extent. The manner of greetings in Southeast Asia looks remarkably similar to the *namaste* of India.

The intrepid traveller Guru Rabindranath Tagore said during his visit to Java in 1927, 'I see India everywhere, but I don't recognize it'. The philosopher, thinker, poet and the cultural ambassador of India had travelled to several Southeast Asian countries and would probably have made a similar observation in all these societies.

The history of Indian influences in Southeast Asia, as gathered through architectural, literary, archaeological and cultural evidence establishes the assimilation of Indian culture with the primordial culture of these Southeast Asian lands from as early as second century AD. The earlier demography of these countries suggests that the culture in these regions was probably more ethnic, rooted in the topography of these areas with clear contours of a folk or tribal nature. The synthesis of a more creative and imaginative Indian artistic influence combined together with the ethnic and tribal culture of these lands created something which was truly Southeast Asian with a strong Indian character.

The empire which built the Myson Valley temples was Champa of Cham people, distinctly belonging to the region, of a stock completely different from Indian and yet it was the Indian cultural influence brought through traders and travellers which created the magnificent edifices of Indian culture. Angkor Wat and Wat Phu temples are creations not of Indian artisans, but a result of the vision of Suryavarman and Jayavarman, Khmer kings belonging to the Indochinese region. Borobudur or Bagan were again created by the people of those areas rather than Indian people.

The central idea, therefore, of the earlier history of Southeast Asia is that it was distinctly Asian and Southeast Asian even though it drew heavily from the Indian cultural and civilizational influences brought by the traders and travellers, as well as the naval flotillas of the Chola empire, which went as far as Vijaynagar in search of riches and new ideas. The traditional Indian influence is reflected not just in culture and civilization, but also in political organization and economic activities during that era. The textiles created a cultural tradition for Indian textiles which introduced several design and artistic innovations, both ways. The concept of *devaraja* (God-king), social hierarchies and the administrative structures were largely shaped by Indian practices.

A seminar organized by the Indian Council for Cultural Relations under the title 'Civilizational Dialogue' in July 2012 clearly brought out that the travel of cultural influence between India and Southeast Asia was not unidirectional from India to Southeast Asia, but several sculptural and architectural ideas have been imbibed by Chola designers from Southeast Asia.

As a result of these historical interactions, India and Southeast Asia share a distinct Asianness which shows itself visibly in the family and social traditions, family hierarchy and order, emphasis on education, religious philosophy and cultural diversity.

Culture has acquired a new prominence in the present times. It has been variously described as soft power leading to cultural diplomacy and creating in the process several misplaced high expectations and misconceptions. Irrespective of these, culture does play the role of a strong bridge of understanding and friendship amongst different societies.

Dialogue amongst civilizations which can only base itself on culture provides the only suitable response to Samuel Huntington's theory of clash of civilizations which was used in the post-9/11 era to explain the growing interstate tensions and conflicts. The theory of clash of civilizations bases itself on the idea of ethnic, religious and cultural identities entering into a contest with each other creating friction, generating heat of religious and ethnic conflicts. The balm of cultural understanding promotes a dialogue which brings these multiple identities from across the globe together into a unified globe with distinction of identities enriching it rather than causing clashes.

Culture has also played the role of soft power to lubricate the process of interstate dialogue by attracting others rather than creating a threat. Hollywood and Bollywood are perhaps the two best examples of such soft power instruments throughout the world. Indian Bollywood actors are a household name in Southeast Asia.

In a general fashion, culture would play a role in the future to strengthen the dialogue between competing parties by introducing a certain benignness of process. The culture would most importantly create a civilizational understanding between people where competition would benefit nations and societies by bringing out their best rather than introduce conflicts amongst societies.

The events organized on the margins of the India-Southeast Asia summit in December 2013, which included a car rally, a shipping expedition, various economic workshops by the chambers of commerce, a conference on civilizational dialogue, an exhibition of archival material of early interactions between India and Southeast Asia, all clearly illustrated the commonality of history between these nations, but more importantly, the possibilities of a strong common future.

Most interestingly, the joint India-ASEAN cultural performance organized at the dinner hosted by the President for the visiting heads of ASEAN states clearly brought out the common traditions of performing arts which have evolved between India and these countries in their own distinct manner, with a strong connection over a millennium of history. Almost all heads of state or government present on the occasion were unanimous in their judgement that the common culture shared between India and the Southeast Asian nations was the strongest assurance of the bright future of India-ASEAN relations in all areas including trade, investments, technology and strategic interests. The common civlizational and cultural history of India and ASEAN member-nations would ensure absence of misunderstanding where such possibilities could arise and further ensure that competitive interests would result in collaboration rather than conflict.

There is no doubt that culture will provide a strong bond in the relations between India and the Southeast Asian nations. The driving forces would be a combination of economic, commercial and strategic interests but the matrix of civilizational ideas will provide succour to these relations in a more abiding manner than anywhere else because of the history of about two millennia.

However, unlike the past, cultural interactions cannot be left anymore to the vicissitudes of trade and travel in view of the more defined geopolitical boundaries as a reality of today. The governments of the day need to make a more determined, focused and conscious effort to ensure that the network of trade, economic and strategic cooperation is built on the basis of sustained exchange of ideas, knowledge, intellect and culture between these countries. As stated by Ambassador Sudhir Devre in his book, *India and South East Asia*, 'knowledge, education and human resource development is a living cultural expression and has been so even in the ancient times of intensive India-Southeast Asia interaction too'.

The revival of Nalanda University through the joint project of ASEAN must therefore be taken to its conclusion to provide the civilizational context to relationships in the contemporary times.

The path of such social-cultural collaboration as included in the India-ASEAN Vision Statement provides a concrete path for the future. These provisions state that

> we will strengthen social-cultural cooperation and promote greater people-to-people interaction through increasing exchanges in culture, education, youth, sports, creative industries, science and technology, information and communication technology and software, human resource development and scholarly exchanges. We will also enhance contacts between parliamentarians, media personnel, academics and Track II institutions such as the network of think tanks. We will encourage the study, documentation and dissemination of knowledge about the civilizational links between ASEA and India.

CHAPTER 16

Ethnic Chinese and Indians in Southeast Asia: A Comparative Study

V. SURYANARAYAN*

A comparative study of Indian and Chinese communities in Southeast Asia is yet to be undertaken by scholars specializing in Southeast Asian Studies. A perusal of the bibliography on the subject shows that there is hardly any creative work in this fascinating area. However, there are a number of scholarly works analysing the problems of the Chinese and the Indian communities in the region as a whole, as well as in individual countries.

The comparative perspective is extremely important for two reasons. Lying to the south of China and east of India, the countries of Southeast Asia are extremely important from the foreign policy perspectives of these two Asian giants. The issue is of crucial importance because China's bilateral relations and, to a lesser extent, India's relations with Southeast Asian countries are rendered complex by the presence of Chinese and Indian minority groups in these countries. Equally significant both China and India are trying to attract the considerable reservoir of capital possessed by these two communities for their economic development.

SEMANTIC CONFUSION

Being Chinese and Indian outside China and India has several complex facets. The commonly used term for these people today is diaspora.

* Prof. V. Suryanarayan, Former Senior Professor and Founding Director, Centre for South and Southeast Asian Studies, University of Madras.

The Singhvi Committee Report also uses this term. The term diaspora is Jewish in origin and does not exactly convey the complexities of these communities. It was used to refer to the Jewish communities 'living in exile outside Palestine' consequent to the seizure of their homeland by foreign powers. The Jews were subjected to persecution and they fanned out to different parts of the world. However, throughout the centuries, they hankered for their homeland. There was a special relationship between the land of Israel and the Jewish people. However, if one analyses the spread of the Chinese and Indian communities abroad, there were several 'pull' and 'push' factors. And what is more, most of them do not want to return to China and India. Regarding the Overseas Chinese Prof. Wang Gung Wu makes an interesting observation. If one subscribes to the view that there is cohesion among them, it would be misleading. The fact is that the Chinese, wherever they go, are easily influenced by the environment. They adapt to new circumstances and thus become very different from other groups settled elsewhere.

Equally unsatisfactory is the term 'Overseas Chinese' and 'Overseas Indians' popularized by political sociologists. The overwhelming majority belongs to the third or fourth generation and has become a permanent feature of the demographic profile of these countries. They would like to be called as Malaysians of Indian origin or Singapore citizens of Chinese origin rather than Overseas Indians or Overseas Chinese. The implication of the latter is that they are only an extension of the people of India or China. The Chinese and the Indians are slowly, but surely, becoming distinct communities, linked with certain cultural affinities with the land of their forefathers, but also different in many respects from these societies. Cultural persistence – retaining many aspects of their culture in an alien environment and adaptation to new surroundings – are twin facets of these dynamic groupings.

Another caveat is necessary. In terms of their legal status, there are important variations among these peoples. They could be categorized into three groups:

1. People of Indian or Chinese origin who have taken citizenship of the countries in which they have settled.
2. All those Indians and Chinese who have neither taken Chinese or Indian citizenship and nor have been granted citizenship of the countries in which they have settled. According to the Singhvi

Committee Report, there are 400,000 people of Indian origin in Myanmar who are stateless. According to official statistics, there are 50,000 ethnic Indians who are stateless in Malaysia. According to Hindu Rights Action Force (HINDRAF) this figure is an underestimate. All of them are born in Myanmar and in Malaysia, and it is inhuman to keep these people stateless. The Government of India must take up this thorny issue with Kuala Lumpur and Yangon and get the problem resolved satisfactorily. As far as Myanmar is concerned, according to media reports, large numbers of Chinese are illegally migrating to Myanmar through the porous China-Myanmar land border.

3. Indians and Chinese, who retain their citizenship and have gone to Southeast Asian countries on employment visas. It should also be pointed out that the existence of two Chinas – PRC and Taiwan – adds a new dimension to the problems of ethnic Chinese in this region.

As far as Southeast Asia is concerned, it is sometimes difficult to identify who is an Indian or who is a Chinese. In Thailand and in the Philippines the Chinese have, over the years, successfully assimilated with the Thais and the Filipinos. Similarly Indian Muslims have found no difficulty in assimilating themselves with the Malays. How can we characterize these people? Thais or Chinese? Chinese or Filipinos? Malays or Indians?

The Chinese and the Indians are not homogeneous communities. The Chinese belong to several linguistic groups – Hokkien, Hakka, Cantonese, Teochew, Hainanese, Kwangsi, etc.; what is more, these dialects are mutually incomprehensible. The attempts made by the Government of Singapore to introduce Mandarin as the common language for all did not initially find favour with many people, who wanted to continue with their dialects. The Indians are also divided on the basis of their religion – Hindus, Christians, Muslims and Sikhs – and on the basis of language – Tamil, Malayalam, Gujarati, Telugu, Sindhi, etc. In Malaysia and Singapore, the term 'Indians' includes Indians, Pakistanis, Sri Lankans and Bangladeshis.

It would be simplistic and naïve to assume that the problems that these people face and what the future holds for them are identical. Their problems are intertwined with the nature of their migration, their social and economic status, the size of the community, educational attainments and the majority-minority syndrome in the countries in which they have settled.

SIGNIFICANT FEATURES

Certain significant features of the two communities should be highlighted in the beginning itself.

1. Ethnic Chinese presence in Southeast Asia is substantial, 35 million, whereas Indians are negligible in numbers, 6 million. Except in Myanmar, Malaysia and Singapore, where Indians constitute 5, 8 and 7.1 per cent respectively, they are a microscopic minority in all other countries.
2. The Chinese constitute 76.0 per cent of the population of Singapore and, therefore, Singapore provides a contrast to other countries. Far from being a minority compelled to adjust to the demands and pressures of the majority community, the Chinese community in Singapore sets the role model for others to follow. However, its location in the midst of the Malay world, noted for xenophobia, compels the political leadership to organize the political culture in such a way that Singapore does not become 'Third China'. In his memoirs, Singapore statesman Lee Kuan Yew mentions how he underlined this reality during his first visit to China in 1976. Lee Kuan Yew declared in the official banquet, 'History brought together Chinese, Malays and Indians in Singapore. We are proud of our heritage. Sharing a common experience, we are developing a distinctive way of life. By geography our future will be more closely interlinked with those of our neigbours in Southeast Asia.' Lee Kuan Yew underscored the problem if China continued to view Singapore as a 'kinsman's country'. To quote Lee, 'The more China embraced us as a "kinsman country", the greater would be our neigbours' suspicions. It was difficult because Singapore's neighbours had significant Chinese minorities who played a disproportionate role in the economy and their economic success had aroused the jealousy and suspicion of the indigenous peoples.
3. On Malaysia's, eve of independence in 1957 the Chinese constituted 39 per cent of the population. But today while the Malays constitute 67 per cent of the population, the Chinese proportion has come down to 27 per cent. Even then it is a large number. The Malaysian government cannot impose restrictions on the Chinese as the Indonesian government does like prohibiting the Chinese from entering the retail trade. It may be recalled that till the downfall of Suharto, the Chinese in Indonesia could not use

Chinese names, there were no Chinese newspapers, no Chinese-medium schools, no Chinese political parties nor could the Chinese celebrate the Chinese New Year. Pragmatic as the Chinese were they accepted their subordinate status in the political life, but sharpened their entrepreneurial skills.

4. Ethnic tensions in Southeast Asia revolve around relations between the indigenous majority and the culturally exclusive and economically powerful Chinese minority groups. Anti-Chinese riots had occurred in all countries, the more significant being anti-Chinese riots in Malaysia in May 1969 and anti-Chinese riots in Indonesia after the downfall of Suharto. Lee Khoon Choy, former Singapore Ambassador to Indonesia has written that the Chinese became the target of attacks because of their relative affluence and close affinity with the Suharto government. At the height of the riots Chinese girls were raped and some of them burnt alive. As recently as May 2014, there were attacks on the ethnic Chinese in Vietnam following strains in the relations with China consequent to the installation of an oil rig in the South China Sea. China immediately sent ships to evacuate the Chinese who wanted to leave Vietnam. The Indians, miniscule in number, are not a factor in ethnic politics. However, recent developments in Malaysia should be a matter of concern. The increasing urbanization of the Indian community following the disintegration of the rubber plantations and their lumpenization has brought severe strains in the relations between the Indian community and the Malay-dominated Malaysian government. The violent Malay-Indian clashes in Kampong Baru in 2001 are a clear illustration of simmering discontent within the Indian community.

CYCLES OF MIGRATION

Migration of Indians to Southeast Asia can be traced back to first century AD, when Indian princes, merchants, poets and artists went to these countries. Their interaction with the local rulers and peoples led to the founding of Indianized empires. The spread of Indian cultural influences led to the enrichment of Southeast Asian countries. Indianized kingdoms like Funan, Sri Kshetra, Pagan, Khemer, Sri Vijaya, Sailendra and Majapahit; the familiar Indo-Sanskritic vocabulary in Thai and Bahasa Indonesia; architectural monuments like Angkor Wat, Borobudur and Lara Djjongrang; literary masterpieces like

Ramkein, *Amaramala*, *Arjuna Vivaha* and *Bharata Yuddha*; the *Wajang Kulit* based on the *Ramayana* and *Mahabharata* themes; the living Hindu traditions in the island of Bali – all these bear testimony to the courage and zeal of Indian princes, priests, poets, merchants and artisans and the ingratiating and assimilable qualities of Southeast Asian peoples. The Indian interaction was in sharp contrast with China's interaction with northern part of Vietnam, which came under direct Chinese domination and was sinicized. One direct consequence of Chinese occupation of Vietnam was the growth of anti-Chinese feeling among the Vietnamese which survives to the present day.

Large-scale migration of Indians and Chinese commenced when the colonial powers extended their influence in Southeast Asia. In some countries, there was shortage of labour; in a few others the indigenous people lacked initiative and enterprise. Under the protective umbrella of the British, Indian labourers migrated to Burma and Malaya. The Chinese under the supervision of the labour contractors or on their own migrated to all countries in the region. The fact that the Chinese and the Indians were industrious and not troublesome, with no apparent interest in local politics, made them desirable colonial subjects. As the colonial rule got consolidated the Chinese became the most dominant group and started controlling trade, business and industry. In the nineteenth and twentieth centuries another class of migrants – lawyers, doctors, teachers and white-collar workers – moved into these countries. The early migrants were birds of passage; but gradually the transient population became permanent settlers. In the post-Independence era Indians and the Chinese – both highly qualified and working class – migrated to these countries, which lacked labour and qualified personnel, with the support and encouragement of the local governments.

RISE OF POLITICAL CONSCIOUSNESS

The Chinese and the Indians were always subjected to pulls and pressures from their homeland. In the beginning it was economic and a large proportion of their savings were remitted to China and India. But with the growth of nationalism, political pulls also started exerting in a big way. Just as Mahatma Gandhi's baptism into politics took place in South Africa in defence of the Indian community, the initial activities of the revolutionary movement in China were related to Chinese communities abroad. Sun Yat Sen himself was a migrant to Honolulu, who had his higher education in Hong Kong. From its inception, the Kuomintang began to enlist the support of the Chinese communities in Southeast Asian countries. The Nationalist Government after the revolution in 1911 started the Ministry of Overseas Chinese; Consulates were opened in Malaya, East Indies and the Philippines. What is more, the new government enunciated a novel principle of citizenship. The doctrine 'once a Chinese, always a Chinese' came into force. It meant that citizenship went by ethnic origin and not by place of birth. It had dangerous implications and naturally was viewed with suspicion by the colonial governments and by Southeast Asian nationalists. The Chinese in Southeast Asia gave massive financial support to the Nanking government during the Sino-Japanese War. Finally the forces opposed to Japan were united and resistance movement against Japan was kept alive in Southeast Asian countries.

Communism also came to Malaya and Singapore from China. It was from among the local Chinese that the Malayan Communist Party (MCP) was able to recruit its revolutionary leadership and militant following. Very few Malays and Indians joined the MCP. In Malay perception the MCP was Malayan only in name, but was Chinese in practice. It was the inability of the MCP to build a multi-racial following that led to its eventual downfall. The powerful ideological support given by the Chinese Communist Party (CCP) during the communist struggle for power created further misgivings among the Malayan nationalists. They viewed the Chinese minority as a potential 'fifth column' of China.

Suspicions about China's expansionist designs and the CCP's linkages with local communist parties stood in the way of normalization of relations between Beijing and anti-communist countries in Southeast Asia. Complicating the situation was the subtle distinction which China made between party-to-party relations and government-to-government relations. For several years, the underground radio stations of pro-China communist parties were broadcasting from southern China. However, with the ascendancy of Deng Xiao Ping support to communist ideology had been put into cold storage by the Chinese leadership.

Compared to the Chinese, political consciousness among the Indians was comparatively less. However, with the growth of the nationalist movement in India, the educated Indians began to take keen interest in the political developments in their motherland. This received a further impetus after Jawaharlal Nehru's vast to Malaya in

1938. During the Second World War, the Indians rallied round the Indian National Army and joined the Azad Hind Fauj in large numbers. The *Thondar Padai* (Comrades Army) sensitized the Indians and gave them the proud feeling that they were in the vanguard of the Indian independence movement.

Unlike China which looked at ethnic Chinese living abroad as Chinese citizens, the Indian nationalist leaders, especially Gandhiji and Nehru, were more sensitive to the cross-currents of international politics and the xenophobic tendencies among the Southeast Asian nationalists. They repeatedly exhorted the Indian communities to identify themselves with the political aspirations of the indigenous peoples. To illustrate, in November 1927, Ganndhiji exhorted the Indians living in Ceylon to co-exist harmoniously with the Sinhalese as 'sugar in milk'. However, the Indian assumption that with the independence of Asian countries a new era of Asian unity would emerge was misplaced. In many countries the newly-independent countries enacted citizenship legislations which discriminated against Indian settlers. Many Indians were rendered stateless. What is more, in their eagerness to introduce a socialist society, the Burmese government nationalized even retail trade which hit the Indian Tamil community very badly. It must, at the same time, be pointed out that because of the personal friendship between Indira Gandhi and Tun Abdul Razak, the problems faced by the Indian workers in Malaysia consequent to the introduction of work permits was amicably settled.

CHINA AND ETHNIC CHINESE IN SOUTHEAST ASIA

Ethnicity is all pervasive in Southeast Asian countries. What is more, the nationalist movements had a strong xenophobic content in Indonesia, Vietnam, Burma and Malaya. The nationalists were not only opposed to the foreign powers, but also to the compradore classes, Indians in Burma and Chinese in all other countries. With independence, the indigenous majority started building the nation on the language and religion of the majority peoples. Affirmative action was introduced to uplift the indigenous peoples. The Chinese and the Indians, most of them belonging to the third or fourth generations, feel that they are being treated as second-class citizens. The educated among them have migrated to greener pastures in Australia, New Zealand, United States and Canada. The Chinese are the worst hit because of the Chinese stranglehold in the economy of many countries. The Chinese businessmen who prospered under the long spell of Suharto regime were referred to as *Cukong*; 'Cu' meaning 'master' and 'Kong' meaning 'Godfather'. One of the notorious *Cukongs* was Liem Sioe Liong, a good friend of the Suharto family. His business interests spread over clove, flour, cement, petroleum, chemicals, property development and banking. He owned the largest business conglomerate in Indonesia. Suharto used Chinese businessmen because they never threatened his position. What Suharto underestimated was the growing opposition from the students and the general public. As Singapore diplomat Lee Khoon Choy vividly describes, the *pribhumis*, people belonging to the lowest strata of society, 'hated the Suharto regime, because it sides with the Cukongs. They hated the Cukongs more, because in their opinion, they were looting the country and exploiting the poorer classes'.

Numerous anti-Chinese riots have taken place in Southeast Asian countries at frequent intervals. The question may be asked: How has the Government of China responded to the crisis situation? Has China been able to protect the interests of ethnic Chinese in Southeast Asian countries? The initial reaction of the Chinese government had been to launch strong protests to the concerned governments. On a few occasions, China appealed to the patriotic sentiments of the Chinese people and requested them to return to China. To evacuate them China sent ships to these countries, but most Chinese preferred to stay on in the Southeast Asian countries. On one occasion, in 1979, the Government of China resorted to punitive military expedition against Vietnam. The reasons for Chinese military action were a combination of several factors: the growing friendship between Hanoi and Moscow, Vietnamese intervention in Cambodia and the forcible ejection of the Hoa people from Vietnam. But the conclusion is inescapable. Whenever and wherever China adopted a strong policy in support of the ethnic Chinese – in Federation of Malaya in 1952, in Indonesia in 1959 and 1965, in Burma and Cambodia in 1966 during the Cultural Revolution and in 1979 in Vietnam – Beijing could not fulfil its objectives. It resulted in strains in China's bilateral relations with these countries. What is more, it made the ethnic Chinese more vulnerable.

Southeast Asian countries have been undergoing remarkable economic transformation during recent years, though the economic miracle suffered serious reverses on a few occasions. What is the role of the Indian minority groups in this economic miracle? The sad fact must be underlined that their role has been negligible. Though the Indian Chettiars played a significant role in the economic development during colonial rule, they preferred to bring back their wealth to India rather than grow roots in the region. The position of the Indians in Malaysia can be understood from the fact that they owned only 1.0 per cent of the national wealth in the 1970s; it went up to 1.5 per cent in the 1980s and it has come down to 1.3 per cent during recent years. While the Malays have improved their status as a result of government intervention, the Chinese still continue to dominate the economy. The Indians remain the Cinderella children of Malaysia. As N.J. Colleta has written, 'Ignored by Government policy, hidden from mainstream Malaysian society, the Indian labour force indeed becomes Malaysia's forgotten people'. The position of the Indian minority in Myanmar is equally pathetic. As Singhvi Committee report mentions, 'A majority of the present day Indian community in Myanmar is not well off. . . . Most of the PIOs are engaged in jobs like domestic help, mechanics and construction workers, while others are engaged in petty trade.' Indian faculty members dominated the education scene during the British period, 'but today there are hardly any Indian students and teachers in Burmese universities'.

ROLE OF ETHNIC CHINESE AND ETHNIC INDIANS IN ECONOMIC DEVELOPMENT OF CHINA AND INDIA

Rapid economic transformation that has taken place in China since Deng Xiao Ping assumed power has been facilitated by the capital investment of the ethnic Chinese living abroad. Detailed statistics are not available but according to informed observers nearly 70 per cent of the foreign direct investment that has gone into China is attributed to the ethnic Chinese living abroad. The contribution made by the Singapore leaders, especially Lee Kuan Yew and Dr. Goh Keng Swee, needs special mention. The Chinese government realized that viewing ethnic Chinese as citizens of China will not serve any purpose and gave up that stance. They were treated as citizens of the countries in which they have settled. Those who have not taken the citizenship of host countries were treated as Chinese nationals. They were advised to abide by the rules and regulations of the host countries. The ethnic Chinese were required to have passports and get visa from Chinese embassies. Equally interesting, the ambivalent policy of party-to-party relations and government-to-government relations was given up.

In his frequent meetings with Deng Xiao Ping, Lee Kuan Yew pointed out that PRC could gain immensely if the capital and entrepreneurial skills of the ethnic Chinese was mobilized for the economic betterment of China. The fact that both Deng and Lee were Hakkas further cemented their friendship. To quote Lee Kuan Yew from his memoirs:

> I told Deng over dinner in 1978 that we, Singapore Chinese, were the descendants of illiterate landless peasants from Guangdeng and Fujian in South China, whereas the scholars, Mandarins and literati had stayed and left their progeny in China. There was nothing that Singapore had done which China could not do, and do better.

Deng Xiao Ping was impressed by the progress that Singapore had made and the orderliness and discipline that chracterized Singapore work ethics. He wanted to replicate the Singapore model in China and invited Goh Keng Swee to advise him on the establishment of export promotion zones.

But there is an apparent danger lurking in China's relations with the ethnic Chinese in Southeast Asia. Can the relations between Beijing and ethnic Chinese be confined only to the economic level? What happens if PRC mobilizes the support of ethnic Chinese for political ends? In this connection it should be mentioned that when the Olympic torch was being taken around the world before the Beijing Olympics, many European countries saw angry protests against China on the issue of human rights violations. But when the Olympic torch reached Southeast Asia ethnic Chinese rallied behind China and held demonstrations in Kuala Lumpur, Bangkok, Jakarta and Saigon. The Chinese prime minister congratulated the ethnic Chinese for displaying their patriotism towards China. It did not lead to any strains in China's bilateral relations because on the issue of Olympic Games the Southeast Asian governments were on the side of China. But on possible issues of dissonance if the ethnic Chinese support China against the local governments the xenophobic nature of indigenous nationalism is likely to come to the fore and harm the interests of both China and the ethnic Chinese. During the recent South China Sea crisis it should be underlined that there was violence against Chinese community in Vietnam and Beijing had to send ships to evacuate them.

Singapore, during recent years, has emerged as the top source of foreign direct investment, investing 5.9 billion US $, which is about one fourth of the total FDI. How much of it comes from ethnic

Indians in Southeast Asia is a moot question. As pointed out earlier, majority of ethnic Indians are not economically well off and do not have the capital and technical knowhow to invest in India. But the capital and enterprise of richer Indians can be mobilized. In this connection it should be mentioned that the richest Malaysian is of Indian origin. The capital of the ethnic Chinese have to be attracted to India. What is more, Chinese entrepreneurial skill can be mobilized for infrastructure development, development of ports and modernization of the aviation sector. What acts as a stumbling block is the big hiatus between promise and implementation. The Government of India must immediately set its house in order so that India can absorb right lessons from the economic transformation that has taken place in Southeast Asian countries.

CONCLUSION

What are the future prospects of ethnic Chinese and ethnic Indians living in Southeast Asian countries? The future would depend upon the goodwill, cooperation and the measures that would be taken to integrate them into host societies. What gives hope is the remarkable resilience displayed by the Chinese and the Indian communities in Southeast Asia.

PART VI

The Road Ahead: Imperative of Interdependence

CHAPTER 17

The Past, Present and Future of India's Ties with its Eastern Neighbourhood

G. PARTHASARATHY*

With its shores washed by the waters of the Indian Ocean, India has historically maintained trade and civilizational ties in an area ranging from the shores of Africa and the Gulf of Oman to its west, to the Straits of Malacca and beyond to its east. Mercifully, its history is not burdened by moves for conquest and domination beyond its shores. Trade ties flourished across India's western shores with countries in the Arab World and East Africa. The great Semitic religions – Judaism, Christianity and Islam – came to India through trade ties, or through refugees fleeing persecution in their homelands. The western land borders of the country, however, faced foreign invasions from across the Hindu Kush Mountains from Afghanistan, Iran, the Arab world and Central Asia. At the same time, centuries of interaction with its north-western neighbourhood left a lasting impact on Indian national life, particularly in northern India.

India's interaction across its eastern neighbourhood was, however, qualitatively different from its historical experiences with countries to its west. Trade links with Myanmar, Thailand, Cambodia and Vietnam expanded from the first century BC. Indian cultural, religious and spiritual influence, based on Vedic (Hindu) texts and Buddhist culture and philosophy, gained growing acceptance and influence in Myanmar, Thailand, Indonesia, Malaysia, Laos and Cambodia,

* Amb. G. Parthasarathy, Former Ambassador of India to Myanmar, High Commissioner to Pakistan and Australia and Joint Secretary in Prime Minister's Office.

together with Buddhist architectural and artistic creations. Indian cultural traditions including dance and music were creatively absorbed in the Indonesian islands of Sumatra, Java, Bali and Sulawesi and extended even to the Philippines. Being amongst the first to free itself from colonial shackles, India played an active role in Indonesia's struggle to end Dutch colonialism and set the stage for progressive decolonization to its east.

While one would have expected India's ties with its Southeast Asian neighbourhood to thrive in the immediate aftermath of independence and the Bandung Conference of 1955, this did not happen, as the entire region got dragged into the vortex of Cold War rivalries. Differences grew not only within the region itself, but also impacted the fashioning of India's own ties with its eastern neighbours. Moreover, whereas the original members of ASEAN moved quickly towards developing market economies, India chose the path of developing a 'socialistic pattern' of society, marked by a quest for 'self-reliance' through a process of 'import substitution'. This resulted not only in a decline in India's share of world trade, but also led to ASEAN members outpacing India in rates of economic growth and excelling over India in human development indicators.

The advent of the Cold War complicated diplomatic relations between India and ASEAN members even before ASEAN was formed. The association of some ASEAN members with SEATO and involvement in the American war in Vietnam was accompanied by India playing an independent and non-aligned role, often viewed with suspicion by the US and its allies in the International Control Commission. The takeover of Tibet by the Peoples' Liberation Army of China in 1949 led to a situation when, for the first time, India's north-eastern frontiers were vulnerable to an attack from across the Himalayas. Differences on demarcation of the Sino-Indian border escalated tensions between India and China, resulting in a short, sharp and serious border conflict in 1962. India moved strategically closer to the Soviet Union, while the founding members of the ASEAN were clearly inclined towards Washington, as they moved towards setting up the institutions for greater regional cooperation in Southeast Asia. Moreover, as the Nixon-Mao entente led to a strategic convergence between the US, China and ASEAN members over the Vietnamese-led overthrow of the Pol Pot regime in Cambodia, India and the ASEAN found themselves on opposite sides over developments in Indo-China.

The end of the Cold War saw a remarkable turnaround in India's policies towards its eastern neighbourhood. The Indian economy went through an unprecedented economic crisis marked by spiralling inflation, falling growth rates and fast depleting foreign exchange reserves in 1990. With the collapse of the Soviet Union, India lost its largest trading, economic and strategic partner. The realization dawned on India that its past economic policies had to be discarded and a process of economic restructuring and liberalization embarked upon. The architect of these changes, then Prime Minister P.V. Narasimha Rao realized that for the Indian economy to grow rapidly, a process of closer economic cooperation and integration with the fast growing economies of East and Southeast Asia was imperative, even as economic liberalization proceeded. This new orientation was what Narasimha Rao characterized as India's new 'Look East' policy (LEP).

As a first step in its LEP, the quest began for a closer partnership with the members of ASEAN, with whom India had no bilateral political differences, or land and maritime border disputes. Moreover, centuries of links with the ASEAN states had been marked by cordiality and shared religious and spiritual experiences and not by any animosities or fears. India's 'Look East' also coincided with a desire by Thailand to 'Look West' and with a new military regime in neighbouring Myanmar – which shares a 1,640-km land border with India – that was seeking to end over forty years of economic isolation. Narasimha Rao's interest in Look East was complemented by his high regard for Singapore's elder statesman Lew Kwan Yew, who, in turn, saw benefit in expanding cooperation with a newly-emerging India. Singapore played a crucial role in persuading some sceptics in ASEAN about the benefits of closer cooperation with India.

These imperatives led to India becoming a sectoral dialogue partner of ASEAN in 1992, with the relationship upgraded to full dialogue partnership in December 1995.This relationship was further upgraded to one involving annual ASEAN-India summit meetings during the annual ASEAN Summit in Phnom Penh in 2002. This move occurred after some concerns in ASEAN, following India's May 1998 nuclear tests, were assuaged. The ASEAN states are members of the 1997 Southeast Asian Nuclear Weapons Free Zone Treaty (SEANWFZ), whose provisions are open for endorsement by the five Nuclear Weapons States, so designated by the NPT. Despite professions of understanding and respect for provisions of this treaty, none of the five 'established' nuclear weapons states have signed the protocol to accede to the provisions of the treaty, quite evidently because of reservations regarding its application to continental shelves and disputes over the South China Sea. While India was not required to do so, it nevertheless expressed its readiness to respect the provisions of the treaty in 1999.

In the early years of its association with ASEAN, India focused attention primarily and almost exclusively on promoting its economic integration with ASEAN members. It followed a similar approach on closer economic integration with genuine market economies like Japan and South Korea. India also sought growing economic interaction with China. Its bilateral trade with China has rapidly expanded, albeit with a growing and perhaps unsustainable trade deficit. Progress was also recorded in cooperation with ASEAN members in combating international terrorism and in extending and expanding bilateral ties with the military establishments of individual ASEAN members.

Given its satellite launch and aero-space capabilities, India can expand cooperation with its ASEAN partners in areas of satellite launching and communications. Bilateral trade with ASEAN members rose significantly, from a mere $12.1 billion in 2003 to $74.9 billion in 2011. A target of $200 billion has been set for ASEAN-India trade by 2022. Progress in boosting foreign direct investment has, however, been uneven and some would aver disappointing. It is, however, expected that as the Indian economy recovers from the downturn it experienced between 2011 and 2013, the prospects for a substantial increase in FDI are bright. While India and ASEAN concluded signed a Free Trade Agreement on trade in goods at the Bangkok Summit in August 2009, the two sides agreed at the ASEAN India Commemorative Summit in December 2012 that an Agreement of Trade in Services and Investments would be finalized and signed in 2014 after ratification by ASEAN member states. Tourism has, in the meantime, also grown substantially.

India's dialogue with ASEAN has included steps for improving connectivity through Myanmar. The implementation of the India-Myanmar-Thailand trilateral highway linking Moreh in India's Manipur state with Mae Sot in Thailand has moved forward with the construction of a road linking Moreh with Tamu and Kalemyo in Myanmar. Moreover, a strategic corridor linking India's landlocked north-eastern states with the Sittwe port in Myanmar, designated as the 'Kaladan Multimodal Transport Corridor', is now under implementation, though it must be acknowledged that progress on this project has been tardy and slow. Discussions have also commenced on the trilateral India-Myanmar-Thailand highway to be extended to Laos, Cambodia and Vietnam. The strategic importance of Myanmar as a link between South and Southeast Asia and between ASEAN and SAARC has been underlined by the establishment of the BIMSTEC grouping linking the littoral and landlocked states of the Bay of Bengal in a sub-regional economic grouping designed to promote trade, investment and communications. Nepal, Bhutan, Bangladesh, India, Myanmar, Thailand and Sri Lanka are members of the BIMSTEC.

Going beyond ASEAN, India has a vital interest in the security of sea lanes beyond the Indian Ocean, in the South China Sea, through which over 44 per cent of its trade flows traverse. India has historically enjoyed a very warm relationship with Japan. India was one of those few countries whose representative opposed provisions in post-war agreements indicting Japan as being unequal and symbolizing a relationship between victors and the vanquished. Relations between India and Japan were cordial and correct throughout the Cold War. Economic ties with Japan have steadily expanded in recent years, with Japan dominating the automobile manufacturing industry in India. Japan is now emerging as India's most important partner in the development of freight and industrial corridors across the country. The New Delhi Metro Rail, built with Japanese assistance, is expected to be the key to India having one of the largest metro networks in the world. The 'Western Dedicated Freight Corridor', the 'Delhi-Mumbai Industrial Corridor' with eight new industrial townships, and the 'Chennai-Bangalore Industrial Corridor', are all mega-projects being undertaken with financing and collaboration from Japan. These projects are expected to transform the industrial landscape of India in the next decade.

New Delhi's security ties with Tokyo have also grown steadily in recent years. A bilateral security pact was inked in 2008, following an expression of resolve to strengthen strategic and global partnership, which was formally established in 2006. The National Security establishments of the two countries have agreed to regular high-level consultations. Japan has participated in the annual India-US Joint Naval exercises, both in the Indian Ocean and off Okinawa. There have also been regular India-Japan bilateral naval exercises off the shores of India and in the South China Sea. Moreover, there are now possibilities of Japan selling defence equipment to India. The expectation is that as India liberalizes its procedures and regulations on foreign direct investment, Japan would emerge as a major investment partner in high-tech and defence-related industries.

Japan is the only country with whom India has a partnership involving meetings at high official levels in which representatives of both the defence and foreign affairs establishments jointly meet. China has, on occasions, voiced concerns about growing defence ties between India and Japan. New Delhi has responded by noting that it would be ready to have joint exercises with China in both the Indian Ocean off India's shores and in the South China Sea, off the shores of China. It appears evident from China's reluctance to accept proposals for joint naval exercises off the coast of India that Beijing would like to be very careful in not raising concerns in its 'all weather friend' Pakistan, given the nature of its close military, nuclear and missile partnership with India's western neighbour. Economic ties with South Korea have also grown rapidly in recent years with the signing of a Comprehensive Economic Cooperation Agreement (CECA).

The signing of the CECA with Japan and South Korea and the extension of the Free Trade Agreement with ASEAN to cover services also, has set the stage for closer integration of the Indian economy with those of ASEAN, Japan and South Korea. China has similarly concluded FTAs with ASEAN and New Zealand. While there has been a proposal for a FTA between India and China, there are concerns in India on the need to proceed with caution in finalizing an FTA with China, given the huge trade deficit that India has with it, and opinions about the need for more transparency of China's trade and economic policies.

In the meantime, an ASEAN-led effort is underway since the ASEAN Phnom Penh Summit in 2012, to develop a Regional Comprehensive Economic Partnership (RCEP) covering India, members of ASEAN, China, Japan, South Korea, Australia and New Zealand. While the ASEAN-led RCEP is still in its very initial stages, the US has embarked on a Trans-Pacific Partnership (TPP). Brunei, Chile, New Zealand and Singapore were original signatories to the TPP in June 2005. The United States has since been joined also by Australia, Peru, Vietnam, Malaysia, Mexico, Canada and Japan, in negotiations for concluding the proposed TPP. Taiwan and South

Korea expressed an interest in joining the grouping in September 2013. Despite initial reservations, China has not ruled out joining the TPP. While a high degree of secrecy has been maintained about the negotiations on the TPP, there are reports which suggest substantial focus on issues like Intellectual Property Rights and government procurement, which go well beyond existing WTO provisions. Given its present economic and developmental priorities, many in India believe that the country would find it difficult to agree to these provisions. It would, however, be difficult to predict just now how India will approach issues of acceding to either the CECA or TPP.

While the focus of what Hillary Clinton described as the Indo-Pacific Region was initially primarily on economic cooperation, there is now a considerable focus of attention on security issues, especially after the establishment of the annual East Asia Summit. The end of the Deng Xiaoping era in China has been followed by an economically vibrant and militarily robust China flexing its muscles across its entire neighbourhood. Having added an aircraft carrier to its fleet to project power, and with a determination to expand its fleet of aircraft carriers, China clearly intends to expand its strategic reach across the Pacific and Indian Oceans. It firmly defines its maritime frontiers unilaterally in the South China Sea, under its 'Nine Dotted Line'. It has militarily seized the Paracel islands from Vietnam and claimed the Spratly Islands, overriding objections from the Philippines, Brunei, Malaysia, Taiwan and Vietnam to conform to its 'Nine Dotted Line'. It has used force to seize the Mischief Reef, located barely 51 km from the Philippines, but 590 km from its Hainan Island. China's extraordinary claims on its maritime borders do not, according to many analysts, conform to the provisions of the UN Convention of the Laws of the Seas (UNCLOS).

China's assertion of its Air Defence Identification Zone (ADIZ) has been challenged by Japan, South Korea and Taiwan. The US has challenged the legality of the ADIZ by sending unarmed B-52 bombers into the zone. But US commercial aircraft have been advised to observe China's requirements. Japan and South Korea have, however, refused to comply with Chinese demands. Chinese threats of overflying the disputed Senkaku Islands have been have been met by Japan scrambling F-15 fighters. The South Koreans have proclaimed: 'We expressed deep regret and reaffirmed our jurisdictional rights to the waters surrounding the (submerged rock) Leodo, would not be affected by neighbouring states' air defence zones'. The Chinese announcement of its ADIZ has exacerbated the existing disputes with South Korea over fishing rights in the Yellow Sea.

US Vice-President Joseph Biden has expressed his solidarity with allies Japan and South Korea over China's maritime boundary claims during his visits to Tokyo and Seoul. The US has also sent P-8 Poseidon Maritime Patrol aircraft to Japan. China's aim is to get Japan to accept that the Senkaku Islands are disputed territory. According to the Hong Kong-based *Asia Weekly*, China sees its maritime boundary in the East China Sea as stretching from the southern-most Japanese Island towards the East Coast of Taiwan and joining the South China Sea. China is now clearly seeking unchallenged access to the Pacific Ocean. In 2009, the Commander of the US Pacific Fleet Admiral Timothy Keating told Indian interlocutors that one of his Chinese counterparts had suggested to him when China acquired aircraft carriers that the US should leave maritime security in the Western Pacific and Indian Oceans to the Chinese navy, with the US confining itself to security of the Eastern Pacific.

The growing presence of the Chinese navy and Beijing's efforts to secure berthing facilities across the Indian Ocean do cause some concern in India. India's own maritime capabilities are being strengthened with the induction of nuclear submarines and aircraft carriers. India has a natural and legitimate interest in ensuring freedom of navigation in the South China Sea, through which over 44 per cent of its international trade traverses. This requires New Delhi to take a greater and continuing interest in joining efforts to see that its freedom of navigation through the international waters of the South China Sea is not adversely affected. There is broad support in India for emphasizing the need for all concerned to ensure that the provisions of the UNCLOS are respected and serve as the basis for resolving differences over maritime boundaries. This has been and will likely remain the basis for India's approach to relations with its ASEAN partners and in its participation in East Asia Summit meetings.

The first years of the twenty-first century were marked by distinct improvement in New Delhi's relations with Beijing. Despite differences over the demarcation of its borders with China, both sides endeavoured to ensure that peace and tranquillity prevailed in the border areas. The high point of efforts to resolve differences on the border issue was the agreement between prime ministers Manmohan Singh and Wen Jiabao in 2005 on the 'Guiding Principles' for a border settlement. These principles state: 'The (Sino-Indian) boundary should be along well defined and easily identifiable geographical features, to be mutually agreed upon'. Moreover, there was specific provision that in arriving at a border settlement, both sides will take into consideration the presence of settled populations. This was tacit acknowledgement that there could be no change in the status of places like the monastery town of Tawang, to which China lays claims.

India's claims, based on historical data, fulfil all the provisions of the 2005 agreement. On its eastern frontiers with China, across the state of Arunachal Pradesh, the Indian view is that the border lies along the watershed of the high Himalayan peaks. On its western borders with China, India has asserted that the border lies on the Indus River Watershed, with the Karakoram Mountains forming the natural boundary. Barely had the ink on the 2005 agreement dried when China upped the ante laying claim to the entire state of Arunachal Pradesh. Intrusions by Chinese forces across what was commonly accepted as being the 'Line of Control' have periodically escalated tensions. While any spillover of these intrusions has been contained by inter-governmental mechanisms to de-escalate the situation, New Delhi does see these incidents as part of a growingly assertive approach by Beijing to issues pertaining to its claims on its maritime and land borders.

India realizes that the strategic environment has changed substantially since the days it embarked on its 'Look East' policies over two decades ago. Happily, with its maritime frontiers on its eastern shores firmly settled, there are no differences on border issues with its ASEAN partners. Trade, travel and investment ties are steadily growing, though many within India and its ASEAN partners will agree that much more could be done to promote a more intensive dialogue on issues from terrorism and piracy to trade, industry, tourism and environment. Moreover, India's ties with partners in northeast Asia, notably Japan and South Korea are rapidly expanding. India has welcomed the readiness of the present generation of Japan's leaders like prime ministers Koizumi and Shinzo Abe to play a more proactive role in fashioning a new security architecture and a stable balance of power in Asia. Japan is seen as a key partner in coming years for the development of infrastructure, transport and industrial corridors and investment in high-tech industries in the country. Moreover, like some of its ASEAN partners, many in India see considerable potential for the development of economic cooperation with Taiwan in select sectors of industrial development.

Across the shores of what former Secretary of State Hillary Clinton described as the 'Indo-Pacific', India sees its 'Look East' policies in coming years as being marked by exciting opportunities for growing economic integration, while resorting to imaginative diplomacy to meet the challenges posed by a growingly powerful and assertive China. While many had predicted that the world order after the collapse of the Soviet Union would be characterized by a United States-dominated unipolar world, what appears to be emerging is a growingly multipolar world order.

CHAPTER 18

The Evolution and Expansion of India's Look East Policy

PRAMIT PAL CHAUDHURI*

India's Look East policy (LEP) began as an attempt to develop an economic relationship with Southeast Asia. Over the years, however, it has slowly grown in both the nature of the economic relationship, the geographical area that it has covered, and increasingly includes security and strategic concerns as well. If Singapore was the focus of the LEP when it was initiated, today the greatest potential of the policy is the burgeoning multi-faceted relationship between India and Japan.

LOOK EAST POLICY'S FIRST PHASE: 1992 TO 2002

Prime Minister P.V. Narasimha Rao announced the LEP in 1992. It had a clear and unambitious agenda of developing a trade and investment relationship between India and the 'tiger economies' of the Association of Southeast Asian Nations; the economically booming nations of Singapore, Malaysia, Thailand and Indonesia were of special interest.

The LEP also reflected Prime Minister Rao's desire to adopt a new market-friendly and export-oriented model of development. The LEP was an external manifestation of the economic liberalization policy adopted by Rao and his then finance minister, Manmohan Singh.

Singh acknowledged this years later when he was prime minister.

* Pramit Pal Chaudhuri, Foreign Editor, *Hindustan Times*; Member, National Security Advisory Board; Member, Aspen Study Group of India; and Senior Associate, Rhodium Group, New York.

The LEP, he said, 'was not merely an external economic policy; it was also a strategic shift in India's vision of the world and India's place in the evolving global economy. . .' (Prime Minister Manmohan Singh, address to Asia Society Corporate Conference, Mumbai, 18 March 2006).

However, the LEP had a limited agenda because the Indian economy remained highly uncompetitive in the international trade arena and struggled to find value-added products to sell to the more advanced economies of Southeast Asia.

There were other developments that stalled progress in the LEP. The Asian financial crisis of 1996, for example, put a question mark over the ASEAN model of development. It also made the region more inward-looking, making outreach to India a lower Southeast Asian priority. This was then followed by the 1998 Pokhran II nuclear tests carried out by India. Though they were eventually lifted, the tests resulted in international sanctions being imposed on India and New Delhi being temporarily politically isolated. But the foreshortened Look East vision was largely the consequence of India's weak economy.

LOOK EAST POLICY'S SECOND PHASE: 2002 TO 2008

The 'second phase' of the LEP was declared by the then Indian foreign minister, Yashwant Sinha. While he was largely interested in defining the policy in a manner that differentiated itself from the previous Rao government, 2002 did mark a shift.

The two key developments were an expansion of the geographical area which the LEP covered so that it included what would generally be called Asia-Pacific – the arc of countries running from Japan to Australia. Sinha said in 2003, 'The first phase of India's Look East policy was ASEAN-centred and focussed primarily on trade and investment linkages. The new phase of this policy is characterized by an expanded definition of East, extending from Australia to East Asia, with ASEAN at its core' (Indian Foreign Minister Yashwant Sinha, 'Resurgent India in Asia', speech at Harvard University, US, 29 September 2003). The then Indian prime minister, Atal Behari Vajpayee, expansively spoke of an Asian Economic Community modelled after the European Union in 2003.

India's formal entry to the East Asian Summit in 2005 was the highlight of the second phase of the Look East, symbolically tying India to the larger Asia-Pacific.

The second was the introduction of a security element to the policy as India expanded its military contacts and counter-terrorism cooperation with these same countries. Sinha cited protecting sea-lanes and coordinating anti-terror actions. In his Harvard speech he spoke of how 'the military contacts and joint exercises that India launched with ASEAN states on a low-key basis in the early 1990s are now expanding into full-fledged cooperation' (ibid.).

The entry of Myanmar into ASEAN in 1991 also opened another security door. 'In recent years, New Delhi has openly indicated that the development of India's Northeast, the containment of insurgencies there are vital interests and a pillar of its Look East policy' (Archana Pandya and David Malone, 'India's Asia Policy: A Late Look East', ISAS Brief No. 2, Institute of South Asian Studies, National University of Singapore, 25 August 2010).

India also expanded its naval outreach into the South China Sea from 2000 onwards, made its first carrier visit to Southeast Asia in 2005, held its first multilateral naval exercises in Northeast Asia in 2007 besides impressing Southeast Asia and the US with its naval humanitarian actions during the 2004 Indian Ocean tsunami crisis.

LOOK EAST POLICY'S THIRD PHASE: 2008 TO THE PRESENT

What defines this phase is the expanded strategic element to the LEP; while economics remained important, security relationships widened. The past few years have seen all of this being embedded by India in a much larger and more ambitious strategic vision. Earlier much of the engagement between India and the other Asian states to its east was a fragmented mix of bilateral initiatives and multilateral activity.

At the heart of this new LEP is a growing Indian concern at the unpredictable and aggressive behaviour it has experienced from China. And the primary consequences is the burgeoning relationship between India and Japan.

Tokyo's entry into the picture elevates the LEP to a different level. It is not merely that Japan, even after decades of stagnant growth and deflation, is wealthier and technologically more advanced than any of the Southeast Asian states. It is also because what Japan's leadership has envisaged is the restructuring of India's economy, including the building of world-class infrastructure and the creation of the export-oriented manufacturing sector that India lacks, and the expansion of its strategic capabilities in areas like weapons manufacture.

Prime Minister Singh, his aides often pointed out, was a long-standing admirer of Japan and added the adjective 'transformational' to his descriptions of India's relations with only two countries: the US and Japan.

Singh declared during Japanese Prime Minister Shinzo Abe's visit to India in January 2014, 'Japan is at the heart of India's Look East policy. It is also a key partner in our economic development and in our quest for a stable, peaceful, stable and prosperous Asia and the world.'

Early Divide. Indian diplomats who claim to have written the first proposals for a LEP say that Japan was always the ultimate target of the policy. Catching the attention and interest of Asia's first industrialized state and economically most advanced nation had always been difficult for India. New Delhi was a poor match for Tokyo given the economic disparities between the two countries, their different Cold War foreign policy fronts and simple geographical distance.

Japan was largely indifferent to even the 1991 economic opening up of India – bilateral trade moved from $3.5 billion to $3.8 billion between 1990 and 2000. Japanese firms found India a difficult business environment and unlike their South Korean counterparts declined to invest in India through much of the first few decades after economic liberalization. As strategic analyst C. Raja Mohan has written, 'Traditionally, India was not part of Japan's conception of Asia' (C. Raja Mohan, 'Is India an East Asian Power? Explaining New Delhi's Security Politics in the Western Pacific', ISAS Working Paper no. 81, Institute of South Asian Studies, National University of Singapore, 11 August 2009).

Abe's Turn. Prime Minister Abe has been probably the longest running and most enthusiastic advocate of a strong Indo-Japanese relationship. He enunciated his view of a common strategic environment, which he dubbed the 'Indo-Pacific' and described as 'the confluence of the two seas', in his first term as Japan's prime minister in a speech before the Indian parliament (Prime Minister Shinzo Abe, 'Confluence of the Two Seas, speech before Indian Parliament, 22 August 2007, http://www.mofa.go.jp/region/asia-paci/pmv0708/speech-2.html.

When he was re-elected with an overwhelming mandate in 2013, Abe immediately sought to implement this earlier policy. India converged in a number of ways with Abe's vision of the future of

Japan. One, because New Delhi had no Second World War legacy issues with Japan, it was the perfect government to legitimize Abe's plans to end the post-war legal and psychological limitations placed on Japan's military and foreign policy.

Two, Abe represented a consensus within the Japanese leadership, following the growing tensions with China over the Senkaku Islands dispute, that building up India as a great power would serve Japan's geopolitical interest to balance China.

Three, successive Japanese governments have seen considerable economic opportunity in helping build India's economic infrastructure and moving Japanese manufacturing plants to the subcontinent. In effect, say Japanese diplomats, it would amount to externalizing the economic stimulus packages that Tokyo had used in the past to revive growth. An estimated 40 per cent of the cost of an industrial corridor in India would go to orders in Japan itself, they say.

On the Ground. Signs of how Tokyo's interest in India is being converted into reality on the ground are growing thick and fast. On the military side, though India and Japan had begun holding naval exercises as early as 2000, it was in 2008 that the two countries signed a 'Joint Statement on the Advancement of the Strategic Global Partnership'. Until then, Japan had signed a similar agreement only with Australia.

India has also upgraded its bilateral naval exercises with Japan to the level it accords the US. India has also committed to buying Japan's first post-war arms export, the US-2 ShinMaywa seaplane, with an expectation that eventually this plane will be manufactured in India.

On the economic side, Japanese investment in India has been growing though India's own economic problems crimped such plans in the second term of the Singh prime ministership. However, Tokyo has extended support in other strategic ways: in the autumn of 2013 the Japanese Ministry of Finance proposed increasing a $15 billion currency to a larger $50 billion arrangement in a successful move to arrest a sudden and sharp fall in the exchange rate of the rupee (http://blogs.hindustantimes.com/foreign-hand/2014/01/31/how-japan-save-the-rupee/).

Another strategic decision was for Japan to use its overseas aid to help build highways, ports and smaller roads to develop India's physical connectivity with Southeast Asia, largely across the border between the northeastern states of India and Myanmar. Among the most dramatic of these projects is the so-called Trilateral Highway that was designed to connect India, Thailand and Myanmar but has since been expanded to bring Vietnam and Cambodia into its reach. These projects are quite overtly designed to reduce Southeast Asia's, and especially Myanmar's, dependence on the Chinese economy and provide an alternative to the comprehensive north-south-running infrastructure that China has built across Upper Burma and the Mekong Valley.

America Wobbles. A key driver in the closer Indo-Japanese relationship – and an unspoken reason why India is attempting to put a stronger strategic overlay to its LEP – is the uncertainties regarding the US.

Following the 2008-9 Lehman Brothers financial crisis and the US decision to withdraw from its twin wars of Iraq and Afghanistan, Washington became increasingly isolationist in its foreign policy stance.

US President Barack Obama with his determined focus on domestic reforms embodied this mindset but polls show it was also reflected among the broader US public. Obama, therefore, set out to develop a partnership with China that was designed to allow the US reduce its military and political commitments in the Asia-Pacific. This so-called G-2 policy unnerved US allies like Japan because it seemed to go hand-in-hand with increased Chinese aggressiveness towards them. The more Washington wooed Beijing, the more it seemed to embolden the Chinese to take a more hawkish position within the region.

Japan became particularly unhappy with the G-2 policy and under Abe it began to assert its own foreign policy, albeit within the US security structure. However, this concern converged with an equally strong Indian sentiment that the US's isolationist tendencies were undermining New Delhi's interests in Afghanistan-Pakistan and knocking down a common view of China that had been seen to underpin the Indo-US strategic partnership.

This combination of US passivity and Chinese aggression was recognized to provide India new avenues for expanding its ties in the region, with Japan being front and centre in this regard.

'We can also thank China's recent assertive behaviour for the strength of the partnerships that we have built with other powers in her vicinity. To some extent the success of our Look East policy is a result of this factor', said the then National Security Advisor Shiv

Shankar Menon in 2014. (Shiv Shankar Menon, India's National Security, 3rd Annual Foreign Policy and National Security Workshop, Institute of Defence Studies and Analysis, 7 May 2014.)

Rest of Asia. This did not mean that the LEP began to overlook India's relations with the ASEAN states. However, it would be correct to say Southeast Asia has begun to be overshadowed by what India has begun doing with Northeast Asia.

In the military sphere, and driven by the China conundrum facing all Asian countries, India signed a Joint Declaration on Strategic Partnership in 2007 with Vietnam.

The other major accomplishment was the signing of the 2009 India-ASEAN Free Trade Agreement which covered manufactured and agricultural goods. This has been partly marred by the failure of ASEAN to follow through with a second FTA that was supposed to provide India the services access that it wanted.

But the ASEAN is proving to have limited strategic capability, largely because its membership has become increasingly divided over how to handle the widening influence of Chinese power. Laos and Cambodia, say diplomats of various Asian countries, are effectively in Beijing's pocket. Vietnam and Indonesia are extremely bellicose about China. However, Malaysia takes a more benign view. ASEAN's internal divisions have meant that the strategic and foreign policy component of the organization's brief is shrinking.

CONCLUSION

The LEP of India, as has been mentioned, has developed an increasingly strategic element to its agenda. This has been spurred by concerns about Chinese power, equal concerns about the US security commitment to the Asia-Pacific, and the increase in Indian economic and military capacity.

The original economic focus of the LEP has hardly gone away, but many of the original accomplishments have become the economic *status quo* between India and Southeast Asia. The shift to investment and infrastructure connectivity is the new economic story – but it has strong overlays of strategic behaviour.

People's Daily, a state-owned Chinese newspaper, suggested that 'LEP' did not mean Look East Policy but perhaps 'Look to encircle China policy'. (Gayatri Lakshminarayan, India Looks East: Encircling China or Enlightened National Interest?, ISAS Brief No. 174, p. 3,

Institute of South Asian Studies, National University of Singapore, 10 November 2010.) This is an exaggeration, but it is safe to say that India's LEP has progressed well beyond merely 'looking'. It is a regional strategic policy that incorporates many facets and has, at its core, a desire to resist attempts by China to follow a path of ultranationalism. Such a policy is difficult and even more so when you are a country with a fledgling strategic culture and considerable domestic concerns.

CHAPTER 19

Towards a Revitalized Look East Policy

SUDHIR T. DEVARE*

An intensified engagement with Southeast and East Asia, re-discovery of this region or a Look East policy – all signify a new trend in India's foreign policy since the early 1990s. It marked a course correction which opened new policy options when the global centre of economic gravity started showing signs of a shift to the East. Geopolitically the timing was opportune, coincided as it did with the end of the Cold War and the emergence of the US as the only superpower (at that time) as also the continuing rise of China. Over the years India's interaction and involvement with this region has increased manifold. There is now institutionalized association at the bilateral and multilateral levels and progress in terms of a regular dialogue. The Look East policy as an instrument of the country's major foreign policy outlook is beginning to come of age.

This is also an appropriate time to evaluate if the above foreign policy direction adopted by India has delivered on its expectations. The foreign policy of any country has among its priority objectives the preservation and maintenance of its security and stability; economic progress and well-being of its people; and sustainable development within the framework of its socio-cultural values and traditions. For India, the East signifies a great deal. India has had civilizational links with this region. Today it is one of the most dynamic regions in terms of economic vitality and growth. Economic liberalization across the region, including in India and the process of globalization are already

* Amb. Sudhir T. Devare, former Secretary, Ministry of External Affairs, former Ambassador of India to Indonesia and the Republic of Korea and former Director-General, Indian Council of World Affairs (ICWA).

leading to a degree of economic integration between India and the countries of the East. Yet the level of integration so far is limited and India, for that matter the whole of South Asia, remains far behind its counterparts in Southeast or Northeast Asia in terms of production networks or supply chain linkages. At the same time the geopolitical situation in the Asia-Pacific continues to be volatile and fluid calling for close monitoring and adjustment of India's defence policies.While there is a broad acknowledgement among the countries of the East of the salience of the Indian Ocean in the politics and economics of the region, so far there is little evidence to suggest that the term 'Indo-Pacific' has come close to replacing 'Asia-Pacific'. Within the country itself the Look East approach seems to have fired imagination in only a few pockets or parts of the society. The northeastern part of the country which shares a common boundary and proximity to Southeast Asia remains far from being closely associated with the policy. Without the involvement of the northeast the whole Look East approach would come to naught. It is therefore about time to analyse in a candid and objective manner how and where the Look East approach has to evolve further and entrench itself in the overall policy calculus, be it external relations, defence, finance, trade, investment, education, culture or tourism. This policy can be expected to deliver on its objectives only if a holistic approach taking into account the totality of the above aspects is followed in its implementation.

A number of developments and factors have impacted and will continue to impact on India's policy to this region. Some of them include:

1. The current geopolitical situation in the region which is marked by an acute political rivalry, if not confrontation, between several regional and global powers. Ironically, this has occurred despite considerable and growing economic interdependence among them.
2. China's growing assertiveness vis-à-vis its neighbours and its aggressive position on the South China Sea issue. China's naval and diplomatic expansion to the Indian Ocean is also a matter of strategic significance.
3. The US which all along had an all-pervasive military and economic presence in the Asia-Pacific (though lately perceived by its allies in the region as a declining interest) has announced a 'rebalancing' or 'pivot' to Asia thus signalling its renewed

resolve for preparedness to deal with a changing politico-security landscape in the region.

4. Security Architecture in the Asia-Pacific: The evolving security architecture in the region which is premised on the needs of security and peace for all is expected to have deep implications in view of the unaccommodating and often confrontational positions of some of the powers in the region. India's stakes in a peaceful and secure environment in the Asia-Pacific and the adjacent Indian Ocean cannot be overemphasized.
5. Regionalism and Economic Integration: The relative success of regionalism in Southeast Asia and progress towards economic integration across the Asia-Pacific in the wake of globalization are positive stories on the Asia-Pacific canvas. The Asia-Pacific Economic Cooperation (APEC) and now the on-going negotiations for a Regional Comprehensive Economic Partnership (RCEP) and Trans-Pacific Partnership (TPP) are important landmarks. India is still not a member of APEC and is not participating in TPP negotiations. Their relevance and impact on India is a subject of considerable importance.
6. India's Look East policy has a major strategic value which has to be recognized within the country itself and for that it is necessary to acknowledge that the policy starts in India's own northeast region and also relates significantly to India's relations with its neighbours such as Bangladesh, Myanmar, Nepal, Bhutan and Sri Lanka. Connectivity has become a watchword which needs to be transformed into development partnership for which efficient implementation of external projects undertaken by India in neighbouring countries of Southeast and South Asia becomes an imperative need.

Over the past two decades India has established institutionalized links with countries of Southeast and East Asia. These linkages include the India-ASEAN Annual Summit meeting, ASEAN Regional Forum (ARF), ASEAN Defence Ministers' Meeting++, East Asia Summit (EAS), etc. India is also the founding member of sub-regional bodies such as BIMSTEC or Mekong-Ganga Cooperation. Besides in South Asia, India is the key player in SAARC. While membership of these regional and sub-regional organizations has enabled India to get closely associated with security and peace issues relating to the region and has also helped to develop closer economic ties there is need to assess if India's engagement so far as expressed in its Look East policy prepares the country to face the kind of challenges listed above. For India, security and peace in the Asia-Pacific is imperative. What happens in Afghanistan post-2014 or in the South China Sea or in the Indian Ocean region can have direct repercussions for India's own security. Any policy which India follows has therefore to help create a secure environment in India's immediate and extended neighbourhood. The Look East policy is expected to serve this very purpose.

CONFLICTS IN THE ASIA-PACIFIC REGION: CHALLENGES BEFORE ASEAN

For the past decade or so, the waters in the South China Sea (SCS) are troubled with China pressing its claims over the entire sea. China's assertive position through its nine-dash proposal with respect to sovereignty over the SCS and provocative actions including placing an oil rig in the Vietnamese economic zone has met with sharp reaction from the other five claimant states, especially Vietnam and the Philippines. The war of words and even skirmishes between the rival claimants have led to a deteriorating situation and an uneasy stalemate in the strategically crucial South China Sea through which vital supplies of oil and natural gas pass to major economies of the Asia-Pacific. India has major stakes in peaceful resolution of the conflict. A substantial proportion of India's trade passes through these waters. India also has oil and natural gas installations in the Vietnamese economic zone. India has made it clear that it believes in the universal rights of free and unimpeded navigation in the seas in accordance with the existing international law.

The growing tension between China and Japan over the disputed islands Senkaku/Diaou in the East China Sea/the Sea of Japan is another cause for anxiety since the two major powers show no sign of accommodation which does not augur well for peace and security in the region.

These developments pose a major challenge to India's policy in the East even as they seem to create divisions within ASEAN on the South China Sea issue. ASEAN is under considerable pressure as no unified position has been arrived at so far. Two years ago at Phnom Penh, the ASEAN for the first time failed to have a joint communique after the foreign ministers' meeting due to sharp differences among themselves on the SCS question. Clearly each of the ASEAN states sees its relationship with China through the prism of its own interest. Efforts to have a binding code of conduct between China and ASEAN have not succeeded despite there the 2002 Manila Declaration to that effect. Indonesia, not being directly involved in the conflict and as the largest country in ASEAN tried to bring about a diplomatic understanding in the last couple of years but could not succeed while China's aggressive position vis-à-vis the Philippines and Vietnam continues to prevail. In the circumstances, the much talked about 'centrality of ASEAN' in the regional arrangements, painstakingly and imaginatively crafted by ASEAN over several years is beginning to be questioned. This notion is actually the bedrock on which peace and security in the Asia-Pacific has been preserved and promoted since the end of the Cold War. Despite its military weakness ASEAN was able to bring together major powers including adversaries to a state of dialogue over the issues of war, peace and economic prosperity. India has all along stood for ASEAN's centrality acknowledging that her footprint in the Asia-Pacific was principally recognized by ASEAN which enabled her to be a participant in the ASEAN-led forums and dialogue partnerships.

EXPECTATIONS FROM INDIA

It is important to consider what contribution India can make to promote security and peace in the region. The countries of the region also have growing expectations from India. Clearly, most countries in the Asia-Pacific would not wish their region to be embroiled in any military conflagration. The costs of such extreme situation would be too high. Even among ASEAN states, some of which are the allies of the US or closely linked to the US defence arrangements, there is evident reluctance to be drawn into a military race. Yet they would not wish to be seen as totally hapless states unable to take any position, howsoever justified legally or morally, because of their weakness. Here India can have a role to play which need not be directed against any specific power. Some of the legitimate defence requirements of states in Southeast Asia can be met by India for which a number of possibilities have existed for a long time. Given the kind of 'security convergence' that exists between India and Southeast Asia it needs to be seen what form of defence cooperation can take shape between the two. There are defence cooperation agreements already signed between India and Indonesia, Vietnam, Singapore, Myanmar,

Thailand, the Philippines and Malaysia. However, the extent of cooperation is still limited except perhaps with Singapore in the naval field and Vietnam with respect to training. Joint production of naval crafts, military aircraft and helicopters, and small arms could be within the scope of joint production. Some of us had equipment of common origin. For example, MIG or Sukhoi aircraft of Russian origin are with Malaysia, Indonesia, Vietnam and India; however, no serious effort has been made to go into collaboration. Perhaps this was because of various prejudices during the Cold War period when India and ASEAN often found themselves on the opposite sides. What happened in the case of aircraft also applied to ships or submarines of British or German or Russian origin. In the meantime local defence industries of ASEAN states like Singapore, Indonesia, Thailand, Malaysia have progressed. Their defence outlays in terms of GDP percentage though relatively small are today sizeable and like India's, are primarily spent on imports from abroad. In India, with a new emphasis on greater private sector participation in the defence sector as well as incentives for foreign direct investment in the defence field (with 49 per cent FDI and in certain high-technology sectors even 100 per cent investment being permitted) it is hoped that indigenous defence production and technology up-gradation would improve. With that there should be much greater scope for collaboration with defence industries in Southeast Asia. This may be possible even with Japan or South Korea which have advanced defence industries though they may have to fulfil their military alliance obligations wherever necessary. It may be recalled that a South Korean shipyard had entered into a collaboration with the Indian Navy as early as in 1987 for joint production of offshore patrol vessels (OPVs).

Maritime security in the Pacific and Indian Oceans has become a primary concern in the region. In view of the continuing tensions in the South China Sea and East Sea between China and five claimant countries of Southeast Asia, and China and Japan there is a growing feeling in the region that India with its large navy might be persuaded to play a more active strategic role. In India, we have often talked of our maritime security zone extending from the Gulf of Aden in the west to the Straits of Malacca and beyond in South China Sea in the east. As stated earlier, India's firm and unequivocal position with respect to openness of international waters for free and unimpeded navigation in accordance with the international law is itself a helpful assurance to the countries in Southeast Asia which are assiduously working towards a binding code of conduct in the face of China's coercive stand on the issue. This would need to be demonstrated from time to time in specific action. For example, India should remain unmoved with regard to its right of exploration and extraction of oil and natural gas in the blocs in Vietnam's economic zone which are contested by China.

THE ROLE OF THE INDIAN NAVY

The Indian Navy is regularly engaged in joint naval exercises with several countries of the Asia-Pacific including China. This is no doubt a useful and necessary expression of showing goodwill as well as deep rooted interests in the region.This practice should be continued and further widened. The navy may also carry on with its coordinated patrolling with neighbouring countries like Indonesia, Thailand, Malaysia, Singapore, etc. Equally importantly India could come up with proposals to support the needs of the littoral countries for keeping the sea lanes of communication safe and secure. For example, under MALSINDO (Malaysia, Singapore and Indonesia naval arrangement to keep the Malacca Straits free and safe) the littoral states are keeping the crucial waterway in the Malacca Straits secure. India's offer of assistance should help these littoral states a great deal.

Similarly, India might also consider assisting Indonesia, another important and friendly neighbour to keep the Straits of Sunda and Lombok safe for navigation. This would go a long way in securing the Indo-Pacific region towards unhindered movement for international shipping. India has a certain geo-strategic advantage in the Indian Ocean due to its location which straddles the SLOCs passing from the Persian Gulf to the Straits of Malacca through which the vital supplies of oil and natural gas pass to the industrialized economies of Northeast and Southeast Asia. This indirectly places a role and responsibility on India with regard to the safety of the ocean space around itself, be it with respect to free passage for shipping; for anti-piracy, counter-terrorism or natural disasters. During the tsunami disaster in 2004 the Indian navy was able to render timely help to Indonesia, Sri Lanka and Thailand. India has extensive interests in the southern Indian Ocean and has built close maritime relations with Mauritius, South Africa and the eastern seaboard of Africa. The Indian navy is a force multiplier and its systematic modernization and expansion is a manifestation of India's well-calibrated policy to the East.

THE CHINA FACTOR

Given the fact that China remains and would continue to be a key factor in India's engagement with the East, it is important to keep in mind that India's own management of its relations with China will impact extensively on the Look East approach. It will not be an exaggeration to state that the progress (or the lack of it) will have considerable effect on the overall security scenario in the Indo-Pacific. China's aggressive build-up including strategic roads or railways in the countries surrounding India or its developing ports in what is often described as 'strings of pearls strategy' in the Indian Ocean is a manifestation of a certain degree of competitiveness for influence in the region. India also had the opportunity to develop some of the strategically located ports in the Indian Ocean and can be in a position to do so even now. How does India respond to the Chinese moves and indeed deals with China' s overall policy towards India will largely determine India's standing in the Asia-Pacific or the larger Indo-Pacific. It remains to be seen if and how the upcoming interactions between China and India at the highest level set the stage for a dialogue based on mutual respect and understanding. If a partnership howsoever unsteady and uncertain to start with, indeed develops between India and China, it could go a long way in creating a more positive landscape in the region.

ASIA-PACIFIC SECURITY ARCHITECTURE

Against this backdrop the question that arises is what kind of security architecture does India envisage in the Asia-Pacific which will be conducive to its Look East policy. Today, there are half a dozen major powers which are simultaneously rising or have already risen in the region. The US has remained the preponderant power with its military alliances in the region even as China has continued to grow exponentially in economic and military terms. For the past two decades countries in the region have benefitted from a relative peace or rather absence of major conflicts. Interestingly, strategic ambivalence is the underlying principle which seems to have been followed by all of them in which they have not allowed their historic rivalries or political animosities to come in the way of economic interdependence. It is this kind of ambivalence or adjustments in relationship, especially between the US and China, that largely has been a balancing factor so far. The recent US decision of 'rebalancing or pivot to Asia' while renewing and strengthening its presence in the Asia-Pacific keeps its multi-dimensional and complex relationship with China on an even keel.

In the evolution of a security architecture in the Asia-Pacific, India could be an important interlocutor. If the differences between China on the one hand and several other countries like Japan, Vietnam, the Philippines on the other continue to widen or the US 'rebalancing' does not progress well, regional balance of power would need to be preserved collectively in which India could contribute usefully. India has strategic partnership with a number of countries in the region including the United States, Japan, Vietnam and others. It also enjoys a cooperative dialogue with ASEAN. India's own management of its difficult relationship with China could be a useful element in this regard.

ECONOMIC DIMENSION

In the initial years of India's Look East approach, while political will on both sides was responsible to bring India and ASEAN closer it was the economic relationship, both at the bilateral level with individual countries as well as at the regional level which led to regular and expanded exchanges. Beginning with full dialogue partnership, the ASEAN-India relationship has evolved into an annual summit-level arrangement where issues of trade, investment, connectivity, education,technology have acquired prominence. ASEAN-India trade has grown at the annual rate of 23 per cent for the past decade and crossed $80 billion in 2012-13. India which had lagged behind in free trade agreements has signed the ASEAN-India FTA in goods and the agreement on services and investments is expected to be signed soon. In the meantime India has also signed Comprehensive Economic Cooperation agreements with Singapore, Malaysia, South Korea and Japan. India's membership of the East Asia Summit (EAS) was an acknowledgement of India's widening 'foot print' on the Asia-Pacific. Currently a Regional Comprehensive Economic Partnership (RCEP) is under negotiation in EAS. India has so far not shown interest in joining the Trans-Pacific Partnership (TPP) agreement presently under discussion with the US in a lead role.

While these steps signify sustained progress towards India's economic engagement with the dynamic region of the Asia-Pacific, it is important to assess how far has India travelled in terms of economic coherence or integration in pursuit of its Look East policy since one of the principal objectives of the latter is to take India to the level of economic development recorded by the Eastern economies. While the growing integration of India with the latter is paying dividends to India's trade and investment with ASEAN the overall economic exchanges are still insignificant as compared to that of China, Japan or South Korea. In terms of linkages to global supply chains or production networks India is far behind the Northeast Asian economic giants. India is still not a member of a major economic grouping, the Asia-Pacific Economic Cooperation (APEC). It is ironical that a major Asian economy is not a participant in the APEC, a forum for open regionalism which accounts for nearly 50 per cent of global trade, investment and technology transfers.

Can India realistically achieve its place as a dynamic economy in the Asia-Pacific without its own economic reforms? India has still a long way to go to create a more liberal tariff regime, ease customs procedures, relax rules of origin with regard to investment regulations in India, to work on regional value chains, etc. Trade facilitation is thus a much needed requirement for the country. Membership of TPP may become important for India in the future if all major economies of Asia join this arrangement. There are reports that China, still not a participant in TPP may be considering joining the negotiations. Moreover, TPP may be a more overarching agreement than even a RCEP or may be WTO plus.

CONNECTIVITY

India is rightfully attaching priority to connectivity between India and Southeast Asia and expects that a number of related projects currently in progress will be completed in the near future. No doubt this will require close monitoring and coordination among various agencies within India and a cooperative arrangement with the concerned countries in Southeast Asia. Timely implementation of infrastructure projects is the key to earn confidence and goodwill of the neighbouring countries, an area in which India still needs to register further progress. Equally, India has to deal with a bigger challenge as to how to transform connectivity into development corridors. Connectivity without substantive development partnership would have little meaning.

REGIONALISM OR SUB-REGIONALISM

One of the main features of Look East policy is that it opened the way for Indian policy makers, officials, corporates, strategic thinkers, etc. to think in regional terms. India's experience in regionalism or regionalization was limited as progress in SAARC had been slow. Even with the European Union it was uneven. Today India's engagement in the Asia-Pacific is extensive, both at the multilateral as well as bilateral level. With ASEAN poised to becoming an ASEAN Economic Community in 2015 and a Security and Social Community soon thereafter India will also require to interact closely with these groupings. India's engagement with a number of ASEAN-centred forums such as the Summit dialogue, ASEAN Regional Forum, ASEAN Defence Ministers' Meeting, etc., call for a specialized approach. India's membership of APEC which needs to be intensively pursued could place India as major multilateral player in the region India's decision to appoint a separate envoy to ASEAN was therefore a timely step. The East Asia Summit (EAS) though potentially a very useful forum is still beset with difficulties because of sharp bilateral differences among many member states. However, important negotiations such as Regional Comprehensive Economic Partnership agreement are being held which will have impact on India's trade and investment regime. In addition, India would need to attach considerable importance to sub-regional organizations/forums such as BIMSTEC, Mekong-Ganga Cooperation, Bangladesh-China-India-Myanmar Initiative, etc. These are more compact arrangements where tangible cooperation in areas such as trade, investment, education, culture, energy, connectivity, tourism, etc., can take place effectively.

Besides pursuing regionalism at the inter-state level, it is equally necessary to establish and strengthen non-governmental exchanges and cooperation with bodies such as Council for Security Cooperation in Asia-Pacific (C-SCAP), ASEAN-India Network of Think-tanks, the ASEAN Centre in India, etc. Academic exchanges between Indian and Southeast and East Asian scholars and institutions also need to be enhanced on a major scale which so far have remained limited. Southeast Asian or for that matter Northeast Asian (China, Japan and Korea) studies in India are far too inadequate and are certainly not commensurate with the importance that India attaches to this region. No policy can succeed or be credible unless it has a substantive and wide-ranging academic and information base. Both government and private institutions have therefore to play an active and expeditious role in this regard.

While multilateralism has been accepted as an indispensable mechanism in promoting India's engagement with the East, the basic need to have strong bilateral ties with the countries of the region cannot be over-emphasized. With Japan there is a new enthusiasm to upgrade the relations substantially at the highest level. With China, too, efforts seem under way on both sides to manage the complex relationship while expanding the economic exchanges. Indo-Korean relations would need to be given further fillip through major investments on both sides.

It is in Southeast Asia that India's bilateralism requires deeper attention and imprint. While this would apply to all countries in the region, one country that may be prioritized for the purpose is Indonesia. This largest state of Southeast Asia shares an extraordinary range of commonalities with India, including size, ethnic diversity, religious plurality, democracy, cultural affinity, developmental needs and independent foreign policy. Through a remarkable coincidence the two countries have now new leaders with a great deal in common. India needs to reach out to Indonesia with respect to developing closer relations. A dynamic India-Indonesia equation has the potential to become the bedrock of India's Look East policy.

INDIA'S NORTHEAST IN LOOK EAST POLICY

The northeast region of India is often described as a gateway to Southeast Asia and a key player in India's Look East policy. With Myanmar opening up after democratization, the northeast's special position as a direct neighbour of Myanmar is further highlighted. After all, Myanmar and India share a common boundary of over 1,600 km in the northeast.

When LEP was initiated the perspective was that a region which has ethnic and historical ties with Southeast Asia should economically integrate with the latter even as the northeast continues to go on integrating politically with the rest of India. But this perspective does not seem to have been achieved over the years. Two decades after India's policy of intensified engagement with the East has been in force there has been little progress to term the northeast as a bridgehead to Southeast Asia. There are internal issues which need to be addressed simultaneously with external ones related to connectivity to Myanmar. The northeast is too diverse to be treated as one entity. Each of the states has its own set of problems and aspirations. Connectivity among the states and with the rest of India is itself still poor. Be it direct trade between the northeast and Southeast Asia, or border trade at the designated check-posts on the India-Myanmar border, or air flights, travel and tourism or investments in the northeast from Southeast Asia there is still a long way to go. It should be however acknowledged that projects for improving road and railway connectivity are progressing. The Kaladan Multi-modal project linking Sittwe port in Myanmar with Mizoram or extension of the Moreh-Tamu-Kalewa road within Myanmar or the Trilateral Highway between India, Myanmar and Thailand are expected to be completed in the coming years. Improved connectivity would no doubt facilitate travel between India and Myanmar and beyond in Southeast Asia and should contribute substantially to greater people-to-people exchanges, trade and investment. However, at present major questions remain. Economic development within northeast itself has lagged behind with the resultant unemployment and social resentment. There is widespread insurgency in some of the northeastern states. Investment in the region from the rest of India has so far been marginal.

Cooperation with Myanmar is also not adequate and uniform. The Myanmar central government's directives are often seen to be not implemented by the local authorities at the border between India and Myanmar. Insurgents from India are still reportedly finding shelter in the areas of Myanmar across the border and operating from there.

Against this background it is not uncommon to find the grievance in the northeast that the region has largely remained outside the country's LEP purview; at best the northeast has become a transit passage. The region which was supposedly the *raison d'être* of the country's policy has not benefitted as expected.

Clearly, if the northeast is to be fully integrated into the LEP, the political issues and misunderstandings which come in the way of India's relations with the neighbours including Bangladesh, Nepal, Myanmar, China and Bhutan will need to be addressed. After all the northeast has close connection to the countries which border individual states. In the meanwhile, within the northeast itself a new paradigm based on development will have to be expanded and sustained which is in contrast to the previous one which looked at the northeast as 'a tribal hill people syndrome' or 'a strategic region because of its proximity to other countries especially China'. The volume of border trade of the northeast with Myanmar or Bangladesh or Nepal is still quite small though it does help border people to some extent. In order that the northeast benefits from its huge natural resources large-scale investments from the rest of the country and improved communications and infrastructure facilities will be necessary. Some of the northeastern states such as Meghalaya, Sikkim, Manipur can also become attractive destinations for education, health care, IT services, etc., for the neighbouring countries like Bangladesh, Myanmar or Nepal.

The BIMSTEC or BCIM sub-regional approach for developmental cooperation can be of significance for the region which will help the latter to become an integral part of the Look East policy.

PEOPLE-TO-PEOPLE EXCHANGES

India's policy of enhanced engagement with the East will get real boost when people-to-people exchanges substantially grow through 'soft power' attributes such as education, Bollywood, tourism, Buddhist heritage travel, health care, cuisine, etc. The electronic and social media will inevitably play a key role in this regard. The Indian diaspora which is present in large numbers in many countries of the East has contributed substantially to developing closer relations between India and the host country. With a broad political consensus within India for this policy and growing democratization across the Asia-Pacific region (with a current exception of Thailand) there should be a better socio-cultural climate for mutual understanding and awareness and resultant interdependence. Therein lie the optimistic prospects for a continued march of India's reinvigorated LEP.

CHAPTER 20

Look East Policy 3.0: The Way Ahead

RAJIV K. BHATIA*

INTRODUCTION

Within a generation India's relationship with Southeast Asia has undergone a visible transformation, gaining in texture, content, range and strength. This has been achieved through the instrumentality of the Look East Policy (LEP) which itself changed over time just as the geostrategic, political and economic environment changed. The policy, often hailed as 'the cornerstone' of India's foreign policy, has been sustained through national consensus among political parties, India Inc., media and civil society.[1] This mix of support explains its rising trajectory, although the policy's underperformance should not be ignored. As one reflects on its future, it appears that LEP is set to make further headway, especially if considered suggestions by experts for its refinement and expansion were to be accepted and acted upon.

While composing this essay, I recalled the year 1985 when I first went to Indonesia to spend over three years there, serving as DCM in the Indian Embassy in Jakarta. I savoured the magic of the journey of India and Indonesia as 'companion souls', as Rabindranath Tagore depicted them. In the early 1990s, working as head of an important division of the Ministry of External Affairs, I witnessed the quiet competition between SAARC and ASEAN to claim Myanmar as a new member, besides participating in the crafting and implementation of India's 'dual track' policy on Myanmar. In the subsequent decade,

* Amb. Rajiv K. Bhatia, Director-General, Indian Council of World Affairs and former Ambassador of India to Myanmar.

I had the privilege to serve as India's Ambassador in Yangon (2002-5), a transformative period for the bilateral relationship. For the past two years, I have been entrusted with the responsibility to manage the Indian Council of World Affairs (ICWA) and shape its track-II initiatives, largely focused on Asia. This institution, translating Jawaharlal Nehru's vision of Asian unity into reality, had helped to organize the Asian Relations Conference. At its historic opening, Nehru, addressing the delegates, said that it was not the invitation from India 'but some deeper urge that brought you here'.[2]

Hence, this analysis will draw from the long experience of a practitioner and a member of India's strategic community as well as from ICWA's comprehensive dialogues, held in recent years, with our partner institutions in China, Japan, Russia, Australia, Indonesia, Vietnam, Myanmar, South Korea and Malaysia. This essay will first delineate briefly the evolution of LEP, pinpointing its key constituents today. It will then examine the changing strategic context, moulded by geopolitical shifts and changing power equations, which motivate policy makers to plan for a far more complex environment in the future. Towards the end, the author will offer a package of ideas and recommendations with a view not only to protecting India's national interests but also for promoting the region's quotient of security, peace and prosperity. While doing so, it would be essential to factor in the impact of the change of government in New Delhi in May 2014.

POLICY EVOLUTION

The '3.0' in the essay's title refers not only to the third decade since Prime Minister Narasimha Rao launched what later came to be known as the LEP; it also points to the third phase of policy which took India's engagement with ASEAN from sectoral dialogue, through full dialogue and summit-level dialogue, to strategic partnership.[3] To be more precise, the third phase began with the ASEAN-India Commemorative Summit in December 2012.

As the engagement deepens further, we need to note that in the present situation and in the foreseeable future, India's strategy towards East Asia is likely to focus as much on ASEAN as on other key role players, namely US, China, Japan, Australia and South Korea.

It will also bring in the maritime dimension within its ambit with greater intensity than before, considering that (a) the notion of inter-linkage of security-development paradigm in the Indian Ocean and the Pacific Ocean has been gaining increasing acceptance, and (b) continuing tensions and the possibility of conflict, by design or accident, in the South China Sea and the East China Sea have made everyone fully aware of their inescapable impact.[4] LEP of the future may, therefore, increasingly be called upon to operate on the larger canvas of the Indo-Pacific Region (IPR) rather than East Asia only.[5]

THREE COMPONENTS

Among various components or constituents of India's engagement with the region, three may be identified as the principal ones. First, interaction and cooperation with ASEAN, both as a regional grouping and bilaterally with its member-states, represent the inner core of this relationship. New Delhi's consistent adherence to 'ASEAN centrality' reflects this as well as its belief that it is a positive concept for the region's interests. However, the emerging fact is that since 2012, ASEAN's unity – and, therefore, its centrality – has been weakened considerably. Paradoxically, this comes at a time when ASEAN is in the final phase of its community-building project, a lengthy process to strengthen its three pillars – political and security, economic, and socio-cultural.[6] Despite ASEAN losing some of its sheen, India should remain its close friend, supporter and partner even as it moves forward to focus on other dimensions of the LEP.

In this context, bilateral relations assume even greater significance than before. While all ten members of ASEAN are important, they are not equally important. One should reckon four of them as especially significant for India: Indonesia – for its size, strategic location, national identity and being a natural, though still reluctant, leader; Singapore – for its unique position, influence in the region and favourable disposition towards India; Vietnam – for its critical role as a nation resolutely committed to defying dominance by others; and Myanmar – for its new-found calibration and capability to balance its relations with China on the one hand, and others, including India, on the other. A fifth country – Thailand – too should be kept within our purview, given the steady expansion of tourism, commercial and cultural cooperation with India, although Bangkok is bound to remain inward looking in the short term.

The second component of LEP is the elaborate framework of sub-regional cooperation India has been able to build through the means of various regional initiatives and groupings such as the Initiative for ASEAN Integration (IAI), Bay of Bengal Initiative for Multi-Sectoral Technical and Economic Cooperation (BIMSTEC), Mekong-Ganga Cooperation (MGC), and Bangladesh-China-India-Myanmar (BCIM) Forum, etc. Projects and programmes in infrastructure development and capacity building have connected us to our immediate neighbours in ASEAN: Cambodia, Laos, Myanmar and Vietnam (CLMV) and Thailand. BIMSTEC brought four other SAARC countries, viz., Bangladesh, Sri Lanka, Bhutan and Nepal into an association that has performed well below par. The newest trend is to bring China and Bangladesh into an equation focused on border development, connectivity projects, facilitation of border trade and planning for development corridors. As prospects for India-China relations appear to be bright in the short to medium term, an initiative like BCIM has the potential to outshine older programmes.

Third, the extra-ASEAN facet of our LEP has undoubtedly gained salience and may do so further in the coming years. This should encourage both our government (and strategic community) to monitor closely and contribute to the development of institutions such as ASEAN Regional Forum (ARF), ASEAN Defence Ministers Meeting+ (ADMM+), ASEAN Maritime Forum (AMF), and East Asia Summit (EAS) as well as the trajectory of India's relations with non-ASEAN powers in the region. The need for reforming and strengthening regional architecture for security – and even economic cooperation – becomes truly significant, perhaps even urgent. What has been happening on this subject, both in the public domain and below the surface, i.e. within the chancelleries, needs to be assessed objectively.

CHANGING POWER DYNAMICS

While contemplating about future contours and directions of the LEP, an accurate reading of the changing relationships among key players in East Asia is indispensable. The seminal development undoubtedly is the strategic contest between the US and China alongside their mutual economic inter-dependence, against the backdrop of power shift from the West to the East as well as Asia's resurgence and the general decline of traditional powers.[7] Much debate goes on about 'the reality' behind China's economic and military rise and diminishing of American power. But the incontrovertible fact remains that the US dominance in Asia is being contested by a China that was never as strong as it is today. China's growing economic and military strength clearly enables it 'to challenge American primacy in Asia'.[8] Near certainty of steady increase in China's comprehensive national power makes it more assertive and other countries more worried. Tackling the question as to what China wants, Hugh White, an eminent Australian scholar, asserts convincingly: 'China's rulers want their country to be wealthy, but they also want it to be strong and respected. They want it to be a leader among nations.'[9]

The strategic response by US to China's changed behaviour appeared in the form of 'pivot/rebalancing to Asia' policy, which has been in the process of evolution in the past four years. It has generated some confidence among American allies and partners; considerable criticism by the Chinese; and widespread anxiety and uncertainty elsewhere. Consequently, experts are engaged in speculation and discussion on a wide array of possibilities ranging from a 'G-2' between US and China, a new cold war in Asia, and even the inevitability of military conflict. Sober voices also suggest the possibility and indeed the desirability of the key nations succeeding in crafting a *modus vivendi* that takes the region towards peace and prosperity for all.

While evaluating reactions in the region to the current phase of US-China rivalry, one is struck by the divisiveness within ASEAN. It is widely perceived as a divided house when it comes to engaging China. Vietnam and Philippines have had public spats with the Chinese; Malaysia, Cambodia and Laos are seen as pro-China; Myanmar is a *sui generis* case; and the remainder are wary and cautious. Indonesia, the largest and the most powerful member-state, took the lead for lowering tensions on the South China Sea dispute and related issues. The unfolding China-ASEAN discussions or negotiations on converting the Declaration of Conduct (DOC) into the Code of Conduct (COC) on South China Sea are watched with deep interest, both within and outside the region. The recent cycle of talks, tensions and disputes on full public display, has been noted. At the time of writing, my perception is that the situation concerning the South China Sea and the East China Sea may get worse before it gets better.

Other key stakeholders from India's perspective are Japan, Australia and South Korea. Japan contributed significantly to China's economic rise, but ironically it has the tensest political relationship with China today. In an interaction with us in April 2014 in Delhi, the head of a premier Japanese think tank frankly confessed that 'Japan does not know how to handle China'. He went on to add that 'China itself does not know what it wants'.[10] South Korea is one country which is most at ease with China's rise. It knows well that concerning its problem no. 1, North Korea, China holds many valuable cards in its hands.[11] As regards Australia, we discovered a significant contradiction during the ICWA dialogue in March 2014 with scholars and officials in Melbourne, Canberra and Sydney: Australia Inc. seemed perfectly happy reaping benefits from China's growing prosperity, whereas the former's strategic community was becoming increasingly nervous about the latter's long-term military prospects, plans and intentions. As a result, Canberra seemed engaged in balancing its relations with China and US.[12]

My recent interaction with Hugh White (referred earlier) unveiled deeper complexities of this subject. In his brilliant book, *The China Choice*, he argues that when it comes to dealing with China, US has only three choices: 'withdraw', 'compete', or 'share'. He recommends the third option, a view that is seriously contested by other experts as well as Australian officials. White maintains that East Asia needs 'A Concert of Asia', i.e. a grouping of Asian great powers, suggesting 'a party of four' – US, China, Japan and India. He excludes Russia, South Korea and Vietnam on the ground that they are 'middle powers', but he adds: 'Only Indonesia has the potential to become a genuine Asian great power eventually – but not before mid-century'.[13] My own considered view is that the US may not choose one of the three options; rather it may prefer a combination of White's second and third options.

We need to bring the US-China equation into India's regional calculus. We in India watch fluctuations in the evolution of this relationship with considerable interest and some anxiety. It is widely recognized that India-US relations stood at 'a plateau' at the time of writing (in June 2014). Most scholars recommend and expect that it would take an upward trajectory from this point onwards. But specifically with regard to East Asia, India has its own way to assess the situation in the long term. It may aptly be claimed that while the US favours a unipolar world and a multi-polar Asia, China craves for a unipolar Asia and a multi-polar world. If so, one should assert that India advocates the idea of a multi-polar Asia within a multi-polar world. Neither hegemony of a single country nor a condominium of G-2 variety nor a cold war between US and China is in Asia's interests.[14]

What is, therefore, needed is an equitable balance among various powers which promotes a constructive partnership, maintenance of peace and security through respect for international law and norms, maritime security and freedom, safety of sea lanes of communication (SLOCs), resolution of disputes through negotiations rather than use of threat or force, and focus on the policy of inclusive economic growth and sustained development. This, in essence, is what India stands for. This strategy will remain at the heart of our future LEP.

IMPLICATIONS/ADVICE FOR INDIA

The foregoing analysis leads us to examine the implications of power dynamics for India.[15] What then is the path New Delhi should choose as it crafts its 'Enhanced Look East Policy'?[16] The first point to stress is that the engagement will now be with the entire region, not just ASEAN. LEP cannot be managed optimally without reference to the considerations and patterns relating to the balance of power which is in a flux. Secondly, while a patently pro-ASEAN route for India is clear, the way to handle major power relationships, especially with the US, China and Japan, will be far more complex and challenging.

In view of my conviction that 'analysis without advice' is an incomplete task, one may first offer the following pointers:

(a) India should improve and further strengthen its relations with the US.
(b) New Delhi should manage ties with China in a manner that economic cooperation grows; peace and tranquillity on the border are ensured; and political-diplomatic competition is kept under check.
(c) India should also take further measures to deepen cooperation with Japan, both in economic and strategic domains – but without choosing Japan over China.[17]
(d) In sum, India needs not only the US, but also both China and Japan.
(e) Conversely, each of the big three – US, China and Japan – needs India even more to promote its interests in Asia (and the world). Developments in the second half of 2014, i.e. Prime Minister Narendra Modi's interactions with the leaders of China, Japan and the US are likely to yield rich dividends for New Delhi.
(f) Finally, India must focus on consolidating and deepening its

strategic partnerships with Australia and South Korea as well as the multi-faceted ties with four countries of ASEAN mentioned earlier – Indonesia, Singapore, Vietnam, and Myanmar.

Flowing from the above, a few actionable recommendations may be put forward, as below:

1. A top priority for India is to focus on developing its engagement with ASEAN to its optimal potential. ASEAN too needs to reciprocate fully as it is a two-way street. The dearth is not of ideas and plans, but perhaps of determination of governments, business communities and other stakeholders to translate proposals, pronouncements and agreements into action – with resoluteness, consistency and speed.
2. We need to streamline the existing regional architecture for dialogue and cooperation, reducing overlapping, raising efficiency, and enhancing deliverability.[18]
3. The need to ensure primacy and effectiveness of EAS should be reflected upon and addressed.[19]
4. Asian Powers in G-20 should expand their dialogue and craft a common approach on international economic, financial and development issues.
5. Parallelism between Regional Comprehensive Economic Partnership (RCEP) and the Trans-Pacific Partnership (TPP) needs to be addressed and resolved. Encouraging convergence and eventual merger of the two processes will help the cause of regional integration.[20]
6. Greater synergy at the level of strategic communities could lay the foundation for a more positive environment and harmonious relationships in East Asia.

CONCLUSION

In the end, it is apparent that India's LEP has come a long way from that day in September 1994 when Prime Minister Narasimha Rao delivered his famous speech at Singapore, delineating his 'vision of a new relationship between India and the Asia-Pacific. . .'.[21] At this point of time, India's engagement with the East Asian region seems set to grow and deepen in a manner that promotes the interests of both sides. On the success of our policy makers, diplomats and other stakeholders as well as their counterparts in the region will depend the journey of LEP in the coming decade.

NOTES

1. Prime Minister Manmohan Singh, Opening Statement by Prime Minister at Plenary Session of India-ASEAN Commemorative Summit, 20 December 2012: 'The breadth and intensity of India's engagement with Southeast Asia is unmatched by any of our other regional relationships'. <http://www.mea.gov.in/Speeches-Statements.htm?dtl/20981/Opening+Statement+by+Prime+Minister+at+Plenary+Session+of+IndiaASEAN+Commemorative+Summit> (accessed on 21 June 2014).
2. At the conference held in March-April 1947, Nehru observed: 'A change is coming over the scene now and Asia is again finding herself. We live in a tremendous age of transition and already the next stage takes shape when Asia takes her rightful place with the other continents.' <http://www.tibetsun.com/news/1947/03/24/pt-jawaharlal-nehrus-speech-at-asian-relations-conference-1947> (accessed on 21 June 2014).
3. 'Vision Statement – ASEAN-India Commemorative Summit, 20 December 2012'. At the ASEAN-India Commemorative Summit on 20 December 2012, leaders announced the establishment of strategic partnership and spelt out their vision in clear terms: 'We will strive towards the full, effective and timely implementation of the ASEAN-India Dialogue relations across the whole spectrum of political and security, economic, socio-cultural and development cooperation. . . .' < http://www.mea.gov.in/bilateral-documents.htm?dtl/20982/Vision+StatementASEANIndia+Commemorative+Summit> (accessed on 21 June 2014).
4. David Brewster, 'Strategic Convergences between India and Australia in Southeast Asia', *Journal of Indian Ocean Studies,* vol. 22, no. 1, April 2014, New Delhi: Society for Indian Ocean Studies, 2014, p. 19. The author argues: 'The Indo-Pacific strategic concept has particular significance for India's potential role in Southeast Asia. This includes India playing a much greater security role in the Pacific Ocean and forming much closer security relationships with US allies such as Australia and Japan and others.'
5. Rory Medcalf, 'Pivoting the Map: Australia's Indo-Pacific System', *Centre of Gravity Series,* ANU, 2012, p. 2. The author states: 'Certainly the Indo-Pacific has gained considerable currency of late. Its acceptance as a distinct biogeographic region in marine science is of long standing. But in geopolitics the term lay dormant for decades until its recent re-emergence in a gathering tempo of speeches, press reports, government documents and think-tank reports.'
6. At a meeting on 22 May 2014 with the ICWA delegation, led by the author, A.K.P. Mochtan, Deputy Secretary-General for ASEAN,

conveyed that with regard to the goal of community-building with its three pillars, ASEAN was moving 'on track' to meet the deadline of December 2015. It planned to be 'a people-oriented, people-centric and rule-based community' (from my personal notes).

7. Hillary Rodham Clinton, *Hard Choices*, (Simon & Schuster, London: 2014), p.66. Referring to US-China ties, the author states: 'This isn't a relationship that fits neatly into categories like friend or rival, and it may never. We are sailing in uncharted waters. Staying on course and avoiding the shoals and whirlpools requires both a true compass and a flexibility to make frequent course corrections, including sometimes painful trade-offs.'
8. Hugh White, *The China Choice* Collingwood: Black Inc., 2012, p. 43.
9. Ibid., pp. 49-50.
10. During a Q & A session at a discussion hosted by the Forum for Strategic Initiatives, 25 April 2014.
11. At an informal conversation on 4 May 2014 with Skand Tayal, former Indian Ambassador to South Korea and author of *India and the Republic of Korea: Engaged Democracies.*
12. Melissa Conley Tyler and Samantha Shearman, 'Australia Re-Discovering the Indo-Pacific', in Rajiv K. Bhatia and Vijay Sakuja (eds.), *Indo-Pacific Region: Political and Strategic Prospects*, New Delhi: ICWA, 2014, p. 38: 'Australia is in a delicate strategic position as it attempts to balance its alliance with the US and its economic relationship with China; it does not want to upset this balance.'
13. Hugh White, *The China Choice*, Collingwood: Black Inc., 2012, p. 144.
14. Arvind Gupta, 'India's Approach to the Asia-Pacific', in S.D. Muni and Vivek Chadha (eds.), *Asian Strategic Review 2014*, New Delhi: Pentagon Press, 2014, p. 215: 'India's strategy should be to seek deeper engagement and economic integration with the Asia-Pacific region. India should be particularly engaged in the security dialogues and processes in the region.'
15. A part of the preceding analysis and this section have been drawn from the Paper entitled 'Geopolitical Shifts in East Asia: An Indian Perspective' which I presented on 21 May 2014 at symposium in Jakarta, hosted by the Indonesian Council on World Affairs.
16. Address by Secretary (East) to International Conference on Cham Civilisation at the Indira Gandhi National Centre for the Arts, New Delhi, 26 April 2014. 'We are now engaged in the formulation of an Enhanced Look East Policy for the new century which fully recognizes the potential of our civilizational outreach, our economic aspirations, our desire for integration and our shared values and objectives.' <http://www.mea.gov.in/Speeches-Statements.htm?dtl/23250/Address+by+Secretary+East+to+International+Conference+on+Cham+Civilisation+at+Indira+Gandhi+National+Centre+for+the+Arts+New+Delhi> (accessed on 21 June 2014).

17. Rajiv Bhatia, 'India's Options: Peace and Conflict in East Asia', *India Writes*, 10 June 2014. 'Just as the US and Japan made China stronger economically, Japan and China can contribute to India's development. However, on the larger political issues, India will surely need to develop an equitable and effective balance of power that encourages nations to resolve their disputes peacefully. New Delhi should find tangible ways to work both with Beijing and Tokyo.' <http://www.indiawrites.org/diplomacy/indias-options-peace-and-conflict-in-east-asia/> (accessed on 21 June 2014).
18. Salman Khurshid, 'Keynote Address', Rajiv K. Bhatia and Vijay Sakhuja, (eds.), *Indo-Pacific Region: Political and Strategic Prospects*, New Delhi: ICWA, 2014, p xii. Khurshid stated: 'The challenge Asia faces is to evolve a transparent, open and balanced regional architecture for itself, both in the economic and security arenas.'
19. As US Secretary of State Hillary Clinton observed: ' I will introduce the two core principles that the Obama Administration will take in its approach to the EAS – first, ASEAN's central role, and second, our desire to see EAS emerge as a forum for substantive engagement on pressing strategic and political issues, including nuclear non-proliferation, maritime security, and climate change.' America's Engagement in the Asia-Pacific' by Hillary Rodham Clinton, Secretary of State, 28 October 2010, pp. 243-52. S.D. Muni and Vivek Chadha (eds.), *Asian Strategic Review 2014*, New Delhi: Pentagon Press, 2014.
20. For an excellent analysis of opportunities and challenges of convergence and progress towards Free Trade Area for Asia-Pacific (FTAAP), please see Sanchita Basu Das's Paper 'Trends in Southeast Asia', #02, ISEAS, Singapore, 2014.
21. Government of India (1996), *P.V. Narasimha Rao: Selected Speeches*, vol. IV (June 1994-June 1995), New Delhi: Ministry of Information and Broadcasting.

Editor's Reflections

A common thread running through most of the essays in this volume, unmistakably, relates to the imperative of our long-term engagement with the Indo-pacific as a means of furthering and securing our strategic, security, political, economic, cultural and other interests in India's extended eastern neighbourhood. The Look East policy (LEP), having acquired critical mass, now in its third decade, has become an integral and irreversible dimension of our foreign policy. The emergence of India as an important Indo-Pacific player offers hitherto unimaginable opportunities, even as it imposes daunting challenges upon us. As we seek to build upon, integrate and consolidate our now greatly expanded ties with the region, we will need to be mindful of nuanced resistance and reservation to India's long-term presence in the region by forces inimical to us. The challenge for Indian diplomacy, in the coming years, will lie in blunting these forces and ensuring that the emerging strategic and economic architecture in this geo-strategic space provides us requisite latitude, role and responsibility commensurate with our strength, size and potential, enjoying the support of the countries of the region. The key for India is to become internally strong and resilient and externally relevant, useful and dependable, making our strength and benign presence count positively in the region.

The essays in this volume, generally, analyse, assess and evaluate the LEP positively, recognizing that while much has been achieved in the past two decades, much more needs to be accomplished to realize the full potential and benefits of this win-win partnership. A common criticism relates to our inability to clearly define and prioritize our long-term objectives; inordinate delays and impediments in taking new policy initiatives; inability to optimally consolidate and build upon past gains; missed opportunities due to policy hiatus, tardy or no meaningful implementation of policy; absence of monitoring and timely course correction; and, of course, slow and less than imaginative reaction/response to important developments in our eastern neighbourhood (e.g. response to the 1997-8 financial crisis, South and East China Sea developments and, possibly, in regard to our meaningful and timely participation in several ASEAN-led fora), leading some to even questioning our seriousness, credibility and capacity. Some scholars, therefore, argue that a totally new look and direction is needed to redefine the LEP, consistent with contemporary realities, imperatives, challenges and opportunities. These experts suggest that in the coming decades greater imagination and vigour will need to be imparted to this partnership; a well-thought out vision, the next steps needed and time bound pro-active road map for the future worked out by making use of the building blocks of the first two decades of LEP. Some very useful, constructive and workable suggestions have been made in the essays which need to be reflected upon for possible implementation.

The need for closer and well-thought out strategic and defence interface comes across strongly in several essays. The implications of the rise of China and her growing assertiveness, the fallout of the East and South China Sea tensions and its implications for India (e.g. freedom and safety of navigation in international waters, unilateral use of force to alter the *status quo*, etc.), maritime security issues, non-traditional security threats, terrorism and transnational crime, energy security, environment, natural disasters and other aspects have been highlighted in the essays with insightful analysis and inputs for possible policy. The changing role of the US and its 'rebalance' policy, Trans-Pacific Partnership, Sino-US rivalry and confrontation, US security commitments in Northeast Asia, Japan's new imperatives, policies, priorities, increasing relevance and strategic convergences with democratic countries like India, recent tensions between ASEAN and China, etc., have also been examined and commented upon, with analysis of possible implications for India and the region. The new Modi government's focus on the Indo-Pacific, especially relations with Japan, RoK, ASEAN, Australia and China, generally welcomed and reciprocated by regional powers that see India as a potentially important player, has also been discussed in some essays. The importance and imperative of normalizing and more pragmatically managing our relations with China comes across in several essays; some believe that such an approach is feasible, even as vexed bi-lateral and other differences with China will continue to remain unresolved in the foreseeable future. They see cautious optimism in China's initial, though as yet untested and tentative, reaction to the new Modi government in India. However, nobody should have any exaggerated expectation of a dramatic or early breakthrough in relations.

Naturally, the important economic and connectivity dimensions of our engagement receive focus in several essays. Some comments candidly reflect on the cost of unfulfilled agenda, targets and goals. Concern has been expressed on the tardy and delayed implementation of agreed programmes. The prospects, potential and options available for India arising out of the multiple free trade/comprehensive economic cooperation agreements (including the India-ASEAN FTA and the proposed Mega-Regional Comprehensive Economic Partnership Agreement) have been comprehensively analysed and commented upon, also bringing into the ambit of discussion issues relating to sub-regional cooperation, the emergence of trade blocs from which India, for now, has been excluded and prospects for new mega trade, investment and technology agreements providing an option for an alternate regional response. The references in some essays to the region's remarkable growth and the need for India to learn from the experience of several rapidly growing economies, even as we proactively promote our own core competencies, are highly instructive.

The section on diaspora, cultural affinities, people-to-people contacts, science and technology, HRD cooperation, India's soft power assets, etc., contain a fascinating discussion on these hitherto little-focused areas of our engagement with this civilizationally integrated region. At least one essay has delved deep into studying the experience of other ethnic immigrant communities in the region compared to the Indian diaspora.

Several essays have attempted to peep into the future and contain practical suggestions for the next steps needed in the coming decades. The 'building blocks' of our engagement in the first two decades of the LEP and the 'road ahead' have been thoughtfully discussed in the essays, particularly in the concluding section. The imperative of broadbasing our relations with the entire Indo-Pacific geographical space in areas such as defence and security, strategic dimensions of our engagement, developing enforceable regional legal instrumentalities for combating trans-national crime and in reinforcing our economic and connectivity ties to make them self-sustaining are, obviously, at the centre of discussion in some of the essays. The priority that the Modi government is expected to accord to the Indo-Pacific space is likely to translate, in concrete terms, to new proactive initiatives to enhance our strategic, security, political, economic, cultural and people-to-people relations with our extended eastern neighbourhood. The reinforced and revitalized LEP, some experts believe, could emerge as a game changer that could catapult India into a major regional and global player in the next decade or so, releasing her hitherto latent potential, straitjacketed so far by subcontinental preoccupations, to a larger canvas.

The message discernable in all essays relates to the enormous benefits, inevitability and irreversibility of our Indo-Pacific engagement. The LEP, now directed at the entire region, is seen as a pillar of our foreign policy and the engagement with the Indo-Pacific our best, albeit somewhat delayed, doubted and underutilized, policy option. The policy derives its strength and rationale not only from external strategic, defence, political, economic, cultural and historical imperatives but also, equally importantly, from history and our domestic compulsions, concerns and requirements of national interest (particularly with regard to the northeast, the Andamans and the southern peninsula which have enjoyed centuries of close traditional and trade links with the Indo-Pacific), a fact that has been highlighted in contemporary discussions and in several essays in this volume.

It is hoped that the reader will be motivated to ask questions, research, comment and write upon some of the aspects of our Indo-Pacific engagement outlined above. That is the purpose of this compilation.

AMAR NATH RAM
Editor

Index